T0385145

BLOOD &
TREASURE

Also by Duncan Weldon

Two Hundred Years of Muddling Through:
The surprising story of Britain's economy
from boom to bust and back again

BLOOD & TREASURE

The Economics of
Conflict from the
Vikings to Ukraine

Duncan Weldon

abacus
books

ABACUS

First published in Great Britain in 2025 by Abacus

1 3 5 7 9 10 8 6 4 2

A CIP catalogue record for this book
is available from the British Library.

Hardback ISBN 978-0-3491-4539-6
Trade paperback ISBN 978-0-3491-4540-2

Typeset in Baskerville by M Rules
Printed and bound in Great Britain by Clays Ltd, Elcograf S.p.A.

Papers used by Abacus are from well-managed forests
and other responsible sources.

Abacus
An imprint of
Little, Brown Book Group
Carmelite House
50 Victoria Embankment
London EC4Y 0DZ

The authorised representative
in the EEA is
Hachette Ireland
8 Castlecourt Centre
Dublin 15, D15 XTP3, Ireland
(email: info@hbgi.ie)

An Hachette UK Company
www.hachette.co.uk

www.littlebrown.co.uk

For Natalie

Contents

Introduction

Sometimes archaeologists get lucky – maybe never more so than when they find what they call a 'hoard'. A hoard, or wealth deposit, is something different from the detritus of everyday life that archaeologists usually deal with. It is a collection of valuable items such as jewellery, silver plate and money, often buried by its owner. Archaeologists love a hoard. The inclusion of coins, which can have the year they were minted stamped on to them, usually makes the items dateable. But while discovering a hoard is great news for an archaeologist, the very existence of such a wealth deposit generally spelled disaster for whoever buried it and failed, for whatever reason, to recover it.

Plotting the date of discovered wealth deposits over time is not a bad indicator of societal stress. There is a significant spike in discovered hoards around Europe from the ninth and tenth centuries – the Viking Age. The existence of boatfuls of marauders prowling the coasts and rivers of the continent clearly left many affluent citizens feeling uneasy. The most spectacular find in China, which contained more than 1.5 tons of bronze coinage, seems to date from the Jin-Song wars of the early thirteenth century when the borders of northern

China were redrawn. Looking back over the centuries of British history, there have been two notable spikes in the burying of wealth that archaeologists have discovered. The first came towards the end of the fourth and beginning of the fifth century AD, at the time of the end of Roman rule in Britain. The second and even larger spike came in the middle of the seventeenth century. This was the era of the British civil wars, a time of chronic instability. This was also the era in which the now common phrase 'blood and treasure' entered into widespread usage. There was so much blood being shed that many chose to bury their treasure.

Wars are hugely expensive, both in human and financial terms. Blood and treasure is the neatest three-word way yet devised that encapsulates a frequently overlooked aspect of history. At first glance you might assume that the study of economics can help us to understand the monetary aspect of this equation but be on far less sure footing when it comes to the matter of human toll. But 'following the money', as I hope to persuade you, is absolutely as useful a device for understanding how and why states have fought wars as it is for understanding how they have paid for them.

War and conflict may sometimes seem like the most irrational aspects of behaviour, and a discipline usually associated with 'utility-maximising actors' – as economists drily refer to human beings – may appear ill-prepared to explain them. But there is far more to economics than the arid textbook approach may suggest. Two economic notions in particular are crucial to understanding conflict and war: incentives and institutions.

A rational look at incentives can often explain even the most seemingly irrational behaviour – and few things are as irrational as war. Crucially, though, incentives are not formed in a vacuum. They are shaped by the wider social, cultural and political context – the kind of things economists call institutions. In economic parlance, an institution is not nec-essarily an organisation with an address and phone number but an expected manner of behaviour. The FBI is obviously an institution, but in economic terms so too is the notion that people should go through their everyday lives without stealing from their neighbours. So institutions can be actual organisa-tions, but also wider forms of behaviour and the general rules of society.

Over time institutions change and incentives change too alongside them. The world of early medieval Europe in which this book opens was very different from that of the 2020s in which it closes. Institutions had changed in almost unrecognisable ways, and with them incentives. Together, though, institutions and incentives shape and explain human behaviour.

Most economists agree that countries' comparative wealth is largely decided by institutions. Some states have developed institutions that support economic growth and higher living standards, others have not. Institutions matter far more than technology, climate or a myriad of other factors in explaining one's life chances.

Over the long span of human history, nothing has shaped institutions – and hence economic outcomes – as much as war and violence. The key institution has been the state, and for almost all of human history making war and preparing to make war – what economic historians call 'the gift of Mars' – has defined states and their development. Warfare is crucial to understanding institutional development, and institutional development is crucial to the central questions of economics. War-making and state-making have developed side by side. What we now call states and nations often developed out of particularly successful warbands.

History, as Arnold Toynbee once noted, risks being 'just one damned fact after another'. Economics and economic thinking provide a framework for considering why things happened as they did, a handy toolkit for explaining what sometimes seems like inexplicable human behaviour and one that stretches well beyond money and production. The social sciences and history are naturally complementary. Social science without history is a dry and often unhelpful theoretical exercise, one that might make sense in a mathematical model or in a textbook but will usually struggle – or even be actively unhelpful – in the real world. But history without social science or theory can often be little more than a list of dates and events. Sometimes an interesting one, but a list nonetheless. Combining the two can allow the reader to understand not only what happened but, crucially, why it happened.

The first states were built by what economic historians politely dub 'violence specialists', and the threat of violence sat behind most forms of economic exchange. It was not long after the agricultural revolution that some bulkier humans realised that while farming was hard work, using threats to take some of the produce of the farmers was an awful lot easier. Those with what economists would call a comparative advantage in violence could live well. The best way for those not endowed with a propensity for violence was to place themselves under the protection of someone who could defend them. From the very beginning, then, violence and conflict have been key to how human society has developed. But even in a pre-modern world, incentives and institutions mattered.

In the modern world the institutions are different but the incentives for war and violence often remain. Over time war and institutions have shaped each other. The development of new weapons or tactics or techniques has forced states to change how they organise themselves and hence the rest of society.

After the military revolution of the sixteenth to seventeenth centuries, war became more expensive. Armies became larger and wars lasted for longer. The costs of fighting, and hence the incentive structures around them, began to change. That changing nature of war led to a change in the nature and size of states.

In the chapters that follow, this book will examine the economics of conflict and war from the Viking Age to the war in Ukraine. It will explain why Genghis Khan should be regarded as the father of globalisation, how New World gold and silver counter-intuitively kept Spain poor, why some economists think of witch trials as a form of 'non-price competition', how pirate captains were pioneers of effective human resources management, how handing out medals hurt the Luftwaffe in the Second World War, and why economic theories helped to create a tragedy in Vietnam. Along the way it considers why some medieval kings were right to arm their soldiers with inferior weapons, takes some management lessons from Joseph Stalin, and asks if a culture of patronage and cronyism helped the Royal Navy rise to greatness.

I hope it will also show both how economics can help understand war and how understanding war can help explain modern economics.

1

Rational Raiders:
The Economics of the Vikings

When someone is known to history as Eric Bloodaxe it is a reasonable guess that they had what might euphemistically be called a 'colourful' career. Eric Bloodaxe was a tenth-century Viking king who ruled Northumbria twice and was very possibly also, at different times, King of Norway and Jarl (Earl) of the Orkney Islands. His other common nickname was *fractrum interfector*, or brother-killer, which gives some clues as to how he might have become King of Norway in the first place. While his rulership of Northumbria can be more securely dated from both contemporary mentions and coin finds, his other reputed adventures appear in much later sagas. Some historians even think that two Eric Bloodaxes, one historical and one legendary, have become merged over the years. If there was indeed not just one but two kings with the name Bloodaxe, that's rather telling about the nature of Viking kingship. Equally telling is the name of a near contemporary, Thorfinn Skullsplitter of Orkney.

The story of Eric, as cobbled together from the scant

surviving contemporary sources and the later semi-legendary tradition, runs something like this. Eric was one of perhaps twenty sons of the rather wonderfully named King Harald Finehair of Norway. He certainly then was not short of brothers to kill. Possibly the oldest son, and apparently his father's favourite, Eric went about securing his inheritance by knocking off his male siblings one by one. He eventually succeeded as King of Norway, but his rule was harsh, unpopular and short-lived. By the time it was ended by revolt he was down to one surviving brother. Exiled from Norway, he crossed the North Sea, possibly ruled the Orkney Islands for a while, and then established himself as a pirate and raider around the Irish Sea. Over the course of perhaps a decade he amassed wealth, reputation and followers – enough that by AD 947 he was able to claim the kingship of Northumbria, ruling a substantial chunk of northern England from York.

Northumbrian politics in the mid-tenth century are best described as messy. From the late ninth century onwards the country now called England had begun to emerge from a fractured conglomeration of smaller kingdoms and statelets. Alfred the Great and his descendants as rulers of Wessex had not only resisted Viking invasions but gradually begun to add to their own realms. The old Anglo-Saxon kingdoms of Mercia and East Anglia and lands ruled for a century or more by Danish settlers in the Midlands had been incorporated into the newly combined country. Northumbria, though, was the tricky bit. The territory was disputed between the English, or West Saxon, kings descended from Alfred and a line of Hiberno-Norse Vikings associated with the Scandinavian-ruled Kingdom of Dublin across the Irish Sea. The people of the region were themselves a mix of long-standing Anglo-Saxon residents coupled with Scandinavian settlers who had been arriving for three or four generations. Henry of Huntingdon, a later chronicler of English history, believed the people of the north waited to see which way the wind would blow before deciding who to back with 'their usual faithlessness'. Which is a harsh judgement, but not an inaccurate one.

Eric Bloodaxe's first spell as king was brief, lasting only until 948 when he was ousted after a year in charge by a revolt of the native English amid a Scottish invasion. But he was a hard man to keep down. By 952 he was, after another spell of raiding around the Irish, Cumbrian and Scottish coasts, ready for another try. The circumstances of his second reign are frustratingly unclear. The *Anglo-Saxon Chronicle* merely tells us that the Northumbrians 'drove out King Olaf and accepted Eric' in 952, but by 954 they had had a change of heart and decided to throw in their lot with Alfred the Great's grandson King Eadred. Henry of Huntingdon's complaints about faithlessness seem more than just a southern anti-northern prejudice. Eric himself died in the immediate aftermath of this second Northumbrian ousting, killed in battle fighting against the Anglo-Saxons in the Pennines.

Even stripped of any mythical elements, the bare facts of Eric's life and name seem to sum up much of what comes to mind at the mention of the word Viking. Here was a career forged on both sides of the North Sea, one that saw Eric at times as a king and at others as a raider but always as a warrior. Eric was a violence specialist, and the leader of other violence specialists.

No one is quite sure why the so-called Viking Age – which lasted from about AD 800 until the eleventh century – started, what exactly it was that prompted young men in Scandinavia to start preying on the coastal communities of the rest of western Europe. Over the years various explanations have been offered, ranging from climate change depressing agricultural yields in Europe's far north and causing an exodus to increased status competition between local Scandinavian rulers leading to their seeking new treasures overseas. Whatever the causes, it soon became apparent that the Vikings, to use the modern and familiar term, were very good at what they did. The Europe of the ninth and tenth centuries was not exactly short of competing violence specialists, so what was it that set these Northmen apart?

It may be that the young men to be found hanging around the coasts of Scandinavia were simply better warriors than those found in Anglo-Saxon England or Frankish France. Take the Anglo-Saxons as an example. Four or so centuries before the Viking Age, the Saxons had been the Vikings of their day, pagans from across the North Sea arriving by boat on the coast of Christian Roman Britain to raid and pillage. By the sixth and seventh centuries the lowlands of Britain, the bit we now call England, were dominated by Anglo-Saxon kingdoms. The single best source we have on the nature of early Saxon kingship is not a straightforward history or a charter or a chronicle but the great epic poem *Beowulf*. It might be set in Scandinavia and feature things such as monsters and dragons which in reality were unlikely to have bothered early medieval kings, but it says something very important about the nature of power in this era. Strip back the verse, cut out the more fantastic elements, and what you have is a simple story of violence specialists and an explanation of how they ruled society. Kings are gold-givers and ring-givers, feasting with their retainers in great wooden mead halls. A successful king is a successful war leader, and great warriors will wish to serve him. Battle is ultimately about seizing booty to be handed out to one's supporters. The more booty one takes, the bigger the warband a leader can gather. And the larger the warband the gold-giver can gather, the more gold he can take to give out. It is, from the point of view of the violence specialists, a virtuous circle. Or rather it is until it isn't. When a king or leader ceases to be a battle winner, their rule will end.

It doesn't take an economist to spot the rather obvious problem with this model of political economy. To retain the support of their warriors and retainers, a king had to keep fighting wars to get more golden rings and other treasures to dish out to their followers. Instability and conflict were built into the system.

This was a world in which the later idea of royal father-to-son succession lines would seem rather quaint. Powerful retainers knew that not only their income but indeed their lives depended on the ability of the king to lead them into battle. In general, they would rather not trust in the lottery of genetics that the current king's son would just so happen to be equally proficient at war as his sire. The death of a king would mean multiple competing claims to the throne.

By the Viking Age, though, things looked rather different. The Anglo-Saxon kingdoms were larger and more stable. They were Christians now. Father-to-son succession was becoming much more common. While wars between the kingdoms and no doubt raids and skirmishes across borders were still relatively frequent, the overall level of violence had almost certainly decreased over the centuries. There are many advantages to shifting to a model of political economy which does not lead to endemic warfare. The one potential downside, as the Anglo-Saxons were about to find out in the 800s, was that this system perhaps produced fewer and less effective violence specialists. Viking Age Scandinavia, by contrast, as the story of Eric Bloodaxe tells us, was still rather closer to the world of *Beowulf*. That world may have been less stable than the Anglo-Saxon England of the late eighth century but it no doubt produced exceptional fighting men.

There was more, though, to Viking success than the possibility that that they had access to a better class of warrior.

The Vikings also appear to have had two crucial comparative advantages for raiding: superior naval technology and, at least for the first century or so, a lack of a Christian faith. Both these advantages can be seen in one of the earliest and most high-profile Viking raids of the period, that on the monastery of Lindisfarne on Holy Island, off the Northumbrian coast, in 793.

Boats have been important in Scandinavia for a long time. It is hard to see how humans could have lived in an area marked by islands, inlets and fjords for any length of time without embracing some type of shipbuilding. Settlements generally grew up either on coasts or lakes and never especially far from the sea. The ships these people built were generally faster, sleeker and lighter than those found elsewhere in Europe — but, at least initially, powered entirely by oars. At some point before the Viking Age the crucial technological breakthrough occurred and the people of Scandinavia began to add sails to their longships.

This dual-propulsion method turned out to be crucial to the success of early Viking raids. Until then, anyone crossing the North Sea by boat would generally have their course set by the prevailing winds, which vary but not by a great deal. A boat leaving Scandinavia and hoping to arrive at Lindisfarne would probably be blown to somewhere off the coast of southern Scotland then make its way south, clinging to the coast, arriving off Lindisfarne a day or two later. That method of travel works but it is almost impossible to arrive by surprise. The Vikings, though, could sail most of the way and then, while still over the horizon, switch from sails to oars for their final approach. In other words, rather than the monks of Lindisfarne having a day or two's warning that some odd-looking ships had arrived to the north and were slowing in their direction, they would have had at most a couple of hours' warning – depending on the weather and visibility – that vessels had appeared near the island and was heading for the beach. Alcuin, a Northumbrian cleric and noted intellectual resident in Charlemagne's France, wrote on hearing of the Lindisfarne raid that 'such a voyage was not thought possible'.

It was not just coasts that were vulnerable to this sort of raiding either. The narrow keels of longships made them river-going as well as ocean-going vessels. Over the course of the Viking Age the rivers of Britain would become highways for raiders, and the Vikings would prowl down the Seine as far as Paris.

Then there was the Heathen-Men's lack of Christianity. By the 790s Christianity was firmly established in western Europe, and with a universal belief in the same God came an almost equally universal respect for the Church and its institutions. It was this faith in the sanctity of religious sites that meant that valuable treasures could be stored in relatively isolated and essentially undefended monasteries and abbeys on islands like Iona or indeed Lindisfarne. It was the Vikings' tendency to attack religious sites which occasioned the loudest outrage from western Europeans rather than the violence of the raids themselves.

It also took a surprisingly long time for the residents of such sites to realise that things had fundamentally changed. Iona Abbey had been founded by St Columba in 563 and it grew into an important centre of Christian learning and teaching for Ireland, Scotland and northern England in the century and a half afterwards. It was first raided in 795: just two years after the raid on Lindisfarne, the Vikings were now active on the other British coast. It was raided again in 802. In 806 the Vikings hit it for a third time, this time killing sixty-eight monks in what subsequently became known as Martyrs' Bay. Remarkably it was only after a fourth raid in 825 created a new set of martyrs that the survivors decided enough was enough and relocated to a hillfort some 20 miles from the sea in Northern Ireland.

When looking back on the first few decades of Viking raids one is sometimes put in mind of the twentieth-century US bank robber Willie Sutton being asked why he robbed banks and reportedly replying 'because that's where the money is'. Why did the Vikings continually raid coastal monasteries? Because not only was there plenty of treasure to take but they were often essentially undefended.

The economics of the early Viking raids, much like the economics of Willie Sutton more than a thousand years later, are not especially interesting. Robbery is very much a zero-sum game: one person (the robber) ends up better off and the other (the robbed) ends up worse off. Or, as in the case of some of the poor monks of Iona, not only worse off financially but also dead in a newly named Martyr's Bay.

Those first few decades of raids focused on moveable wealth such as coins, silver plate, jewellery, gold – essentially anything that could be put in a sack and moved by a boat. But as time passed not only did the Vikings become more ambitious but the economics of the situation became much more interesting. By Eric Bloodaxe's time, more than a century and a half after the Lindisfarne raid, the Vikings were not just raiders – although they still, like our old friend Eric, did a fair amount of that. By the tenth century they were more than occasional pirates, they were settlers and invaders too. In the 860s Viking tactics in Britain began to change. 865 saw the landing of what the Anglo-Saxons dubbed the Great Heathen Army. This was no mere raiding force content to throw a gold-encrusted church altar into a bag and carry it off to a waiting longship. This was, as its name suggests, an army come to conquer.

Modern scholars tend to put the size of this so-called Great

Army of invading Northmen in the low thousands. Essentially an army in the early medieval period was roughly comparable in size to the away-fans crowd at a Premier League football match. They were certainly larger numbers than what had come before. That called for a change in defence strategy: dealing with a couple of boats full of armed raiders is one thing, dealing with several thousand armed invaders setting up camp on your land is another. The initial response was the obvious one: raise a few thousand armed men of your own and try to drive them off. But when that failed, the rulers faced with Viking incursions switched tactics and tried something new: paying them to stop. The payments, later generally known as 'Danegeld', transformed both the situation and the economics.

Danegeld and the notion of paying tribute to raiders in the hope they would discontinue acquired a negative reputation. Rudyard Kipling went as far as to commit the arguments against paying such blackmail to verse, writing:

> *It is wrong to put temptation in the path of any nation,*
> *For fear they should succumb and go astray;*
> *So when you are requested to pay up or be molested,*
> *you will find it better policy to say:*
> *'We never pay any-one Dane-geld,*
> *No matter how trifling the cost:*
> *For the end of that game is oppression and shame,*
> *and the nation that plays it is lost.'*

The advice never to give in to bullies is, however, rather easy to hand out when one is not being bullied oneself. Faced with the Viking threat the decision to begin handing over cash in the face of their menaces was an entirely rational one. Alfred the Great is nowadays generally associated with a firm policy of resisting Viking aggression. That is fair, but for much of his reign he recognised that paying tribute was the more sensible approach. Between the late ninth century and the mid-eleventh, English kings frequently found themselves handing over not insubstantial sums. Nor were they alone in so doing. Across the Channel, Frankish kings regularly ignored the later advice of Kipling, as did rulers as far away as the modern Baltic states, the modern Low Countries, the Iberian Peninsula and into modern Russia and Ukraine.

One might assume that handing out large sums of wealth in the face of threats is a net negative for an economy. But that assumption is not necessarily correct. In as much as the data can be reconstructed, the Viking Age is not associated with any decline in economic activity around Europe or even in the North Sea region most exposed to the Viking phenomenon. Indeed, quite the opposite is the case: it would appear that growth in output, trade and population was robust in the ninth to eleventh centuries and very possibly faster than in the couple of centuries before. It may well be the case that the appearance of Viking armies and tribute payments was accompanied not by an economic downturn but by an upswing in activity.

Understanding why requires stepping back a few paces and grasping two fundamentals of the economics of the early medieval world and tribute payment in general. Take 991 as an example. In that year the Danes won a great victory over the Anglo-Saxons at the Battle of Maldon, itself later encapsulated in yet another epic poem of the era. After the Danes asked for their, by now customary, payment of tribute, the Anglo-Saxon leader Byrhtnoth refused, no doubt later endearing himself to Rudyard Kipling. Sadly, this did not do him much good. The Danes won the subsequent battle, Byrhtnoth was killed in the fighting and England agreed to make a payment of 3,300 kilograms of silver.

But what happened to that silver? The Vikings did not

simply bury it like a pirate in a modern children's cartoon. Like a gold-giving Beowulf, much of the wealth was distributed among the members of the Viking force. And they will have used it to purchase goods and services. The crucial thing is that many of those goods and services will have been bought from the people paying the tribute.

As economists came to realise in the twentieth century, the economics of tribute payments is rather more complex than often assumed. In the aftermath of the First World War, when Germany found herself paying steep reparations to Britain, France and the other victorious Allies, John Maynard Keynes and Bertil Ohlin, a Swedish theorist, found themselves debating the impact of this so-called 'transfer problem'. And while the politics and context of Weimar Germany paying war reparations and an early medieval king handing over Danegeld may seem very different, the raw economics of this fiscal transfer from one country to another are not *that* different.

Nowadays it is generally recognised in international macroeconomics that a transfer of financial resources will usually be followed, to a greater or lesser degree, by a transfer in real resources. That is to say that the transfer of over 3,000 kilograms of silver from Anglo-Saxon England to a Danish army will have been followed by the transfer of large quantities of other goods from Anglo-Saxon England to the Scandinavians as that silver was used to purchase goods and services.

In a medieval context these transfers become especially interesting. Unlike a modern economy, the medieval world generally ran, in technical economic terms, well below capacity. The typical inhabitant of medieval Europe, and the vast majority of the population, lived in the countryside and worked in agriculture. They were not part of, in modern terms, a monetised economy. That is to say, they did not work for a wage and then use that cash to purchase things for themselves and their family. Instead, they directly consumed most of what they produced and produced most of what they consumed. Some production in excess of personal consumption was required – to make payments, probably in kind or via compulsory labour, to landlords or to sell – but the amounts were small. Modern business and economic principles such as profit maximisation were not only far from their mind but totally alien to it. If an economy is operating well below potential, as early medieval societies generally did, then an increase in tax can actually stimulate more economic output. So to go back through the steps, if the King of England decided to make a payment to the Danes, then he needed to raise the money by increasing taxes on his subjects. Presented with a higher tax bill than the year before, those subjects might understandably grumble a bit, but would have to work more days than they desired to meet that increased demand. The surplus coming from the countryside would rise.

In other words, tribute payments in the medieval world were not simply a dead weight loss. Instead, by increasing the tax demands on agricultural workers, they may have stimulated more production and led to an increase in economic output. Of course, neither the king forced into making humiliating payments in the face of menaces or the peasant forced into working more days each year would think this increase in output something to celebrate. But, in raw economic terms, the appearance of large groups of foreign violence special-ists demanding Danegeld was not necessarily a completely bad thing.

But this is not the only, nor the most interesting, aspect of the economics of the Vikings. Paying the Danegeld or attempting to fight off the invaders were not the only strategies available to early medieval rulers. The third approach, and one which became common around northern Europe, was a technique familiar to rulers of ancient China: 'use barbarians to fight barbarians'. In slightly drier language, settle a bunch of foreign violence specialists in a coastal area and hope they will deter other foreign violence specialists from trying their luck. It was just such a strategy that led to the origins of the Duchy of Normandy in northern France, and it was a version of this approach that saw early-eleventh-century English kings hiring armies of mercenary Vikings.

All of which leads neatly to a theory associated with the American economist Mancur Olson. One of the founding fathers of institutional economics, he had much to say on the nature of banditry, and the Vikings are in many regards some of history's most successful bandits. Olson's crucial distinction was between a roving bandit and a stationary bandit. Both are still bandits, as the name implies, but their incentives differ sharply. Roving bandits – say, a bunch of Vikings in a ship – are simply out to grab what they can carry and make their way home with no regard for the damage done to those robbed. Being raided by roving bandits, as the monks of Lindisfarne or Iona could no doubt attest, was not an especially pleasant experience. But once a bandit becomes more settled and starts to put down roots, things begin to change. Grabbing the treasure of a monastery and carrying it back to Scandinavia was a lucrative business, but in the long run the rights to levy taxes on, say, the peasants of Normandy and claim some of their surplus production was even more lucrative. Stationary bandits, who intend to stick around for a long time, have no incentive to kill the goose that lays the golden eggs. If anything, they would rather that goose became fatter and healthier and laid a few more golden eggs.

While most people would prefer to be robbed by no kind of bandit at all, given the choice, a stationary one is far preferable to a roving one. Over time stationary bandits begin to look a lot like states. Incentivised as they are to see their new domains prosper, they begin to provide what economists call 'public goods' such as law and order. Poachers, after all, tend to make for excellent gamekeepers. Over the longer run, Vikings proved to be excellent state builders. Perhaps the greatest example of this can be seen in the famous year of 1066. That year saw three competing claimants to the English throne and all of them – Harold Godwinson, the leader of an Anglo-Danish great house; Harald Hardrada, the King of Norway; and William, Duke of the Northmen, settled in coastal France – were to a greater or lesser degree varieties of what earlier Anglo-Saxons would have seen as Vikings.

2

Genghis Khan, Father
of Globalisation

Very few historians would dispute the notion that Genghis
Khan has a decent claim to be regarded as one of the most
significant figures in global history. He created what was then
the largest empire the world had ever seen, and which is still,
depending on how one accounts for it, the second or third
largest. But the Great Khan's legacy stretches well outside
military or even political history. If asked to make a list of truly
influential figures in global economic history, many would
plump for a major theorist such as Adam Smith, the pioneer of
modern economic thinking, or one of the great innovators such
as Robert Stephenson, inventor of the steam engine. A strong
case can be made, though, that Genghis Khan's economic
legacy dwarfs that of almost any other individual. His political
and economic unification of Eurasia makes him the father of
globalisation. And, perhaps inadvertently, the grandfather of
the industrial revolution.

Like the Vikings before them, the Mongols became the
most successful and feared violence specialists of their day.

Also like the Vikings before them, they made the transition from roving to stationary bandits and had a lasting impact on the societies they interacted with. But they did this on a far grander and more unified scale. Understanding the Mongol Empire means understanding the nature, social organisation and resulting economics of the Eurasian Steppe, which stretches for around 5,000 miles from the mouth of the Danube to the Pacific Ocean, from modern-day Hungary all the way to China. It is the largest area of continuous grassland in the world and much of it is semi-arid with long dry summers and thunderstorms in the relatively mild winters. Unlike most of the areas it borders, the soil and climate are unsuited to large-scale agriculture. The major population centres of Eurasia have long been distributed as they are now, with concentrations in the extreme west and east, modern-day Europe and China, and to the south in the Middle East – all areas better able to support more pro-ductive agriculture and hence higher human populations. The settled societies that border the Steppe have regarded it in different ways. At times it has seemed to be an almost impassable desert of grass, the effective edge of the world. At other points, though, it has been more like an ocean, difficult to cross if one does not know what one is doing but capable of linking otherwise distant locations.

The climate and geography of the Steppe are not suited to the sedentary, agricultural populations found elsewhere in Eurasia. The agricultural revolutions, based on the mass culti-vation of grains in western Eurasia and rice in eastern Eurasia, never really happened in the Steppe. Rather than settled communities based initially on hamlets and villages – some of which later grew into towns and eventually cities – social organisation at the time of the Great Khan's birth looked much as it would have done two or even three thousand years before. Communities lived in nomadic groups which moved over the course of the year and based their living standards on hunting and herding.

It is perhaps no surprise that such a different basis of production from that found in western and eastern Eurasia led to the formation of very different models of social organisation. Hunting and herding do not generate as high a surplus as settled agriculture. That lower surplus cannot sustain the kind of large elites to be found in Europe and China. Society on the Steppe was less stratified with relatively smaller elites. Twelfth-century Mongolia lacked anything like the large aristocracies of western Europe or the Mandarin class of contemporary China. Tribes had leaders, of course, and those leaders were no doubt better off than the typical herder or hunter, but the scale of difference in life experiences was much lower. In settled societies, centres of population can become the building blocks of larger political units. At a very basic level, the elite of one village can come to dominate those of a neighbouring one. Keep doing that for a few generations and you have something which starts to look like a small kingdom. That process, though, is much trickier in an environment where the centres of population are not stationary but constantly on the move. Tribal confederations do emerge, but they also have a tendency to splinter.

The crucial thing to grasp about the nature of Steppe society is that it does not exist in a vacuum. The peoples of the great Eurasian plain have long interacted with those around them. Sometimes that interaction has taken the form of trade with the Steppe people providing meat or leather or animal pelts in return for the produce of settled agriculture or manufactured goods. At other times it has had a more distinctly violent edge, with people from the Steppe taking what they require rather than bartering for it. But whether through raiding or trading, the people of the Steppe have always sought access to the goods produced by settled societies around them.

This was the world into which Temujin, known to history as Genghis Khan, was born at some point in the late 1150s or early 1160s. The circumstances of his birth and adolescence were marked by what could at best be described as mixed blessings. On the one hand, he was the son of a chieftain and the descendant of a particularly revered war leader. But on the other, his father died while he was still a child, and he and his family were left on the Steppe by their tribe in exile. The first couple of decades of Temujin's life are hard to reconstruct and it is likely he spent some of that time in service to the Jin dynasty in China. The historical record becomes clearer in the mid-1190s. By then Temujin was back on the Steppe and leading a group of warriors. By the very early 1200s he had become sole ruler of the eastern Steppe, and he took the title Genghis Khan around 1206. More than eight hundred years later, the exact meaning of this title is still disputed. Some contend it has no real meaning and was simply a name; others claim that the word Genghis has some connotation of strength or righteousness; some linguists see a Turkic root and believe it may translate as something like 'master of the ocean'. Given that the people of Eurasia believed an ocean surrounded what they thought was the world's sole landmass, this could be taken to mean 'universal ruler'. If this is indeed the meaning of the term, it would have seemed an outrageous boast in 1206, but by the time of his death in 1227 it would have sounded rather less ridiculous. Within two decades of uniting the people of Mongolia, Genghis Khan had conquered northern China and expanded westwards as far as modern-day Georgia and Ukraine. By the beginning of the fourteenth century, his successors ruled all of the territory stretching from modern China to modern

Hungary, as far south as into present-day Iran, Iraq and Turkey and as far north as the Baltic shores of Russia.

All of which poses two questions. What was it that made Mongol armies so staggeringly successful? And how were Genghis Khan and his successors able to organise a previously disparate group of nomadic tribes into a world-conquering empire? The answers to both are closely related: the Great Khan and his successors showed a shrewd understanding of incentives and used this understanding to create and shape lasting institutions.

Central to Mongol warfare and central to life on the Steppe in general was the horse. The horse was the great enabler of the nomadic lifestyle, the crucial tool that allowed herding and hunting to work. The people of the Steppe learned to ride from an early age and spent hours every day of their lives in the saddle. Their horsemanship was without parallel. But so too was the raw number of horses they controlled. In 1206 when he was proclaimed Genghis Khan, Temujin ruled around a million people, but perhaps five million horses. By the year 1300 the Mongol Empire controlled around ten million horses – something like half of all the horses to be found on earth.

Horsemanship goes some of the way to explain both the tactical success Mongol armies regularly enjoyed on the battlefield and the strategic mobility which regularly confounded their opponents. But the easy availability of fresh remounts was probably the larger factor. For every soldier in the Khan's armies there were perhaps as many as twenty horses. That allowed their armies to advance at a pace of up to 50 or 60 miles a day, at a time when their enemies would struggle to manage 10.

The bulk of the Mongol armies took the form of mounted horse archers, able to fire quickly and accurately without dismounting. They could use their superior speed and mobility to control the pace of an engagement, firing repeated volleys until the enemy was disordered and only then moving in for the kill.

But while the Mongols were the masters of this form of warfare in the thirteenth and fourteenth centuries, it was historically nothing new. Hordes of well-mounted horse archers from the Steppe had been known to both the Roman Empire and Qin dynasty China. An army of Genghis Khan's Mongols was not that different, on the battlefield, from Attila's Huns some 750 years previously.

Explanations of imperial success in the pre-industrial world which rely on some form of tactical innovation or piece of military technology or even some sort of gift for warfare among a particular people are never likely to be the whole story. The Mongol's endowment with half of the world's horse population is a necessary criterion, but not a sufficient one, to explain what they achieved. Understanding the empire that Genghis built means looking away from the battlefield.

Genghis Khan certainly had a talent for war. But he had an even more impressive gift for organisation. His truly great talent was to form a political union in the most difficult of circumstances. The methods through which he achieved this have sometimes been thought of as a form of social revolution on the Steppe. Fundamentally, and unusually for his time, the Great Khan was a true meritocrat. Promotion in the empire which he built was open to all those with talent, as long as they stayed loyal.

Specialisation in violence came naturally on the Steppe. Life there bred people good on a horse and good with a bow, and the weak were even less likely to survive than in more settled societies. But the potential rewards available to these violence specialists were relatively low. As already noted, herding and hunting simply do not generate much in the way of economic surplus. Raiding one's more settled neighbours could prove to be more lucrative, but also came with more danger. Genghis Khan showed that uniting the existing nomadic tribes and pooling their resources could hugely expand the potential pool of rewards open to these Steppe violence specialists.

The first step was to break down the old traditional structures based on family ties and kinship groups. In return for accepting a place in an agreed hierarchy, potential followers would have access to new rewards. This eventually became a formal system. At the very top of society under the so-called *khubi*, the rulers of distant parts of the empire were entitled to formal shares of each other's booty. So the ruler of Mongol China would send porcelain and medicine west to Persia, while whoever happened to be ruling Persia would send back in return spices, jewels and pearls. As well as moving horizontally between the leaders at the top, booty cascaded vertically down through the ranks with each warrior being entitled to their own share based on their rank and performance.

In economic terms, the Mongol tribes were benefiting from an economy of scale. While any individual tribe had been able to raid and take booty from its neighbours, the power of all the tribes united together was worth far more than the sum of their parts. Mongol society was reorganised into groups of around one thousand people from previously different tribes breaking old traditional links and reordering kinship groups.

All Mongol men aged between sixteen and sixty were potentially subject to military conscription. The Great Khan could put an army of perhaps 100,000 in the field, a very large number for its time but still one dwarfed by the number of subject peoples. In effect, society was transformed from small tribes of hunters and herdsmen who occasionally raided their neighbours into a cohesive confederation which specialised not in hunting or herding, but in extracting payments from neighbours and subjects. Given access to 100,000 mounted and effective violence specialists and half the world's horses, the Mongols proceeded to build their empire.

The nature of imperial Mongol rule varied from location to location and geography to geography, but the empire is best thought of as one based on tribute. Unlike, say, the earlier Roman Empire or the later British Empire, Genghis Khan and his successors were not primarily interested in the control of territory, nor did they move around Eurasia appointing colonial administrators to rule subject peoples. Indeed, the best way to conceive of the empire is as akin to a mafia protection racket. Peoples who had been 'conquered' – that is to say, militarily defeated but not necessarily occupied – were expected to make regular payments of tribute and as long as these payments continued to flow could go about things much as they wanted. For example, in the areas that are now modern-day Russia and Ukraine, native princes and bishops continued to rule and religion was fundamentally unchanged as long as those rulers kept up their regular extortion payments to the Mongol overlords. This was the time still spoken of in Russia as being 'under the Tartar yoke'. By contrast, large swathes of China and Iran were subject to more traditional direct imperial rule, although in both cases with a great deal of involvement from former members of the local elite.

The new imperial overlords also showed an unusual degree of openness to ideas from their subject people and the ability to combine them in pragmatic ways. Take something as straightforward as setting the date. Running an empire that stretches for the best part of 5,000 miles and includes dozens of different peoples and calendar systems makes administration difficult. Kublai Khan established the Academy for Calendrical Studies with experts drawn from across his territories to establish tables of dating equivalence and then used Chinese technology to have the results mass-printed and distributed.

In warfare too the Mongols were open to new ideas. Their form of mass cavalry army was ideal for the kind of fighting that took place on the Steppe and proved capable of beating the then conventional armies of their Middle Eastern, Chinese or European enemies. But it was generally incapable of overcoming fortifications or castles. Not even a horseman bred in the saddle with access to twenty remounts can leap over a castle wall. So Mongol armies routinely brought Chinese engineers and practitioners of siege-craft along with them. Local labourers would be put to work under these engineers to produce the catapults and trebuchets needed to overcome European or Persian defences.

Both the process of Mongol conquest and subsequent Mongol rule could be brutal. Their invasions of China in the early thirteenth century may have killed between twenty and forty million people, perhaps a quarter of the population. A look back over their law codes shows the death penalty as surprisingly ubiquitous. Even common theft was a capital offence. Nor was the concept of booty limited to goods such as spices, agricultural produce or precious metals. Common people might find themselves enslaved. And at times Mongol armies showed a certain habit for rounding up craftsmen, doctors, astronomers, mathematicians, translators and anyone who might prove useful to be reallocated across the empire. That openness to new knowledge and ideas was not necessarily always beneficial to the people who happened to know something useful.

None of this should come as a surprise; the people who tend to primarily benefit from a mafia protection racket are, after all, the members of the mafia. But, as anyone who has watched more than a few episodes of *The Sopranos* knows, there are some benefits to the 'protection' provided by gangsters. Marco Polo, who visited the empire during Kublai Khan's rule, was struck by the provision of a form of social insurance against crop failures and natural disasters – something mostly lacking in the Europe of his day. As he wrote, 'if the people are afflicted by any dearth through unfavourable seasons or storms, or locusts, or any like calamity, no taxes are exacted for that year or he causes them to be supplied with corn of his own for food and seed'. Like any successful set of stationary bandits, the Mongols realised that it was in their own long-term interest for the people they were robbing to prosper.

But social insurance was not the only silver lining to the, admittedly rather large, cloud of Mongol rule. Genghis Khan and his successors took public order and security seriously. Trade routes were patrolled by the equivalent of a mounted police force and there were provisions in the legal codes for returning stolen goods. They even organised a kind of lost and found service for goods travelling along the old Silk Road.

The political unification of Eurasia under Genghis Khan and his successors led to a profound economic change. Modern economic historians looking back on the era now sometimes refer to a Pax Mongolia, a century or so of relative peace between 1250 and 1350 during which travel between China and Europe was reasonably safe.

The nomadic people of the Steppe had always been involved in trade; exchanging animals and animal products for craft items or grain had been at the core of their existence for thousands of years before the Khan's empire arose. As rulers of Eurasia they took trade promotion seriously too, not just by providing security on the trade routes, but through actively seeking to boost the social standing of merchants and to attract new ones. In Mongol China the official standing of merchants was raised to among the highest of all professions, just below that of government officials. Merchants served as import functionaries in the empire, often acting as key advisers to war leaders when dealing with foreign powers or local people. At first contact with new merchants from a potential new trading partner it was customary to pay two or even three times as much as goods were worth in the hope of encouraging repeat business.

Nor was this the limit of their efforts at trade promotion. To speed communication within their empire and improve imperial rule and coordination, the *yam* postal system was put in place. Every 20 to 30 miles a station was built containing fresh horses; messengers could ride at the gallop between stations knowing a fresh remount would be available. By the 1300s, this system had been opened up to merchants too. Once again, Marco Polo was impressed: 'at each of these stations used by the messengers there is a large and handsome building with fine beds and all other necessary articles'.

There was also the creation of something like a common currency across the empire. The use of Chinese paper money was expanded and the law stated that (and this will come as no surprise to anyone paying attention to Mongol legal codes) the penalty for refusing to accept it was death. Weights and measures too were standardised across the empire, further aiding trade.

Marco Polo may have been the most famous European visitor to China in this era, but he was far from alone. The combination of security, infrastructure and an openness to trade created the first great era of globalisation. A Florentine commercial handbook written in the early 1340s noted that the land route from Crimea to Beijing was 'perfectly safe, whether by day or by night'. Although the journey may have been safe it was hardly short: it would still take between eight and eleven months to make. Given the distances involved, only goods with a very high ratio of value to weight made the trek from one end of the Mongol Empire to the other. Spices, silk, furs and slaves would move very long distances, but it does appear there were fairly extensive regional markets for bulkier and lower-value items such as grain, olive oil and timber. While detailed economic statistics for the thirteenth and fourteenth centuries are obviously lacking, it is notable that by the end of Mongol rule even small towns and villages were now paying their tribute in the form of silver rather than goods. That suggests they were closely tied into a trading system to earn the silver in the first place and points to the benefits of the Pax Mongolia being experienced down to the local level.

If one did have the time to spend the best part of two years on a round trip from Europe to China, the rewards were immense. The Florentine handbook reckoned that travel costs, custom duties and purchasing expenses for a typical trade caravan making the journey from one end of Eurasia to another might amount to 3,500 florins but that the resulting haul could be sold in Europe for more like 25,000 florins. Given those potential returns, it is unsurprising that many made the journey. The experience of making vast riches through long-distance trade in the thirteenth and fourteenth centuries was to prove very important to European developments in later years. It elevated the status of merchants and increased the amount of capital at their disposal. It may well be that without the Mongol-induced trade boom of this time there would have been no later voyages by the likes of Vasco da Gama and Christopher Columbus.

Nor was it just goods on the move; ideas flowed both ways too. Chinese doctors, for example, learned surgical techniques first practised in the Middle East, while their Middle Eastern equivalents learned from Chinese advances in pharmacology. Less helpfully for future human happiness, it was during this time that the Chinese invention of gunpowder first made its way to Europe.

The actual number of people and the volume of goods on the move were much smaller in this first stage of globalisation than in subsequent ones. Political unification and the security it provided was important, but transport costs remained pro-hibitive compared to later centuries. The impact, though, was profound – especially if one looks to how it differed at the two far ends of Eurasia.

Medieval Europe was close enough to benefit from the enhanced trade but distant enough to be spared conquest and incorporation into the Mongol protection racket. Mongol forces did push into Europe from the 1220s to the 1240s and while light reconnaissance units may have made it as far as modern-day Germany, most of the fighting took place in Hungary and Croatia. At the Battle of Mohi, fought in 1241 in the Kingdom of Hungary, a conventional European force of armoured, mounted knights accompanied by footmen with crossbows and melee weapons suffered around ten thousand casualties, perhaps half their overall size, while facing a smaller Mongol army. European military tactics were simply unable to cope with an enemy so different from anything they had fought for centuries. A fully armoured knight, as we will see in later chapters, could be a terrifying opponent on the battlefield. But if the enemy used superior mobility to hold their distance while continually firing arrows, then they could be of little use.

The Mongols won many such victories over the Europeans, but Europe was never conquered by them. The reason for the ultimate failure of the invasions of the west is sometimes blamed on the death of a Khan requiring the invading forces to head back to the centre to dispute the succession. This, though, is deeply unsatisfying. It begs the rather obvious question, why didn't they keep coming back? The real reason

Europe was never conquered or subject to large tribute payments is simply that it was too far from the Mongol centre of power. Armies operating in Hungary were at the edge of their logistical train and the further west they headed the less conducive the territory was to their mounted tactics.

While the ten thousand dead at Mohi would no doubt question this judgement, Europe in general got to experience the upsides of the Pax Mongolia and the booming of long-term trade without the downsides of being directly incorporated into the system.

The story was very different at the eastern end of Eurasia. As viewed through a Chinese lens, the Pax Mongolia was far less beneficial. The initial conquest was catastrophic, with millions killed. It took Chinese agriculture several generations to recover from the death of workers and the conversion of much previously agricultural land into grazing and hunting grounds for their new overlords. For the better part of 150 years they were subject to tax and tribute payments. What is more, as one of the most advanced societies on earth at the time, they gained far less from the exchange of ideas. The so-called Four Great Inventions – gunpowder, the compass, paper-making and printing – spread from China to the rest of Eurasia. It is hard to think of anything on that scale that was gained in return.

This differing impact of the Pax Mongolia would have important consequences in the centuries that followed. It left western Eurasia, and in particular Europe, economically stronger and more outward-looking after seeing the potential riches to be found abroad. But it left China both weakened and more understandably suspicious of those from outside its borders.

Being the father of the first great age of globalisation and helping to set Europe and China on paths that would define the following centuries of global economic history are surely enough to stake Genghis Khan's claim as one of the most significant figures in global economic history.

And he almost certainly played a rather inadvertent role in the industrial revolution, the defining moment of global economic take-off, too. For it was not just goods, people and ideas moving along the old Silk Road, it was disease as well. The Pax Mongolia created what one letter writer has dubbed 'a Trans-Eurasian common market in microbes'. The disease we now call the Black Death made its way along the Silk Road from China to Crimea, where it probably boarded a Genoese vessel and found its way to Europe. Between 1348 and 1351, something like twenty-five million Europeans out of a total population of eighty million died. While the short-term consequences, in both human and economic terms, were no doubt catastrophic, one impact was of lasting importance: the death of quarter of the population left Europe short of workers. That increased the bargaining power of labour and sent wages on an upwards course. Faced with rising labour costs, Europeans increasingly looked for ways to substitute capital for workers. The end result, a few centuries later, was something we now call the industrial revolution.

3

Why Medieval Rulers Were Right to Choose Inferior Weapons

If life is a lottery, then Edward III, Duke of Bar, seemed to be born one of its winners. In general, the prospects for anyone drawing their first breath in modern-day France in the year 1377 were not especially good. Overall life expectancy was forty. And that was not just because of a very high infant mortality rate; even someone surviving until the age of twenty could probably only expect another twenty-five years of life. Those years would generally be filled with hard work, no real prospect of social or economic advancement and certainly no hope of a comfortable retirement. But Edward was born into the nobility. He could realistically expect not only a longer life, but a healthier and more fulfilling one with a real prospect of potential advancement.

His childhood and adolescence saw him prepared for his role in life. He would have learned to read and write not only in French but in Latin as well. But while he would have enjoyed an existence of almost unimaginable luxury and culture compared to the peasants working the farms of his great estates, he was also raised to be a violence specialist. The nobility of fourteenth- and fifteenth-century western Europe had access to great levels of wealth and enjoyed a powerful position within society. But they also owed an obligation to their king to lead men into battle on his behalf.

By the end of his twenties Edward had fought in a dozen battles as part of the ongoing war between England and France. By 1415, at the age of thirty-eight – a veritable old man by the standards of the time – he was an experienced soldier. At the Battle of Agincourt that year he commanded one of the three divisions of the French army. At that battle he would have worn the finest armour available – a full plate suit, almost certainly crafted in Italy or Germany – while many of the men of his division would have had to make do with perhaps a helmet or shield and maybe a chainmail tunic or a leather jerkin. Quite how much that impressive suit of armour would have cost is hard to estimate. The Europe of this time was not monetised like the modern world; that is to say, not every item could necessarily be bought or sold for a certain value. But if such a suit of armour had been available to the wider peasantry, it may well have cost something like five hundred times their annual income; the well-bred and well-fed charger on which he was mounted was probably worth an additional two hundred peasants' annual incomes. When the European nobility of the later medieval period went to war, they certainly did not do so on the cheap.

In the end, this lavish spending did him no good. On 25 October 1415 – St Crispin's Day, as fans of Shakespeare will know – Edward fell on the field of Agincourt while fighting a numerically inferior English army. He was not alone: two of his brothers also perished that day, as did the Constable of France, the Master of the Royal Household, two other dukes, five counts and ninety barons. It was the single bloodiest day the French nobility has ever suffered.

We do not know precisely who killed Edward at Agincourt but we know he was felled by an arrow fired from an English longbow, and we can reasonably guess that whoever fired it almost certainly could not read English, let alone Latin.

Missile (as opposed to melee) weapons have always had a place on the battlefield. They offer the rather obvious advantage that you can engage your opponent without standing right next to them. Over the long span of recorded human military history, at least some component of every army has usually been equipped with them. But for a few centuries after the year 600 or so they seem to have become less common in western European armies. While some lightly equipped skirmishers may have been armed with a short bow or a sling, the nature of battle had begun to change. Shields became larger and heavier – they were much more difficult to penetrate with missile weapons, particularly if the opposing infantry bunched together forming a shield wall and protected each other with their shields. Melee weapons dominated the battlefields of the west in the seventh to tenth centuries, as Europe's closely formed bodies of infantry and later cavalry clashed in vicious hand-to-hand fighting.

But from the late 900s onwards, missile weapons began to reappear in greater numbers on western European battlefields. Especially common was the crossbow. While the Romans had been familiar with crossbows, there were almost no references to them in European literature from the fifth to the tenth centuries. They appear to have dropped out of fashion and then been rediscovered just before the turn of the first millennium. They began to reappear in large numbers in late tenth-century France and many were certainly present in William the Conqueror's army at the Battle of Hastings in 1066, as shown on the Bayeux Tapestry.

Compared to the humble bow, the crossbow seems to offer

many advantages. Like a bow, the basic principle is to use an elastic drawstring to propel a projectile forward with great force. In the case of the crossbow, however, a winch can be used to pull back the string and a lock employed to keep this in place, maintaining the tension before it is fired. It would take someone with almost superhuman levels of strength to be able to fire an arrow from a common bow at any sort of range with the level of force required to be able to penetrate heavy armour. But the introduction of the winch changed the physics. Someone of moderate strength could wind up a crossbow to the point where it fired with enough force to penetrate armour at a couple of hundred metres. And because a mechanical lock rather than raw human effort was maintaining the tension, a crossbow-armed soldier could devote more effort to aiming before loosing their shot.

The weapon was a potential game-changer in European warfare. Following the French lead, crossbowmen began to appear in armies across the continent. As might be imagined, the weapon was not initially very popular with noblemen. The best armour that money could buy was no longer adequate protection against a weapon that could be wielded by a peasant.

Crossbows provoked strong feelings. In 1096, Pope Urban II went as far as to ban their use against fellow Christians on pain of excommunication and eternal damnation. No one paid much attention. Indeed, papal armies regularly used crossbows when fighting fellow Christian Italians. The crossbow was here to stay and it became more and more common across Europe. All the way until the introduction of handheld gunpowder weapons in the fifteenth and sixteenth centuries, specialised companies of crossbowmen, especially from Italy and the Low Countries, were available to hire.

But Edward of Bar was not killed by a crossbow in 1415, he

was killed by a longbow. By 1415, this had been the distinctive English weapon for more than two centuries.

Whereas a typical shortbow measures perhaps 2 feet 6 inches to 3 feet long, the longbow, as its name suggests, is longer. Much longer. The examples recovered from the evacuation of the sunken *Mary Rose*, a Tudor warship, ranged from 6 feet 2 inches to 6 feet 11 inches in length, with an average of six and a half feet. Or in other words, considerably longer than the average person at the time. Holding such a long weapon at arm's length and then drawing the string all the way back would allow a missile to be fired with incredible levels of power.

The longbow appeared to offer many advantages over the more common crossbow. It achieved a higher rate of armour penetration and at slightly longer ranges. But the really big advantage lay in the rate of fire. A well-trained crossbowman could fire perhaps twice a minute, but an experienced long-bowman could fire an aimed shot every five or so seconds. Stacked against those advantages was one considerable disad-vantage: while pretty much anyone could be taught to use a crossbow relatively quickly – hence the noble outrage at their widespread introduction – learning to use a longbow took a lot of effort.

Longbows had been around for a long time by the Battle of Agincourt. The oldest examples found by archaeologists are in fact more than four thousand years old. But their widespread use in English armies was more recent. The Welsh had put them to good use even as they were conquered by Norman England. The Welsh use was certainly enough to impress the English kings and by the thirteenth century they had become the standard English missile weapon.

Training longbowmen was no easy matter. Archaeologists can recognise the skeletons of longbow archers by their enlarged left arms and wrists and oversized right fingers.

Mastering the weapon took hours of practice each week, practice so intense it changed the shape of one's body. The development of that practice can be traced back through English law codes. Initially, that training must have led to some rather unfortunate accidents: a law from the time of Henry I (King of England from 1100 to 1135) specifically absolved anyone from a charge of murder if they accidentally killed someone while practising with a longbow. The Assize of Arms of 1252 encouraged all Englishmen to own and train with one and made it compulsory for anyone worth more than 40 shillings. Edward I (1272–1307) went even further and banned any sport except archery on Sundays. In 1363, Edward III seemed to encourage this beyond Sundays with a declaration that 'Every man, if he be able bodied shall upon holidays, make use in his games of bows and arrows, and so learn and practise archery'. Legally, at least, longbowmanship was certainly the national pastime. Further encouragement to practise archery came from local nobles regularly organising archery contests, often with large financial prizes.

The national pastime was put to good use in many battles over this period, against both the French and the Scottish. In 1333, at Halidon Hill, eight thousand English soldiers faced fifteen thousand Scots. The result was a massacre. Of the Scottish. At that battle, King Edward III of England arranged his army at the top of the hill. As the larger Scottish army began to advance, the English fired down volley after volley of arrows. As one modern historian put it, they rained down arrows 'as thickly as the rays in sunlight hitting the Scots in such a way that they struck them down in hordes and thinning them to the point of defeat'. After the Scots had suffered many casualties and become disordered, the English charged downhill and routed them. The Scottish dead numbered in the thousands, while just fourteen Englishmen perished.

Nor are Halidon Hill and Agincourt isolated examples. Between 1298 and 1453 the English fought twenty-five major battles against either the French or Scottish, with a major battle being defined as having at least five thousand participants. In more than half of those battles the English were outnumbered, sometimes by a ratio of five or six to one, and yet the English emerged victorious in eighteen of those encounters.

At Crécy in 1346, an English army of fourteen thousand, including eleven thousand longbowmen, faced a French army of thirty thousand, with perhaps twelve thousand crossbowmen, many of them Italian mercenaries. The battle began with a ranged missile duel but very quickly the longbow's superior rate of fire proved telling and the French infantry were forced to pull back. The French attempted a cavalry charge with their mounted knights, but it proved no more effective in the face of repeated volleys of arrows. One estimate puts the French dead at ten thousand, including 1,200 knights and eleven princes of France. The English dead numbered in the hundreds.

It is therefore hard to avoid the conclusion that the longbow was a vastly superior weapon to the crossbow. That has certainly become the consensus view of later historians who have subsequently puzzled over the question: if the longbow was so obviously superior, why did the French and Scottish not adopt its use?

Most of the obvious possible answers can be dismissed. It might be argued that learning to use the longbow was simply too much effort. There is absolutely no doubt that becoming proficient with the longbow took an awful lot more time than becoming proficient with a crossbow. But there is equally no doubt that the effort was worth it. Fourteenth-century Englishmen possessed no comparative advantage over their contemporary Scottish or French opponents in terms of physical size or ability to train. Had the French or Scottish kings wanted their own longbowmen, they could have produced them.

Some have argued that the longbow's initial use in Wales reflected its usefulness as a hunting weapon in forested areas. That may well be true, but it still does not resolve the puzzle. Over the period of the bow's dominance, most of its users were English, not Welsh. The geography of northern England is not radically different from that of southern Scotland, nor is that of south-east England from north-west France. And anyway, decades of royal legislation show that longbow skills can be taught and learned.

It could perhaps be argued that maybe the French and Scottish failed to see that the longbow was the superior weapon – they did not deliberately choose the inferior option, they simply made a mistake. This too seems unlikely. The so-called Hundred Years' War between England and France actually lasted longer than a century and that should be enough time to learn. Furthermore, historical documents from both France and Scotland show that their nobility were acutely aware of the power of the longbow.

Another possibility is that longbows were simply too expensive. But the price of a crossbow was roughly six times as high as that of a longbow. The longbow was not only the superior weapon, it was much cheaper.

Two economists, Douglas W. Allen and Peter T. Leeson, have presented the best answer to the puzzle, one that steps back from the battlefield and looks at institutions and incentives.

To be truly effective, they argue, the longbow needed to be used en masse. To gain the advantages of the superiority of the longbow, an army needed a great many longbowmen firing volleys in unison. But it is very clear that given a free choice, not many private individuals would choose to gain the necessary skills to use them. People presumably had other things to do with their Sundays, enjoyed other sports and did not want to deform their left arms and right hands. Gaining access to the necessary number of skilled archers required something like that seen in England: a centralised, top-down, state-driven agenda to create a culture of archery. The real choice faced by rulers was not 'Do I want a few longbowmen in my army?' but 'Do I want to inculcate a culture of archery throughout my realm?'

Impacting on that choice was a crucial feature of longbows. They were both cheap and easy to make. It seems likely that most English longbowmen made their own; given access to some decent wood and enough time it would not have proved too difficult. By contrast, producing a crossbow was not only more expensive, it also required more specialist skills. A typical yeoman farmer of the thirteenth or fourteenth century could certainly craft their own longbow. They probably could not manufacture their own crossbow.

This, then, is the real crux of the problem. Choosing between the longbow and the crossbow was not simply a case of picking a weapon for the battlefield. It was about deciding whether or not you wanted a significant proportion of your adult male population to be trained in the use of a powerful weapon which they would be able to produce for themselves relatively easily. That the kings of England made a different choice from the kings of France or Scotland tells us something interesting about the institutional framework in which they operated. In this case, institutions had driven the selection of a particular technology.

Medieval kings faced two potential kinds of threat: an external threat from their neighbours and a potential internal threat from their nobles and vassals. In making the longbow-versus-crossbow choice they were really making an implicit trade-off between internal and external security. Opting for the longbow, with its eminently superior battlefield performance, offered a boost to external security, especially if your neighbours were still using the crossbow. But that increase in external security came at a potential cost to internal security. Any noble wishing to rise against you would now have access to a large body of men trained at your encouragement and able to provide themselves with the necessary tools to dominate the battlefield. By contrast, opting for the crossbow did come with a real cost in terms of external security and inferior battlefield performance, but it also increased internal security by denying nobles access to trained longbowmen.

Whether a ruler would prioritise internal or external security depended on their incentives. Who did they really fear most? Their own nobles or their neighbours?

The more stable the institutions of the kingdom were, the more likely it was able to adopt the superior military technology. If one was attempting to describe the France of the fourteenth and fifteenth centuries, 'stable' is hardly the first word one would reach for. It is worth remembering that English kings were fighting the Hundred Years' War not in their capacity as kings of England, but in their role as dukes of Aquitaine and claimants for the throne of France. In the words of one modern historian, the France of this era was more a nation of principalities than a kingdom; 'the land was divided into loose and shifting territories that had little or no allegiance to any central authority, ruled across large swathes by noblemen who were little more than warlords'. Sometimes some of these nobles even changed sides and threw in their lot with the English. Large and rich areas of the country such as Brittany and Flanders were semi-independent. In other words, looking at the institutional structure of their domains, any sensible French monarch was incentivised to prioritise internal security.

They, or at least the people around them, also seemed to have been aware of this. Charles VI (King of France from 1380 to 1422) did briefly decide to experiment with the longbow before swiftly shifting back to the crossbow. As the contemporary chronicler Juvénal des Ursins wrote in 1430:

> After a short period of time, French Archers became so proficient in archery that they overcame their fear of shooting the English, and they all started practising archery and crossbow shooting. And in fact, if they got together they would have been more powerful than princes and nobles, and the King declared that such practice should stop. And there should only be a certain number of archers.

Scotland too was marked by dynastic instability, to which can be added a geography which makes centralising power difficult – ruling the Highlands has troubled leaders for the better part of 2,000 years at least – and the added schism between speakers of Gaelic and English hardly helped. The process by which Robert the Bruce became king began with thirteen competing claimants. Indeed, several of the major battles of this period were not really between England and Scotland, but between competing Scottish claimants for their throne, one of whom was backed by England.

Calling the England of this era 'stable' may be too much of a stretch, but it was without doubt more stable than its near rivals. Its borders were at least settled and had been for a long time and, with the important exception of Wales, no territory ruled by the English kings wished to break away. The Great Charter (known as Magna Carta) of 1215 had formalised the duties and obligations of the king and their leading nobles towards each other. Two sets of civil wars (the First and Second Barons Wars), fought over just such issues, showed that writing something down did not necessarily make it true, but from around 1300 until around 1450, the real century and a half of the longbow's total dominance of western European warfare, English domestic politics were in the main stable. Compellingly for the theory on internal v. external security trade-offs in weapons selection, the longer that period of relative stability lasted, the higher the proportion of longbowmen in English armies. In the early 1300s they made up around 10 per cent of the typical English army, but that had risen above 50 per cent by the middle of the century.

Choosing an obviously inferior weapon may seem like completely irrational behaviour. But if a ruler faced an unstable domestic set of institutions, and choosing the superior weapon would weaken their internal security, it suddenly becomes very rational indeed. The incentives of rulers are shaped by the threats they actually face, and which are more pressing. For the kings of both Scotland and France, who always had to keep one wary eye on their own nobles, the price of an inferior battlefield performance against the English was one worth paying. When it comes to working out what someone's incentives are, the economic notion of 'revealed preference' is especially useful. If you want to know what someone thinks, look at what they do.

By 1450 or so, the age of the longbow was coming to an end. The heavy plate armour worn by the elite of an army was now mostly steel rather than iron. Even a well-trained longbowman would struggle to penetrate it. And it was at this time, too, that England's domestic stability began to unravel. The Wars of the Roses, a series of English civil wars lasting from the 1450s until the 1480s, would provide plenty of evidence that French chroniclers had been right and that giving nobles access to trained longbowmen could make some powerful enemies of the Crown. The kind of noble casualty lists that the French had racked up at Agincourt and Crécy would be repeated in England in subsequent battles at St Albans, Towton and Bosworth.

4

How Gold and Silver
Made Spain Poor

Philip II of Spain really was the first person of whom you could say that he ruled an empire over which the sun never set. King of Spain from 1556, he was also King of Portugal, Naples and Sicily, and from 1554 until 1558, via his marriage to Mary I, King of England too. That was on top of his titles as Duke of Milan and Lord of the Seventeen Provinces of the Netherlands. All of that would be a big enough domain for most rulers and more than enough to guarantee his slot in the history books. But Philip inherited the Spanish Crown just as it was completing the conquest of central America begun under his father. In 1565 Spanish forces crossed the Pacific from Mexico and began their conquest of an archipelago that was to be named in honour of their distant king: the Philippines. Once a handful of possessions on the North African coast were added to the total, Philip found himself ruling an empire that stretched over five continents.

Much of this was a dynastic accident. Philip's father, Charles, had found himself – via a series of rather unlikely

chances and unfortunate early deaths – the heir to all four
of his grandfathers. Under Charles, later known as Charles
the Great, the various lands across Europe ruled by the
different branches of the Habsburg family would be united.
He was simultaneously King of a newly united Spain, having
inherited both the Aragonese and Castilian thrones, and
the Holy Roman Emperor of Germany. This was to prove a
solid basis for a bid for Habsburg mastery in Europe in the
first half of the sixteenth century, one that would continue
under Philip.

Unfortunately for the Habsburg family in the long run,
the clan drew the wrong lessons from the potential power
of this united inheritance. While all European royal houses
engaged in a fair bit of inter-marrying, the Habsburgs were
to take this to extremes. The seating plans at a sixteenth- or
seventeenth-century Habsburg marriage ceremony would
be relatively simple to draw up; there would certainly be no
need to divide the party into the family of the groom and
the family of the bride. The last Habsburg King of Spain,
Charles II, died heirless in 1700. His own parents were uncle
and niece and both themselves born to first cousins. He had
an underbite so large that he struggled to chew and a tongue
so large he struggled to talk. After his death the coroner
noted that 'his heart was the size of a peppercorn, his lungs
corroded, his intestines rotten and gangrenous; he had a
single testicle, black as coal'. Unsurprisingly his own rule was
not especially successful.

Back in the 1550s the eventual results of this interbreed-
ing lay in the future. Philip ascended to his thrones as the
ruler of a leading world power and one that seemed ideally
placed to reap the benefits of the European discoveries in
the Americas.

In the 1550s, anyone taking an educated guess at which

areas of Europe would emerge as the global economic winners in later centuries would likely point to Philip's core domains. The most straightforward reason to think that in the future the Mediterranean would be Europe's centre of economic gravity was that it always had been, and there seemed no reason for things to change. The climate was able to support a relatively intense level of highly productive agriculture. The sea itself and the long coastlines around it lowered transport costs and increased communication speed, which allowed for a high level of trade and interconnectedness. It is no surprise to economic geographers that European urbanism began around the shores of the Mediterranean. By the sixteenth century there were no doubt some challenges to this historic position. The rise of Islam and the Arab conquest of much of North Africa – and, for several centuries, large parts of the Iberian Peninsula itself – had challenged the notion of 'a middle sea'. North–south trade from Italy to North Africa was no longer anything of the magnitude it had been in the days of the Roman Empire. But, and especially in the western Mediterranean, trade did continue to flourish. In the 1550s, Italy was the richest point in Europe and much of Italy was ruled by Philip. Income per head in Spain was higher than in France or England or Germany.

What was new in the 1550s compared to a century earlier was that Philip was not just ruling the most economically prosperous part of Europe, he had also inherited new territories, complete with a series of silver mines across the Atlantic.

Columbus's expedition to the New World had been partially funded by the Spanish Crown and had sailed from Spanish ports. Columbus 'discovered' the New World in 1492; the Spanish conquest began in 1493, just a year after Columbus's famous journey. It was astonishingly rapid, although initially did not appear to herald much in the way of economic change.

The conquistadors who headed from the Old World to the New have been succinctly described as fighting for glory, God and gold. The 1490s and 1500s witnessed the Spanish conquest of the Caribbean, which may have brought some fleeting glory to the Spanish Crown but came with little gold. The sparsely populated and economically underdeveloped islands of the region were not too costly to conquer but nor did conquering them bring much benefit – at least initially.

Things began to change as the Spanish moved into central America itself. There they encountered something rather different from the scattered tribes and villages of the Caribbean islands – the empires and cities of the Aztecs and Incas. Although the scale of the wars against these peoples was much larger than the battles fought in the first two decades of the conquest, the techniques were remarkably similar. Relatively small bands of Spaniards, equipped with modern weapons, allied themselves with other native groups against the local dominant powers.

Gunpowder and gunpowder weapons tend to be over-emphasised as factors in Spain's astonishing success. And 'astonishing' really is the only word that fits. Only around three thousand Spanish soldiers (or at least mostly Spanish soldiers – a fair few adventurers from other European states managed to tag along) were involved in the two-year conquest of the Aztec Empire – which could theoretically muster 300,000 warriors – between 1519 and 1521. In the case of the Incas, a decade later, another three thousand Spaniards were able to conquer an empire with perhaps 100,000 warriors. Gunpowder was not the decisive factor on the battlefield. Early modern firearms, which were both slow to load and terribly inaccurate, played a largely psychological role in Spanish tactical victories through causing loud noises and smoke; more decisive was the humble crossbow and the wide use of steel armour by the Spanish soldiers which native weapons struggled to penetrate.

Far more important than anything that happened on the battlefield was the Europeans' real secret weapon: smallpox. The natives of the Americas had no resistance to the smallpox virus which the Europeans, accidentally, brought to the continent. The death toll is still unclear but estimates of 25 to 40 per cent of the native population in the first few decades after contact are credible. Better weapons gave the smaller Spanish forces an advantage in any tactical engagement, but it was the pandemics that sounded the death knell for Aztec and Inca resistance.

And dwelling on those small bands of Spanish outnumbered up to a hundred to one misses another crucial factor: the conquerors had local allies, and lots of them – perhaps 100,000 in the case of the war against the Aztecs. Both the Aztec and Inca 'empires', despite being sedentary, looked more like the Mongol example of tribute-taking than the classical western Eurasian model of formal conquest on the lines of Rome or Persia. Both proved to be strangely fragile, with tribute-paying subject peoples happy, at least at first, to throw in their lot with the new Spanish rivals.

And they, together with later expansion into South America, appeared to offer potentially large rewards. The Inca emperor Atahualpa was captured by the Spanish in 1533 and they demanded he fill a large room in his palace once with gold and twice with silver in return for his freedom. He complied, handing over almost 40,000lb of precious metals. The Spanish killed him anyway. Gold often seemed to oust glory and God in the years of the conquest.

More significant than the immediate booty of war was the potential exploitation of the region. The Spanish were quick to put the remaining native population to work in the silver mines of the region, beginning a large flow of the metal back to Europe which would, at least on the face of it, enrich the Habsburg monarchs for centuries to come.

And yet despite this bountiful inheritance Philip is known to economic historians as the 'borrower from hell'. Four times during his forty-year reign he defaulted on his large debts. Understanding how the most politically and militarily powerful state in Europe, one that ruled a global empire bringing in huge amounts of precious metals, got itself into this position means looking at how that flow of New World silver was not an unmitigated economic gain, and delving into the institutions of early modern Spain.

Economists, left to their own devices, are capable of spoiling almost anything – including children's stories. Take J. R. R. Tolkien's *The Hobbit* as an example. At the end of the tale, the dragon Smaug, who has been sitting on a huge and wondrous pile of gold, is killed and everyone – at least until the Lord of the Rings picks up the story – lives happily ever after. The natural worry of an economist, on hearing of these developments, is to fret about what that sudden injection of gold means for the economy of Middle-earth. Early modern Europe is perhaps the best possible answer.

The quantity theory of money, although only really formalised in the twentieth century, is perhaps the oldest known theory of macroeconomics. Copernicus was certainly aware of it as early as the 1510s. In its modern mathematical form it is often expressed as $MV = PT$, where M means the total amount of money in circulation, V is the velocity of that money – a measure of how often it is being used – P is the overall economy price level and T is the total number of transactions in the economy. To oversimplify by assuming that the velocity of money and the number of transactions do not change much, then the theory states that if the amount of money in an economy doubles then so too will prices. More money is available but as production has not increased there is no more stuff to buy, so the price of stuff in general will rise in line with the amount of money.

In reality, things are more complicated. The velocity of money and the level of transactions have an annoying habit of changing quite regularly. But the straightforward insight that a large injection of new money into an economy will likely push up prices is an important one. The death of Smaug would have almost certainly led to a rising price level in Lake-town. And the discovery of New World silver did much the same in early modern Europe.

Economic historians call the time from the end of the fifteenth century to the middle of the seventeenth the European Price Revolution, or sometimes simply the Spanish Price Revolution. In those 150 years, the price level across the continent rose by about six times. That actually only works out as an annual inflation rate of around 1.2 per cent, which to modern ears sounds very low indeed, but this was new. Before the price revolution there had, of course, been inflation. But there had been deflation, or falling prices, too. Good harvests, bad harvests and changing fashions had caused prices to shift but in general the overall price level had stayed reasonably constant. What was new in the sixteenth century was a *sustained* rise in the price level overall. The best explanation for this change is to be found in the increasing supply of silver and gold. The pick-up in the amount of silver in the European economy pre-dates Columbus's voyages. Production at central European silver mines in places like Hungary began to rise in the 1470s, injecting new money into the European economy. But then, from the 1540s onwards, this trend was supercharged by the inflow of cheaply mined silver from Peru and Mexico. For those on fixed incomes, such as some landlords with fixed rents or many of the minor clergy on a fixed salary, a century and a half of rising prices meant a century and a half of falling real income. For the rulers of early modern states, the price revolution meant a rising cost of doing business.

But while Spain was at the centre of the European Price Revolution, it did affect states across Europe. The price revolution alone cannot explain why Spain became such a bad debtor. To understand why Spain was different, one needs to understand what was different about the institutions of Spain.

Governing an early modern monarchy, even a supposedly absolutist one, was always a bargaining process. The king might claim a divine mandate but getting anything done required buy-in from other powerful figures and groups. The nature of those who had to be bargained with varied by country – it might be powerful nobles with their own retainers and soldiers, it might be wealthy merchants and trade guilds with financial muscle, or it might be the leadership of the Church able to exercise moral suasion.

At one extreme can be found the early Dutch Republic, which broke away from Spanish Habsburg control following the Eighty Years' War for Independence, which began under Philip II and lasted into the mid-seventeenth century. The early Dutch state was an alliance of local notables and wealthy trade-focused cities. Nothing shows this more clearly than their navy. The Dutch fleet that swept the Spanish from the North Sea and preyed on Spanish commerce across the oceans during their long war for independence was not actually one navy at all; rather it was five separate navies, one for each maritime province, each with their own ships, admiralty and officers.

At first glance, a state so fragmented that it did not even have a unified navy might appear weak. But, over the longer term, the wider buy-in from elites – and especially commercial interests – in a state like the Dutch Republic was to prove an important source of economic, and ultimately military, strength.

In the final analysis, state capacity – the ability to actually get things done – matters. And counter-intuitive as it might sound, early modern states that constructed themselves as a bargaining process between different interest groups tended to have more capacity than 'absolutist' peers. The very existence of a system of checks and balances and a sense that there were at least some rules to the game allowed states like the Dutch – and soon their rivals across the North Sea in England – to raise a higher level of taxation. The Dutch, for example, were able by 1600 to extract the equivalent of 76 grams of silver per resident in overall taxation against around 60 for Spain.

Perhaps the best measure of the extent of the bargaining process in early modern states is to look at parliamentary activity. Of course, one needs to be careful to remember that none of the states under discussion were anywhere close to being democratic. Parliaments brought together powerful nobles, senior clerics and the most wealthy and powerful commoners and in no sense even attempted to speak for the bulk of the people.

The Dutch Parliament met in eighty of the hundred years from 1500 to 1599, while the English Parliament sat for sixty-seven of those years. The picture for Spain is more complex. While the monarchies were united in the person of first Charles and then Philip, the underlying kingdoms were not. Each continued to have its own institutions and parliaments. That of Aragon, for example, met for just nineteen years in the sixteenth century while that of Valencia sat for just twelve. Even more striking than the absolute difference in the level of parliamentary sittings between Spain and her northern European peers is the trend. While the Dutch and English

Parliaments sat in more years in the following century, those of Spain sat in fewer.

The principal purpose of monarchs calling parliaments was to raise funds. Taxation, in general, required their consent. As time went on, though, the Spanish monarchs seemed to have less and less need to call them – despite ever-rising expenses. The answer to this quandary is to be found in those very same New World silver mines that were fuelling the price revolution.

The key point to grasp about those New World colonies is that they were held as the personal possessions of, and were directly accountable to, the Habsburg monarchs as individuals with the various local parliaments of their many individual kingdoms having no formal institutional role in their governance. It was not the Habsburg domains that had found a new source of wealth but the Habsburg rulers themselves. That distinction mattered because it suddenly handed those rulers access to new sources of funds that could be spent with no need to seek the agreement of existing local elites. The bargaining process that characterised early modern states was circumvented in Spain and Charles, Philip and their successors – at least temporarily – had far more freedom of action in pursuing whatever course of policy they desired. One major reason that parliaments met less frequently in the Iberian realms as the years rolled by was that the king did not seem to need them any more. Or at least initially.

The main business of the early modern state, like that of the medieval kingdoms it had evolved from, was war. And war, during the era of Charles and Philip, was becoming ever pricier. This was a time some historians have dubbed the military revolution, though while the nature of European warfare was almost certainly shifting, the exact nature of the revolution – much like discussion of the later industrial revolution – remains disputed.

One approach emphasises the role of man-portable gun-powder weapons. Gunpowder had probably first made its way down the Silk Road to Europe in the thirteenth or fourteenth century and, like many other things, Genghis Khan probably deserves the ultimate credit for this. Certainly early cannons were in use in sieges by the 1380s, and by the late fourteenth and early fifteenth centuries 'hand cannons', as they were initially known, were appearing on the battlefield. Such weapons, being slow to load and very inaccurate, were how-ever no real substitute for either the crossbow or, in the case of England, the longbow. But by the late fifteenth century, on the eve of Columbus's voyages, the technology had begun to improve. Handguns, or 'arquebuses', were now becoming an increasingly common feature of both European and Ottoman Turkish armies.

In many aspects the bow still seemed to have the edge. While an early modern firearm could theoretically propel a bullet up to 400 or 500 yards (easily outranging even the most skilled archer) they were not accurate at much above 75 to 100 yards. More importantly, they could rarely manage more than one or two shots a minute. They did have the potential to pierce heavy armour at greater ranges – not to mention a terrifying noise that could frighten less experienced troops – but they were at first regarded as a supplement to other missile weapons rather than a replacement for them.

The Spanish were among the first western Europeans to begin to change that. During a long series of wars for control of the Italian Peninsula fought, mostly, against France between the 1490s and the 1560s, Spanish tactics began to change. Much like during the Hundred Years' War of a century before, mounted heavily armoured cavalry – by now generally referred to as gendarmes rather knights – were a core strength of the French forces. Given that Spain, unlike England, had not gone down the road of longbow specialisation, firearms and arquebuses seemed to offer the best counter to this. In the decades before the 1490s, soldiers armed with arquebuses tended to operate as skirmishers, moving forward in relatively small, loose groups dashing off a few shots and then running back to the safety of their own lines. In the 1490s and early 1500s, though, Spanish armies won a series of tactical victories over their opponents by switching tack. Wherever possible they would group larger bodies of firearm-equipped soldiers behind fortifications and force the other side to attack towards them. They defeated not only the famed French heavy cavalry but also, on numerous occasions, the mercenary Swiss heavy infantry – then reputed to be the finest heavy infantry in Europe and usually armed with long pikes – who contributed to the French forces in Italy.

Of course fighting from behind fortifications, even temporary ones, was not always possible. And loosely formed groups of skirmishers were vulnerable in the open. The Spanish practice, under Gonzalo de Córdoba – a veteran of many previous wars, known as the Great Captain – was to group together firearm-equipped soldiers with sword-equipped men for close-in fighting and, crucially, men armed with pikes. A formed body of pikemen, armed with spears perhaps 14 to 18 feet long, were seen as the best protection for foot soldiers against cavalry. Even the bravest of cavalrymen would think twice before charging home into a line of spear points arrayed by steady soldiers standing shoulder to shoulder, and many horses would simply refuse to do so, not matter how well bred or trained. Other European armies and generals had taken to using pikes in the decades before the 1490s but Córdoba's genius was to permanently attach the pike to the shot in units known as columns – or in Spanish, *colunelas*. King Ferdinand, Charles's predecessor as ruler of Aragon, named twenty officers to the new rank of head of column (*cabo de colunela*) in 1505 as he officially created these new permanent units. In 1508 the title was shortened to the now familiar one of colonel.

It was this new combination of firearms and protecting pikemen that began to change the nature of European battles. If cavalry could no longer be relied on to charge home and break up enemy infantry then, while they still had a role because of superior mobility, they could certainly no longer dominate battles in the way they had in earlier centuries. Grouping large numbers of arquebuses together also helped get over their inherent inaccuracy: a single arquebus might struggle to hit a man at 100 to 150 yards but a few hundred of them firing at a mass of opponents grouped together at the same range would almost certainly hit something.

In the decades that followed the 1500s other European powers followed the Spanish lead. And as they did so the size of armies began to increase. Firearms, like the crossbow before them, required little in the way of training, and as they came to dominate the battlefield – especially as loading times and accuracy slowly improved – generals found they needed ever more men equipped with them. Spain is the leading example of this. In the 1470s it maintained an army of around 30,000. By the 1620s that had grown to more like 300,000. The population of Spain itself over the same period that the army expanded by a multiple of ten times rose from perhaps 6.8 million to around 8.5 million. While the exact timings and the different tactical drivers of the military revolution remain a matter for debate, there can be no doubt that the scale – and expense – of European warfare underwent a step change in the century and a half after the discovery of the Americas. And at the same time an artillery revolution was taking place as the quality, range and weight of fire of cannons improved at so rapid a pace as to render earlier fortifications and castles almost useless. That too added to the cost of war as a successful monarch would now require not only a large siege train of cannon and trained artillery men but also to invest in improving their own fortifications in order to protect their lands from potential invaders.

In the 1550s Spain was spending around 1.5 to 2 million ducats a year on its military. By the 1590s that had risen to 6 million ducats. Indeed between 1566 and 1596, Philip II spent a grand total of 163 million ducats on all items, excluding debt interest payments, of which a staggering 144.3 million ducats – or 88.5 per cent of all spending – was on his military. One driver of this was the ongoing revolt in the Netherlands. But to that can be added a series of wars against France, a long war with England – including the sinking of a fabulously expensive Armada – and an ongoing conflict with the Ottoman Empire in the Mediterranean. The crucial point is that while some of these wars may have been forced on Spain, a great many of them were wars of choice. And the monarch could more easily make the choice for war because he did not need, it seemed, to summon a parliament to fund it. While the English Parliament could – and did – regularly restrain the ambitions of English monarchs by holding tightly on to the purse strings, the Spanish monarchs, because of the bounty of American silver, seemed to face no such check.

Philip's issue was that even his American riches proved unable to fund his ambitions. One option, which he frequently resorted to, was to borrow to make good the gap. Often he did this in the form of short-term loans known as *asientos*, with interest rates of up to 20 per cent. Philip's real problem was that longer-term debt, which would almost certainly have attracted a lower rate of interest, would have had to be backed by a regular schedule of taxation to prove his ability to meet the scheduled payments, and authorising regular long-term taxation would have involved summoning parliaments. But Philip, accustomed to personal rule, was always reluctant to do this. Another option he frequently pursued to pay for his ever-grander geopolitical schemes was the sale of tax exemptions or local monopolies to various nobles, merchants and clerics with access to ready cash. Reluctant to share decision-making and used to getting his own way, Philip took to either expensive short-term borrowing or raising cash quickly by ultimately harming his ability to extract more tax in the future. Both might have seemed like a good idea, or even the easy option, in the short term, but both were ruinous in the long run. Hence his four defaults in as many decades.

Natural resources may seem like a bounty from on high for a nation – or in this case a line of monarchs – but the complex interaction of institutions and incentives can serve to make them actively harmful to future growth. Philip had the misfortune to hold grand geopolitical visions at a time when warfare was becoming ever more expensive. But he had the double misfortune that Spain possessed an institutional set-up in which there was no group that could restrain his ambitions. What is more, the seemingly easy availability of vast fortunes on the other side of the Atlantic acted as a drain on the European Habsburg economies. Some of the most skilled merchants and entrepreneurs, who otherwise might have helped Spain develop economically, sought their fortune on the other side of the world. Investing (if that is the word) in searching for the mythical city of El Dorado, rumoured to be full of gold, seemed at times to be a far better use of money than the rather humdrum work of increasing agricultural yields in Spain itself.

In other European states the rising burden of military expenditure as the military revolution unfolded meant that rulers had to summon parliaments more frequently to raise the necessary revenues. Ultimately, as institutions developed, the state itself seemed to become more powerful. The existence of parliamentary checks and balances helped achieve a wider political buy-in from an ever-growing circle of local elites. That not only allowed easier access to lower-cost borrowing when necessary – as lenders were reasonably certain the state would be able to raise the taxes required to meet the payments and so there was less risk involved – it also allowed the state to take on new powers. If local elites were reasonably sure they could restrain the power of the state if needed, and those powers would not be turned on them, then they were much happier for such powers to exist in the first place. Spain, where New World riches seemed to offer the monarch much more freedom of action in the short run, was much slower to develop such institutions than many of her rivals. The result was that the supposed short-term freedom of action for her rulers actually reduced their power in the long run.

In the six decades after Philip's death, Spain defaulted six more times. The ultimate result of the conquest of the Americas was a weak tax base, high debts, unsustainable public finances and an institutional structure much less useful in the longer run than those developed by Spain's rivals. Strikingly, income per head in Spain was 10 per cent lower 150 years after Columbus's voyages than before. Rather than enriching Spain, American silver helped to make it poorer.

5

Understanding Hysteria: The Economics of Witch Trials

Not all conflict or mass violence is the result of war between states or rival warlords. The witch mania that swept across Europe in the sixteenth and early seventeenth centuries saw around sixty thousand people – most of them women aged over forty – executed on trumped-up charges of sorcery. Economics, which is often associated with rationality and logic, might seem like a poor tool to try and understand what looks to modern eyes like an outbreak of hysteria. But even in something as vicious as the mass killing of innocent women, the role of institutions and incentives played a large role. Economics cannot explain away what happened and it certainly cannot justify it, but it can help us to understand why so many supposed witches were sent to their deaths in a comparatively short period of time.

The best place to start is with Heinrich Kramer, a cruel man in a cruel era. If any single individual deserves responsibility for kickstarting the witch panic of the 1500s it is this man, who saw witches everywhere.

The fear of witches was not a new phenomenon in early modern Europe and occasional flare-ups of witch mania had occurred in local areas for centuries. But by the 1480s, when Kramer emerged as a man with power, belief in witches was by no means universal among clerics. The Catholic Church was far more concerned by heresy, or what it saw as aberrant forms of Christianity, than it was with the supernatural. Indeed, the origins of the inquisition are to be found in efforts to root out those with unsound doctrines, often very violently, rather than in hunting for witches. Nevertheless, believing in witches – or indeed werewolves, which one British publication of the 1630s confidently proclaimed could be found in the Low Countries – was not that unusual. But the Church itself did not take an especially strong collective stance. While references to witches can be found in the scriptures, not much emphasis was generally placed on them.

Kramer was born some time around 1430 and ended up becoming a friar in the Dominican Order. He carved out a reputation for eloquence in preaching and tireless work, became favoured by the Archbishop of Salzburg and by the mid-1470s had been appointed as the inquisitor responsible for Tyrol, Salzburg, Bohemia and Moravia – at that time all part of the collection of states and statelets known as the Holy Roman Empire in what is now Germany, Austria and the Czech Republic. His official remit was to hunt for heretics, but Kramer became increasingly concerned by witchcraft. Indeed to his mind the region was rife with it. The problem for Kramer was that not only did the various local authorities tend to disagree with him, they also did not recognise his authority to prosecute such cases.

In 1484 Pope Innocent VIII issued a papal bull, or declaration, known as *Summis Desiderantes Affectibus,* specifically covering witchcraft and Kramer's authority. Innocent's motivations for taking such a step may well have been primarily political. Inquisitors such as Kramer reported far more directly to the Pope in Rome than did local bishops and archbishops and much of the bull was simply concerned with restating the authority of Kramer to take whatever steps he believed were necessary. But even if the intention was simply an administrative clearing up of reporting lines, what really mattered was the explicit papal recognition that not only did witchcraft exist but that Kramer's agents had approval for 'correcting, imprisoning, punishing and chastising' such witches.

The next year Kramer attempted to put his restated authority to work and held a witch trial in Innsbruck in the Tyrol. It did not go well. He browbeat the local bishop into allowing him to engage in a series of prosecutions and two things became apparent very quickly: first, he only seemed interested in prosecuting women, and second, he showed rather too keen an interest in questioning them on their sexuality and sexual proclivities. He took against a certain Helena Scheuberin, the wife of a prosperous burgher and a woman known for speaking her mind. She attended a sermon of his which appears to have consisted mostly of ranting about witchcraft and understandably enough decided she would rather not attend any more. Kramer took this as evidence that she herself was guilty. He later argued that at the sermon in question he had merely been explaining a technique of striking a pail of milk 'in order to gain knowledge of a sorceress who had taken milk from cows'. It is not hard to imagine why Frau Scheuberin decided she had better things to do with her time.

Scheuberin and thirteen others were accused of witchcraft by Kramer and charged with, among other crimes, having used magic to kill a knight called Jörg Spiess. Kramer, though, failed to produce any evidence of this and eventually the trial was quashed on procedural grounds and the local bishop asked

Kramer to leave his jurisdiction. He did not take this well. Chastised, he moved to Cologne and began penning his most notorious work.

Malleus Maleficarum (the 'Hammer of Witches') is a deeply strange and unpleasant work. Partly self-justification, partly a legal work and partly a practical guide to spotting and punishing witches, it seeks to define witchcraft – still only a nebulous concept at the time – as a form of heresy, which was a specific and recognised offence, and to argue that therefore witches should be prosecuted by both the clerical and secular courts and authorities. What is more, perhaps reflecting on the failed trial and the procedural objections he had encountered in Innsbruck, Kramer was keen to argue that torture to extract confessions was the simplest way to proceed. Also in keeping with his previous form, the work makes clear that it is mostly dealing with witches rather than wizards, as women, being more lustful, are more likely to consort with devils. 'And blessed be the Highest', it says, 'who has so far preserved the male sex from so great a crime: for since He was willing to be born and to suffer for us, therefore, He has granted to men the privilege.' The sexual overtones are not exactly subtle. Witches, argued Kramer, sometimes collect male organs 'as many as twenty or thirty members together, and put them in a bird's nest, or shut them in a box, where they move themselves like living members, and eat oats and corn'. This strange combination of procedural guide and tales of boxes of penises moving around and eating oats somehow became a bestseller with somewhere between thirty and fifty editions going to press over the following century and a half. That helped provide the impetus – and the techniques – for the resulting waves of witch trials.

Of course the tale of one very odd individual and the rather dark book he wrote cannot explain why a process was kicked off which saw tens of thousands of innocent women being grimly executed. There had been manuscripts on witchcraft before Kramer picked up his quill. This is where economics becomes useful in providing the wider context to the witch mania of the sixteenth century, and in particular in terms of understanding why *Malleus Maleficarum* was such a runaway publishing success. The broader economic and demographic context to the sixteenth century and the rather innocuously named concept of 'non-price competition' provides one of the best explanations for the terror that was to follow.

Kramer was definitely lucky in his timing. He penned his work in 1486, just as printing was taking off as big business in Europe. Johannes Gutenberg had invented his moveable type method for printing a few decades before. The ability to print a work rather than relying on having it copied out by hand revolutionised how information spread. In the fifty or so years after 1450 around nine million copies of works were printed. In the entire span of human history until that point, it is doubtful that more than a million works had been committed to paper. In the following century a further 200 million books and pamphlets would go to press. In economic terms, the cost of spreading information was dropping rapidly.

But although printing was clearly a much easier way to reproduce a work than copying it out by hand, it was still neither necessarily straightforward or cheap. Each page had to be handset by skilled artisans, a process that could take up to half a day per page of text. Once all the other tasks – such as setting the ink, physically turning the press and hanging the sheets up to dry, let alone binding them together – are taken into account then one starts to get a sense of the costs involved in printing an early modern book. The cost structure of the industry made the choice of exactly what to publish a crucial one if early printers were going to stay in business. One could not employ a team of craftsmen for a whole month to lay out a sixty-page book if one was not reasonably certain it would sell well. It is no surprise that much of early European publishing focused on the Bible – it was a reliable bestseller. Added to this was the lack of any real sort of copyright protection, especially across international borders. The easiest way to succeed as a printer was to look at what other printers were selling and simply print more of that. If a book did well then it would tend to do very well indeed, as other print shops followed the lead of their rivals and peers. *Malleus Maleficarum*, with its strange tales of oat-eating penises, sold well.

But even if *Malleus Maleficarum* was a necessary factor in the witch craze that followed, by providing both a practical guide to spotting witches and a toolbox for dealing with them, its sales alone were not necessarily a sufficient factor. For that, one needs to look at the bigger picture.

It does not get any bigger than the climate. Europe, in the centuries after the 1300s, was undergoing what is now known as the Little Ice Age. Temperatures dropped by around one degree on average and rainfall became more common. Winters often became spectacularly harsh; in the 1650s, for example, a Swedish army was able to march on Copenhagen across a frozen sea. The evidence for this cool period comes from a variety of sources. The logbooks of ships contain regular temperature readings. More conclusively, analysis of ice cores in glaciers and tree rings has provided proper scientific readings on temperatures. They are also reflected in the art of the period. An analysis carried out in 1970 on 12,000 artworks held in European and American museums and galleries painted between 1400 and 1967 found a spike in the number of depictions of cloudy skies and darkness in the years between 1600 and 1649. That correlates rather well with what climate historians dub the Grindelwald Fluctuation.

While it may sound like the name of a poor-quality thriller, the Grindelwald Fluctuation actually takes its name from the Grindelwald glaciers in Switzerland. Analysis of the ice core there suggests that an especially intensive cooling period took place between the 1560s and 1630s during which the temperature dropped by up to two degrees. In other words, at the height of the European witch mania, it was especially cold.

That matters because extreme temperature changes tend to be associated with crop failures, rising hunger and falling living standards – the kind of background that makes the search for someone to blame more likely. Not only did witch trials rise in these years, so too did pogroms against Jews.

This broader cold period, stretching back before the Grindelwald Fluctuation, had already had an impact on Europe's demographics. Weaker agricultural productivity had lowered crop yields and resulted in lower living standards and, as is often the case at a time of lower income per head, the average age of marriage had begun to rise. Lack of money tends to mean people delay getting wed until they can afford it, if they ever do. In much of northern Europe the average age of first marriage for women rose from around twenty to more like twenty-five over the course of the sixteenth century. This led to a rising proportion of unmarried women in the population. As the Protestant Reformation played out across parts of Germany, Switzerland and Britain and the convents closed, that share grew ever larger. Over the course of the century the share of unmarried women among all adults rose from around 10 per cent to an average of closer to 20 per cent across northern Europe and as high as 30 per cent in some regions. Older unmarried women were often perceived as a burden to their community: with no direct descendants to cater for them, ensuring they were fed became the responsibility of the community as a whole.

One partial explanation for the witch craze is that it was simply an excuse, at a time when climate change had pushed down living standards in general and when there were more unmarried women than ever before, for poverty-stricken locals to get rid of older women. Fewer mouths to feed could raise living standards for the survivors. By this telling, *Malleus Maleficarum*, the work of Kramer and Pope Innocent's papal bull, was simply a convenient cover for actions driven by poverty. One modern study of 'witch' killings in rural Tanzania from the 1980s to 2000s has found a strong correlation with rainfall levels. Heavy rain, which lowers crop yields, is strongly associated with the murder of 'witches' – usually elderly female relatives living with their family, killed by family members – but not with other types of violent crimes.

Those more modern Tanzanian witch killings provide another possible explanation for the surge in witch trials in early modern Europe. It is especially striking that witch killing in Tanzania is almost exclusively a phenomenon found in the countryside and villages rather than urban areas. In other words, it happens where the power of the state is weakest. Something similar may have been happening in the Europe of the sixteenth century. One analysis of witch trials in France in this period compared the incidence of witch killing to the tax receipts taken by central government from each locality. In general, areas from which the state took less tax than expected relative to local wealth tended to carry out more witch trials. The state's inability to extract as much in the way of tax as it desired could be read as a proxy for relative state capacity and power. In other words, witch trials could be seen as reflecting the relative weakness of the early modern state and be driven by local outbreaks of hysteria – or poverty-induced strategies to get rid of perceived burdens on the community.

The weather, falling living standards, perhaps weak state

capacity and almost certainly changing demographic patterns all contributed to the wave of witch trials in the sixteenth century, but another factor may well have played a more prominent role: the Reformation and Counter-Reformation.

The single bestselling author of the sixteenth century was Martin Luther, the father of the Protestant Reformation which tore Catholic Europe apart between the 1510s and the 1550s. Both the Protestant Reformation and the resulting Catholic Counter-Reformation are of course usually thought of in doctrinal terms, as a battle of ideas about the shape Christian belief should take, what the forms of worship should be and how the Church itself should be structured. In a deeply religious continent, as Europe no doubt was in the sixteenth century, debates which can sound esoteric to modern ears held a great deal of power. It was a time when many believed that getting this wrong could lead to eternal damnation. But this battle between traditional Catholicism and the newer Protestant Churches can also be analysed as an economic battle, one in which the Protestant and Catholic Churches were engaged in a fight to be the religious service provider of choice to Europe's consumers.

Analysed as a business, it is hard to conclude that the Catholic Church in the years around 1500 was anything but a spectacularly successful one. Its share of the western European religious marketplace was approaching 100 per cent. Its chief competitive strategy when it came to rivals was what one economic history paper has called, rather meekly, 'coercive exclusion'. That is to say, adherents to any rival creed were either compelled to adopt Catholicism or simply annihilated. When belief in Catharism, a dualist form of Christianity originating in the Balkans, took off in Languedoc in France in the early thirteenth century, the response was a crusade against it – one that killed at least 200,000 people and perhaps as many as a million. The inquisition had been formed to stamp out heresy and protect the Pope's effective monopoly on European religious belief.

When Martin Luther published his ninety-five theses challenging the power of the Pope and the practices of the Church, the Catholic establishment sought initially to reuse the same technique of coercive exclusion. Luther was excommunicated from the Church and the Pope published a bull renouncing Luther's beliefs as heresy. Charles V, the then Holy Roman Emperor and King of Spain just about to see the silver taps of central America turned on, condemned Luther, banned possession of his books – or anything arguing along similar lines – and offered a reward for his arrest.

But this time coercive exclusion failed. While Spain, Portugal and the various Italian states broadly followed the Pope's edict, in Luther's own home region, loyalty to Rome seemed to run less deep. Many nobles and princes, not to mention many prosperous merchants, city burghers and poorer peasants, across the German lands found Luther's case to be irresistible. Many statelets either effectively ignored the official condemnation of Lutheranism or even refused to publish it. And without the support of local princes the Catholic inquisition could not operate in vast swathes of modern Germany.

Things became more serious for the Catholic Church following the Peace of Augsburg in 1555 which ended a revolt of predominantly Protestant princes against Charles as Holy Roman Emperor. That treaty formally decriminalised Lutheranism in the Holy Roman Empire and gave each local ruler the choice over whether his realm would be Lutheran or Catholic. Via the doctrine of *cuius regio, eius religio* – whose realm, his religion – each local magnate was free to pick their own faith and those who happened to live in their territory were expected to comply.

A series of civil wars in France led to a similar outcome. The Edict of Saint-Germain of 1562 effectively allowed for Protestants to reside in France. England under Henry VIII joined the swing towards Protestantism, although mainly for reasons of divorce and dynastic politics.

By the 1560s, then, coercive exclusion – a successful strategy for the Catholic Church for centuries – had clearly failed, and it now faced an active competitor in the European religious market for the first time since the sixth century. As a result it had to find a new technique. The answer both the Catholic and Protestant Churches settled on was one familiar to businesses throughout history: actively try to present yourself as the more attractive option.

This competition to dominate Europe's religious market took many forms. Some Protestant Churches emphasised the potential financial savings associated with their own straightforward 10 per cent tithe on incomes compared to the bewildering array of taxes, tithes and indulgences associated with Catholicism. Both Churches began to offer more schools to potential and current believers, with Catholic efforts spearheaded by the Jesuit order. The Catholic Church went as far as to attempt a modest rebranding with its Tridentine reforms which increased the number of canonisations to cater to the noted popularity of saints with the laity.

Outside the direct competition on costs and tithes, all of these strategies are what economists typically call non-price competition. For modern businesses such practices typically focus on things like advertising, brand awareness and customer service levels. For the early modern Church, however, things were somewhat different. The grimmest form of non-price competition between the competing denominations was found in dealing with supposed witches.

As strange as it may sound, the persecution of witches

functioned much like a form of advertising in the battle for religious market dominance. Belief in them was widespread, even before *Malleus Maleficarum* rolled off the presses. In most villages one could quite easily find a handful of people – mostly older women – widely considered to be witches. But if the supply of 'witches' did not vary much across early modern Europe, the incidence of witch trials certainly did. What is striking is how comparatively rare such trials were in areas loyal to Catholicism, such as Spain or Italy, and how comparatively common they became where the market for religion was most contested – especially in Germany, Switzerland and some regions of France.

The key elements to grasp are that witch trials were both a time-consuming process and one that generated a great deal of publicity. Word of an impending investigation would quickly spread to neighbouring towns and villages and both the trial itself and any subsequent execution would be public affairs attracting large crowds. Hundreds, and sometimes thousands, would attend the grisly killings and hear sermons from the prosecutors. Even those who missed out on the public spectacle would often get a taste of what had unfolded from the production of woodcuts. Sometimes a woodcut was not enough. In Schongau, following the execution of a dozen witches, the priest who had overseen the trial ordered that 'a lasting monument of the trials should be erected in some public place'.

Energetically rooting out witches was a clear sign to locals that the prosecuting Church had their best interests at heart. In religiously divided areas the notion that, say, the Catholic Church was better able to handle the witch threat than their Lutheran rivals was as good a reason as any other to stay loyal to, or to return to, the old faith.

Time and time again across the German lands, islands of Catholic faith cut off among Protestant seas would be especially enthusiastic witch hunters. In Cologne, for example, the ruling Catholic Ferdinand von Wittelsbach found himself surrounded by Lutherans and Calvinists and so, in the 1620s, unleashed the full power of the microstate in attempting 'a final solution' to the witch problem. Across the Rhine in Lorraine, now part of France, in another fiercely contested zone, historians note a 'combative' attitude to witches and a soaring number of trials.

Protestants, or at least those near particularly zealous witch-hunting Catholics, did not feel they could afford to be outdone. The clergy in Lutheran Saxe-Coburg, for example, 'tried to stimulate more arrests of witches in the late 1620s by pointing to the example of their Catholic neighbours in Wurzburg'. Following on from von Wittelsbach's trials in Cologne, Protestants were impressed. Those in Wertheim petitioned their prince in 1628 to increase his own persecutions in response. In Livonia, on the Baltic coast, Swedish Lutherans oversaw an anti-witch campaign 'to dissuade citizens from returning to Catholicism'.

If witch trials were a form of advertising, though, it was one to use selectively. For a start, it was costly, so it was mostly deployed where the religious authorities thought those high costs would bring the greatest benefits – that is to say in areas where faiths competed.

One paper by two economic historians has sought to quantify this effect by gathering data on forty thousand witch trials between 1300 and 1850. The first thing that leaps out of the data is the staggering variation in witch executions across Europe. In Italy, for example, the death rate per million from being executed for witchcraft over the entire sample period was just five. In Germany, though, it was 574, more than a hundred times as high. In Switzerland it was an almost unbelievable 5,691. One was clearly better off being a single, older woman in Italy than in Switzerland during this period.

The authors then compared the incidence of witch trials and executions to episodes of 'confessional battle activity' over both different geographies and time. Confessional battle – defined here as periods of intense competition between competing faiths – really took off after 1520 and the beginning of the Reformation. It subsided for a while before spiking to ever higher levels after 1555, with a brief period of relative religious peace from around 1585 to 1615. The Thirty Years' War, fought between 1618 and 1648 on broadly confessional lines (although with some exceptions – France, for example, mostly sided with the Protestant powers), saw confessional conflict rise to new highs before finally dwindling off after 1650. The pattern of witch trials over time closely tracks this, with a delay of a few years. Ninety per cent of all confessional battles and two thirds of all witch trials took place between 1550 and 1650. What is more, the geography of confessional conflict and locations of witch trials tally together well. Prosaic as it may sound, witch trials probably were a form of 'non-price competition'.

One mystery not fully solved by the authors is the lingering persistence of witch mania, even after religious conflict began to abate. After the horrors of the Thirty Years' War, which killed perhaps 4.5 to 8 million, a broad religious peace came to Europe. Sovereigns mostly no longer had the right to change the religion of their people and the geography of European Protestantism and Catholicism settled into the shape it still roughly holds to this day. But the trials continued, at a lower level, and did not fall back to their 1550 level until just after 1700 – a good five decades after the end of major religious strife. It may be, as the authors put it in very economic language, that 'owing to religious suppliers' provision of witch trials for more than a century, religious consumers became accustomed to witch trial activity'. Eventually, the spread of science and the wider Enlightenment reduced belief in the supernatural, and that consumer demand began to dissipate.

Witch mania may seem about as far from the rational world of economics as one can go. But even the most irrational of behaviours – and there can be few things as irrational as the mass killing of innocent women – can at least be better understood if put into the context of incentives and institutions. Why were so many women put to death in such a short time in early modern Europe? Because the incentive structures of one major dominant type of institution – the early modern Churches – made carrying out such trials and executions in their interests.

6

How Warfare Made the Renaissance

The notion that war and violence can serve as a driver of economic and technological progress is far from new. Harry Lime, the villainous antagonist of *The Third Man*, Graham Greene's superb post-war thriller, famously made just such a case with his wonderful line: 'In Italy for thirty years under the Borgias, they had warfare, terror, murder, bloodshed, they produced Michelangelo, da Vinci and the Renaissance. In Switzerland, they had brotherly love, five hundred years of democracy and peace, what did they produce? The cuckoo clock.' He was broadly right on the link between Italian warfare and the great scientific and cultural awakening that now tends to get dubbed the Renaissance. But not for the reasons he probably suspected.

It is worth starting, though, with the notion that Switzerland enjoyed five hundred years of democracy and brotherly love. While they might be now popularly associated with cuckoo clocks, fancy watches and banking, until the early nineteenth century the Swiss were better known for their army. It was the

Swiss who, as we have seen, reintroduced the pike to European warfare and for a time in the late fifteenth and early sixteenth centuries were widely regarded as the finest heavy infantry in Europe. Swiss mercenaries continued to serve many sovereigns across Europe in later centuries too. The massacre of Louis XVI's Swiss Guard was a turning point in the French Revolution in 1792. Nowadays only the Pope maintains a Swiss Guard but as late as the early 1800s they could be found serving the Spanish, the French, the Dutch and various German states.

But Lime was both right and wrong in far more interesting ways when it comes to Italy. Italy had been racked by conflict in the Middle Ages, but interestingly enough those wars were not especially vicious. Indeed for more than a century they tended to generate a great deal of treasure but not much blood.

Federico da Montefeltro is an interesting character to begin with. Born in 1422 as an illegitimate son to the count of the tiny statelet of Urbino in the Italian Marche, he was legitimised as his father's natural son and heir by the Pope at the age of two. Or at least that is the official story. Some still insist, as they did at the time, that his supposed 'father' was actually his grandfather who, lacking a male heir, took one of his daughter's children as his own. He spent time as a child living in Venice as a hostage to ensure his father's – or perhaps grandfather's – good behaviour and embarked at the age of sixteen on a career in soldiering.

He took to it. Over the following four and a half decades – before his death to a fever in 1482 – he commanded mercenary armies fighting for, at various times, most of the major states of the Italian Peninsula. The Pope, then ruler of the Temporal Papal States in central Italy as well as head of the Church, was an employer on multiple occasions, but so too were Venice, Florence, Milan, the Kingdom of Naples and a handful of smaller city-states and duchies. He never lost a war. He became Duke of Urbino after the death of his half-brother (in which he may have played a role) and was one of the figures who inspired Niccolò Machiavelli to write *The Prince* in 1513 (although the book itself would not circulate until two decades later).

Soldiering made Montefeltro a fortune. At a time when to possess a total stockpile of around 20,000 ducats was regarded as wealthy he earned perhaps 50,000 each year during his decades of active campaigning. And it was a fortune that he mostly ploughed back into the arts and culture. Nowadays he is usually remembered as, in the words of one recent biography, 'the light of Italy'. He assembled the most comprehensive library found outside the Vatican, paid for the training of a young painter called Raphael and commissioned works that can be found in the New York Metropolitan Museum of Art. His patronage spread far beyond Italy. The great Flemish painter Justus painted twenty-eight portraits for his collection. And nor was it just painters who benefited from his support. As Montefeltro himself put it, 'we deem as worthy of honour and commendation men gifted with ingenuity and remarkable skill, and particularly those prized by both the ancients and moderns, as has been the skill of architecture, founded upon the arts of arithmetic and geometry'. Architects, painters, sculptors and writers as well as mathematicians and what we would now call scientists and philosophers all benefited from his immense generosity. For those on the receiving end of such treatment, the appeal ran far beyond the (large) sums of cash involved. Working for Montefeltro also came with access to his library, connections to the Pope and a chance to mingle at one of Europe's leading cultural centres. His fame reached as far as England, where King Edward IV made him a Knight of the Garter despite his never leaving Italy.

Montefeltro would be a fascinating figure in any era, but what makes him most interesting is that in his time he was far from alone. He may be the brightest example but late medieval Italy was chockful of wealthy soldiers of fortune acting as patrons to the arts and learning. It was their wealth, taken from war, that helped to fund the flowering of knowledge which transformed late medieval Italy into Renaissance Italy.

To understand how this happened requires a look at the unique features of the economy and state structures of the Italian Peninsula in this period. The institutional framework created the right set of incentives to channel the spoils of war into expanding human knowledge.

Medieval Italy was unlike much of the rest of Europe. It was both politically fragmented and rich. As already noted, southern Europe – and in particular the areas bordering on the Mediterranean – was the economic heartland of Europe in the medieval era and Italy sat at the centre of this. Partially this reflected the long path of history. It had for centuries sat at the centre of the Roman economic system and even a thousand years after that empire's fall (or at least the fall of the western part of it) that legacy mattered. But from the thirteenth century onwards, trade played a major role in powering forward Italian prosperity. It is no surprise that the Black Death arrived in Europe on a Genoese ship, that Marco Polo was Italian or that the early trade manuals on how to profit from the reopened Silk Road were written in Florence, Turin and Milan. Italians dominated the trade routes between western Eurasia and North Africa and the east. Spices from Asia arrived in Europe, before Columbus and da Gama reshaped the world, either along the Silk Road or via trading vessels plying the routes across the Indian Ocean into Egypt, and from there Italian middlemen took over.

The economic geography of Italy looked rather different

from that elsewhere in Europe too. In particular it was both populous and relatively urbanised. In 1400 the population of the Italian Peninsula was around 8 million, compared to just 2.7 million in England and Wales. But while only two English towns had more than 10,000 inhabitants, twelve did in northern and central Italy alone. Adding on those in the east and south, where urbanism was less spectacular but still well above the European norm, takes the total to eighteen. In other words, Italy had around three times the number of people in England and Wales but ten times the number of large settlements. And some of those settlements truly were cities rather than just large towns. In the mid-medieval period, Venice, Milan and Naples were three of just five cities in Europe to boast more than 100,000 inhabitants.

Italy, as the Austrian statesman Metternich would famously say centuries later, was 'a geographical expression'. While residents of Milan and Venice and Naples shared a broadly similar (although not yet identical) language and an increasingly common culture, they lived in different states. The big five Italian powers – Venice, Milan, Florence, the Papal States and the Kingdom of Naples – were joined by a bewildering array of smaller statelets, independent duchies and city-states. And they possessed a wide variety of governance models. The Kingdom of Naples, which ruled much of the south of the peninsula as well as eventually the island of Sicily, was, as its name rather suggests, a kingdom much like those that could be found elsewhere in western Eurasia. The Papal States, which at this time stretched well beyond the city of Rome to cover much of central Italy, were ruled by the Pope but were effectively another form of kingdom, albeit one with their monarch picked by cardinals. After that, though, things become more complicated. Some states, like Milan, were hereditary duchies but many, such as Venice, Florence and Genoa, were republics controlled by wealthy local oligopolies. Not even the various republics were in any way what we would recognise as democracies. Voting rights were restricted to a narrow circle of the ultra-wealthy. But they were, in economic terms, at least closer to being the kind of open-access orders capable of creating a greater deal of buy-in from important elites.

What was strikingly different about Italy, as compared to much of the rest of Europe at that time, was the relative lack of power – outside Naples and the Papal States anyway – of the kind of feudal, settled, landowning nobility that dominated the politics of much of the rest of the continent. The really powerful movers and shakers in Venice or Milan or Florence were wealthy merchants, and increasingly bankers, rather than people who happened to own a lot of land because their ancestors had been especially successful violence specialists. Banking grew hand in hand with rising trade. Those importing or exporting goods needed access to financial services such as bills of exchange and credit to ease the flow of physical goods. Exchanging bits of paper was certainly much easier than lugging around chests full of gold and silver. Much of the gains of rising Italian prosperity in the fourteenth and fifteenth centuries flowed to commercial interests, to the upper stratum of what we might think of as a rising commercial class, rather than to the owners of land.

This picture of an urbanised, prosperous and in some cases relatively open and proto-democratic form of governance might sound almost idyllic – especially when one adds in pleasant weather and reasonably high agricultural yields. But it was also a time marked by war. A great deal of war. In fact warfare was an almost constant state of affairs in medieval Italy.

The lack of a central governing authority meant that the various states of the peninsula existed in a state of almost constant tension with each other. As the fortunes of the various states waxed and waned over time, their relative strength would vary. As one state became more powerful it would seek to expand its influence and territory at the expense of its rivals until, generally, a powerful enough coalition came together to put it back in its place. Alliances shifted rapidly, and sometimes to a bewildering degree. Take, as an example, the War of the League of Cambrai (1508–16). The League of Cambrai was formed in 1508 amid growing concerns over the rising power of Venice, which not only dominated its corner of north-eastern Italy but also ruled an empire that stretched out into the eastern Mediterranean and Balkans. It brought together the Papal States, the Duchy of Ferrara, the Holy Roman Empire, France and Spain to confront the Most Serene Republic. A series of victories in 1509 and 1510 for the forces of the League, though, quickly changed the calculus. The allies began to worry that the end result would not just be a diminished Venice but a more powerful and lasting French presence in Italy. So in 1510, Spain and the Holy Roman Empire left the war and the Papal States – one of the original orchestrators of the whole scheme – switched sides to fight alongside the Venetians. In 1511 the Pope organised the Holy League bringing Spain and the Holy Roman Empire back into the war, but this time on the side of Venice. The year 1513 saw yet another diplomatic turnaround with Milan joining the Holy League but Venice – the initial target of the war – switching over to fight alongside the French. Keeping track of exactly who was an ally and who was an enemy was never straightforward in Italian politics.

What is most interesting about Italian warfare, though, is not its persistence but its nature. For a start, in striking contrast to elsewhere in Europe, territorial change was more likely to come before a conflict than after it – it was more often a cause of war than a consequence. Often territory would be purchased or would change hands through the luck of inheritance, triggering insecurity and conflict. The result of wars and defeat was more often a large financial payment than the loss of territory. The indemnities paid by defeated rivals could be very large indeed. Pisa, in 1364, paid the victorious Florentines 100,000 florins, the equivalent of around one year of normal income for the city-state. The Pisans got off lightly. When Venice defeated Padua in 1373, they asked for 250,000 ducats as the price of peace – around nine times Padua's annual fiscal revenues. Florence itself was forced to pay 250,000 florins – a whole year's revenue – to the Pope after losing the War of the Eight Saints in 1378.

But even more striking than the typical peace terms in these wars was how they were fought and by whom. For a region racked by warfare for more than a century, there were surprisingly few battles. This was most unusual in warfare at the time. From the fall of the Western Roman Empire in the fifth century AD all the way up to the early modern period, it often makes little sense to talk of western Eurasian military 'strategy'. The leaders of armies thought of their job in relatively simple terms: to seek battle with their opponents, ideally via the most direct means possible. Harrying, or raiding and ravaging the enemy's lands, was mostly about forcing battle. If the attacker had an obviously superior force then the defender would be, understandably, reluctant to take the field. Pillaging the countryside could force the issue; a lord who could not protect his peasants would not be a lord for long. But the point was to force battle.

In Italy, though, warfare was different. That was mostly because of who was fighting it: professionals. In medieval England or France an army would generally consist of a core of experienced fighters based around the monarch, their lords and leading nobles and their own retainers, supplemented by peasants raised for the campaign. As we have seen, in the case of English peasants armed with longbows, that could be a powerful force. But the social structure of much of medieval Italy was rather different. Wealth was increasingly based on banking, trade and commerce rather than land, and political power, even in the kingdoms and duchies, was increasingly held by the wealthy. Cities rather than the countryside were dominant. While the various local leaders and statelets did possess their own retainers and militias it was all on a much smaller scale. If soldiers were needed for a campaign, the usual response was to hire them.

In economic terms, it is perhaps best to think of Italy in these periods as enjoying what Adam Smith would later call the fruits of the division of labour. In theory, and usually in practice too, as economies become richer and larger the division of labour – with each person carrying out increasingly specialised tasks – becomes more evident. This tends to drive up productivity and make economies even richer. It is fairly obvious that a small agricultural community of, say, twenty peasants where everyone tills their own fields, makes their own clothes, shoes their own horses etc. will have a lower level of output per head than a community of one thousand where some will work as specialised blacksmiths, some in producing clothes, some as bakers and some as farmers. In medieval Italy, warfare was increasingly something left to the experts. The oligarchs ruling Venice could concentrate on their shipping and banking businesses and if they had to fight a war with Florence they would simply bring in some hired help.

For a long time these hired hands were often foreigners. One of the most famous of the fourteenth century was John Hawkwood, who was born in Essex but eventually buried in a cathedral in Florence. He learned his trade soldiering in the Hundred Years' War and probably fought at both Crécy and Poitiers before eventually joining a mercenary band known as the White Company and making his way to Italy. He rose to be captain of this body of experienced soldiers and over the course of three or so decades fought for a variety of Italian states. Employment opportunities and offers were never short on the ground for soldiers in the Italy of that time.

By the fifteenth century the mercenaries were more likely to be Italian, although Germans and Swiss were still commonplace. This was the world Federico da Montefeltro was born into.

Mercenaries seemed to offer many advantages to the Italian states. For a start, they allowed for the division of labour. But more generally at a time when weapons were becoming more complex – with crossbows slowly giving way to handguns – hiring professionals seemed to make sense. These bands of soldiers, which could easily number into the thousands, would generally consist of some combination of light infantry men armed with either a crossbow or a handgun together with a mounted contingent of fully armoured heavy knights. They became known as condottieri, the word originating from the Italian term for a contract. They would sign on with one state or another for a year at a time, or for the duration of a campaign.

But while this all seemed to make sense for the Italian states, whose social structure precluded raising armies in the traditional European manner, the incentives of the employer and the employees were not especially well aligned.

The condottieri captains were loyal to themselves and their men rather than any specific employer. They might be signed on to campaign for Venice one year, but the next year they could be working for Milan or Florence. Agreeing to fight for, say, Venice in return for a large upfront sum immediately and the promise of more if victory was won was all well and good. And the prospect of more cash if they performed well should, in theory, have helped align the incentives of the state and the condottieri band in question. But that prospect of a higher payout had to be set against the very real risk of death or serious injury in the event of heavy fighting.

The so-called great captains of the period, men such as Federico da Montefeltro in the fifteenth century or Prospero Colonna and Vitellozzo Vitelli in the early sixteenth, became very interested in strategy and looking back into the accounts of classical warfare in the age of Greece and Rome, before 'strategy' had simply consisted of 'find the enemy and fight them'. They told themselves and (one imagines) their employers that the key to victory lay not in simply fighting a battle against the enemy but rather in manoeuvre and cunning. An army could be outwitted by a complex series of feigned advances and retreats and forced into a position from which they had little chance of victory and might as well surrender without any need for a major engagement. As one military historian of the period has sarcastically put it, 'their campaigns might be described with much justice as the painstaking avoidance of battle'.

Maybe some condottieri captains did genuinely believe their own spin – that manoeuvre trumped battle in the end – but either way, it certainly aligned with their own incentive structure and reduced the potential downside of being a mercenary, i.e. getting killed or crippled. Rather than seeking out the enemy, rival hired bands would often simply march around the countryside purposefully avoiding each other for much of the time, sometimes by explicit agreement. As Machiavelli was to put it, 'these men ... turned war into a technique for wasting so much time that when two states made war, both of them generally lost'. As chancellor of Florence towards the end of the period under discussion, Machiavelli made great efforts to organise a citizen militia and reduce the state's reliance on hired help. While completely aware that his trained peasants and townspeople would be far less experienced and poorly trained compared to the hired condottieri, he also understood that they would at least be incentivised to fight to defend their homes and territory.

But Machiavelli's revelations on the problems of using mercenaries, which are to be found in both *The Prince* and *The Art of War*, came very late. For much of the fourteenth, all of the fifteenth and a good proportion of the early sixteenth centuries the wars of Italy were fought by the condottieri, and even if both states somehow managed to lose, it was the condottieri who were the real victors.

A century and a half of warfare created many condottieri fortunes and, as in the case of Federico da Montefeltro, much of the wealth was ploughed into the cultural and artistic revival known to history as the Renaissance. To understand why this wealth was routed into the arts and culture, one needs to understand the nature of Italian wealth during this period and its underlying distribution – something which was very much shaped by the political geography of the region.

The great fortunes being made in the period came from two sources: the flourishing of trade into western Eurasia (in which Italians generally enjoyed a profitable role as middlemen) and the extensive military campaigns that enriched a growing class of professional mercenaries who were increasingly Italian in origin. Rather than being concentrated within a very small nobility, the wealth of Italy was in the hands of a wider range of potential consumers, there was a surprising amount of social mobility (or at least a reasonably rich person had a chance of becoming super rich to a much greater extent than in, say, England or France), and the wealth was geographically spread across the fragmented peninsula rather than being concentrated in a dominant capital, as was the case in Paris or London.

What is more, warfare added to that economic redistribution by enriching a class of professional soldiers, and in
particular their commanders. That tended to lead to even
more geographic redistribution. Middle-ranking towns such
as Ferrara, Mantua and Montefeltro's Urbino, where prominent condottieri were based, saw their own wealth rise, paid
for by the fees of Venice, Milan and Florence. Warfare, in the
words of one economic historian, 'was an economic activity
that redistributed wealth in Italy in a way that did not happen
elsewhere in Europe'.

It also mattered that the recipients of this wealth were generally not from long-established great families, secure in their
social position. A relatively minor nobleman, or even an illegitimate son such as Montefeltro, could suddenly find themselves
rich beyond their wildest dreams. One strategy to mark out
their newfound social position, and seemingly to secure it, was
a technique that crops up again and again in economic history
at times of rapid economic redistribution and the making of
new fortunes: conspicuous consumption.

It was not simply a case of wanting to spend this newfound
wealth – that would not do. Instead it had to be spent in the
most ostentatious way possible to mark out to neighbours and
peers just how wealthy one now was. In medieval Italy, Ferraris
and Rolexes were not available, but portraits by Raphael and
ceiling paintings by Michelangelo were.

The political, geographic and economic structure of Italy
in the fourteenth and fifteenth centuries made warfare a
constant in life. The lack of a dominant power meant that
maintaining the balance of power between two dozen competing states and statelets would see a great deal of conflict.
But the economic and social structures of Italy meant that
raising armies in the traditional way, common across the rest
of Europe, was not an option. The incentives and institutions

of the medieval Italian states created a great demand for mercenaries. That space was originally filled by foreigners, but as the market for professional soldiers went from strength to strength, the supply of native Italians willing to specialise in violence rose sharply.

That institutional set-up meant that much of the booming wealth of the region, enriched by foreign trade, was redistributed by warfare both geographically (away from the great cities and into smaller towns) and into the hands of a rising class of great captains. Those great captains, the commanders of the condottieri companies, had more wealth than they could ever realistically spend on common and necessary items and every incentive to spend it in the most conspicuous manner possible to show off their good fortune and cement their initially uncertain social position. Nothing said 'I have made it' in medieval Italy quite as clearly as hanging a brand-new da Vinci in your hall. The nature of Italian warfare created the demand for a luxury goods market on a scale that had not been seen in Europe for centuries, and meeting the demands of that market saw the flowering of artistic creativity that was the Renaissance.

The historical moment could not last for ever, though. Beginning in the 1490s, the neighbouring and unified regional powers began to take a more lasting interest in events in Italy. From the 1490s to the 1550s – a period known as the Great Italian Wars – Italy was one of the major battlegrounds in a multi-decade confrontation between the rulers of France and the Habsburg rulers of Spain and the German lands. With the presence of large foreign armies – French, Spanish and German – on Italian soil, the nature of Italian warfare began to change. The commanders of these foreign forces had no time or patience for the subtle manoeuvre warfare of the condottieri, nor did they have the incentive. A French or Spanish commander who purposefully avoided battle would not be rewarded by their king.

With the arrival of foreign armies, the era of the condottieri was coming to an end. And as that era ended, so too did the demand in one of the largest luxury goods markets the world had ever seen.

7

How Pirates Understood
Incentives

Blackbeard, or Edward Teach, is probably history's most notorious pirate. He was originally from Bristol, and when Robert
Newton, a fellow West Countryman, was cast to play him in
1952's *Blackbeard the Pirate* he exaggerated his own accent. The
result, more than seventy years later, is that if asked to adopt
'a pirate voice', most people will fall into an English West
Country twang. At least two more films and three TV series
have followed Blackbeard's career since the 1960s and he may
have been the inspiration for Jack Sparrow in *Pirates of the
Caribbean*. But for all Teach's celebrity, which certainly makes
for fun cinema, his near contemporary Black Bart is the far
more interesting figure.

Bartholomew Roberts has also attracted writers of fiction
over the years – he is one of four real pirates who merits a
mention in *Treasure Island* and is the probable inspiration for
the Dread Pirate Roberts in *The Princess Bride* – but unlike
Teach, Roberts came from Wales. It is hard to imagine Jack
Sparrow with a Welsh accent. Born John Roberts in the early

1680s, the man who would become known as Black Bart went to sea aged around thirteen in 1695, and then essentially vanishes from history until 1718, by which point he was mate on a sloop operating out of Barbados. Approaching forty and with two and a half decades at sea, he was reportedly by then an experienced navigator.

In 1719 he was on board the slave ship *Princess* when she was taken by pirates off the coast of modern-day Ghana. It was at this point that his life took an unexpected turn. Roberts, along with several other members of the captured crew, was forced to join the pirates. This was something that was far from unusual. Pirate vessels only rarely had enough spare hands to crew a prize, so the crew of a captured vessel would often be asked to volunteer their services or be pressed into service. What was more unusual was Roberts's rapid ascent in his new job. The captain of the pirates who had taken the *Princess*, Howell Davis, was a fellow Welshman. Indeed, like Roberts, he was from Pembrokeshire. Davis quickly took a shine to Roberts, valuing his excellent navigational skills and appreciating the ability to converse with him in Welsh and lend some privacy to their discussions.

According to one history, written shortly after his death, Roberts was initially reluctant to embrace his career change but then took a different view. He apparently stated: 'In an honest service there is thin commons, low wages and hard labour. In this, plenty and satiety, pleasure and ease, liberty and power; and who would not balance creditor on this side, when all the hazard that is run for it, at worst is only a sour look or two at choking? No, a merry life and a short one shall be my motto.'

As a second mate on a merchant ship, Roberts earned around £4 a month and had almost no chance of promotion to captain. In the meritocratic world of piracy, the sky was the limit. Just a few short weeks after the taking of the *Princess*, Roberts was on board the pirate vessel *Royal Rover* when it docked at the Portuguese-controlled island of Príncipe in the Gulf of Guinea. By flying the colours of a British man-of-war the *Rover* was able to enter the harbour, and being an inventive sort of fellow, Captain Davis quickly came up with a plan to make some cash during their stay. They would invite the governor over to the ship for dinner and then hold him hostage until a ransom was paid. Sadly for Davis the Portuguese worked out that something was amiss. On his way to the governor's house for pre-dinner drinks, Davis was ambushed and killed by the Portuguese authorities.

It was time for the pirates to elect – as was their way – a new captain. The man they chose was Roberts, who had only been recruited – and possibly reluctantly at that – a few weeks before. It seems that his excellent navigational skills were recognised and valued by his new colleagues and his forceful personality no doubt played a role.

If Roberts had indeed wished for 'a merry life and a short one', he got his desire. Over the next three years he sailed the coasts of Africa and the Americas and took a staggering 470 merchant ships as prizes – an average of around three per week. He was killed in battle with the Royal Navy as a very rich man in 1722. He was not yet forty.

Roberts was clearly a skilled seafarer and navigator and an excellent leader of men. But what is more surprising is that he, even if he would not have put it in these terms, showed an innate understanding of incentives. His crew stayed loyal because their incentives were well aligned by his pirate code and he demonstrated a keen awareness of the power of signalling and at least a rudimentary grasp of game theory. The striking thing, though, is that Roberts was far from unique in this. Odd as it may sound, there is a great deal modern managers could learn from the pirates of the late seventeenth and early eighteenth centuries.

But before dwelling on how pirates fundamentally understood modern management techniques better than many supposedly modern managers, it is worth putting Roberts, Teach and all the rest into their wider economic context.

Piracy is as old as maritime trade and travel itself. Herodotus writes of the pirates that preyed on shipping between ancient Greece and Egypt in the fifth century BC, more than a thousand years before Roberts hoisted the black flag. Pirates pop up in Homer's *Odyssey*, written three centuries before that. But the eight or so decades between the 1650s and the 1720s are often dubbed the Golden Age of Piracy. This was the era of both Roberts and Teach.

One reason for that, at least initially, was the end of the European wars of religion in the 1650s; they had begun with the Reformation in the early sixteenth century. With relative peace on the continent following the end of the Thirty Years' War in 1648, the European powers were able to devote more time and energy to building up their colonial holdings. As global trade (especially seaborne trade) began to rise again, the opportunities for plunder rose with it. But just as important as the expanding volume of trade was the nature of that trade. This was the time of mercantilism, and the shape of that economic system was one important catalyst for rising piracy.

Mercantilism does not have a healthy reputation in economic circles. Indeed *The Wealth of Nations*, Adam Smith's landmark publication of the 1770s and arguably the first modern work of economics, was essentially an evidenced diatribe against the whole notion. But from the sixteenth to the eighteenth centuries, and arguably well into the nineteenth, it was the organising principle for most nations.

At its heart mercantilism is a simple idea, the notion that the key to accumulating state power is the control of more resources and in particular precious metals – seen by many as the only 'real' type of money. Trade with foreigners was something to worry about. If a state's people bought goods from a neighbour, then they would be forced to pay for those goods using either gold or silver – which would result in precious metals leaving one country and going to another. If English people, for example, were to buy French wine then the total stock of gold and silver in England would fall and the total stock in France would rise. This, according to mercantilist logic, would leave France in a stronger relative position to England. This was a horribly zero-sum way of looking at the world – where anything that made one country better off was assumed to make another worse off. The idea of mutually beneficial trade that would enrich both parties was seen as utopian at best and downright dangerous at worst. As one early mercantilist text, published in England in 1549, put it, 'we must always take heed that we buy no more from strangers than we sell them, for so should we impoverish ourselves and enrich them'. Economic policy, itself an anachronistic term in this context, was not really about the economy as such but about protecting and, ideally, expanding the power of the state itself. The key was to run a surplus of exports over imports which would lead to bullion flowing to the trade surplus country. Of course, as critics were to later point out, it was logically impossible that every country could simultaneously run such a surplus.

England, along with some of the Italian city-states, was an early adopter of the system. But from the 1650s onwards it would spread across much of the rest of Europe. In France it was most associated with the programmes of Jean-Baptiste Colbert, controller-general of the finances from the 1660s to the 1680s, to the extent that it is sometimes called Colbertism.

The typical mercantilist policy package consisted of high tariffs to keep out imports, perhaps subsidies to domestic exporters to win in foreign bullion and – the crucial part for piracy – regulations specifying that colonies could only trade with the mother country and so-called navigation acts preventing such trade being carried in foreign vessels.

Spain, as we have seen, had by the 1650s built up a large colonial empire in the Americas, one that shipped silver, tobacco, coffee, sugar and other highly prized and valuable goods back to Spain and one which, guided by mercantilist logic, sought to keep foreigners out of the business entirely. Beginning before the so-called golden age, rival states realised that encouraging corsairs to attack Spanish shipping was in their interest. Thus was born the letter of marque, an effective licence issued by one state allowing piracy. Beginning with France, and then copied by England and the Netherlands and later still others, the European states began issuing pirates with a letter giving them official sanction to raid the shipping of enemy nations.

The mere possession of a letter of marque did not lessen the dangers of such a career. The Spanish, or whoever else, tended to try buccaneers as criminals, and usually execute them, regardless of whether or not they were in possession of such a document. Those who did have the letters were technically known as privateers but the distinction between a privateer and a pirate was very much in the eye of the beholder. However, such a letter did allow the goods taken in a raid to be sold in the ports of the state issuing them.

For the issuing state, the letters of marque were a low-cost way of waging war. The costs of outfitting and crewing the privateer vessel were outsourced, as was the risk of losses. In addition, the inflow of cheap (stolen) goods was seen as beneficial to the economy and to the power of the issuing state. Privateering was to last a remarkably long time. It was not until the Declaration of Paris in 1856 that the European states renounced it as a tool of war, and even fourteen years after that Prussia essentially resorted to it during the Franco-Prussian conflict of 1870 through the use of what it called 'a volunteer navy'.

Even during periods of peace, when letters of marque were not being issued, rival colonial powers, guided by mercantilist logic, were often happy to at least turn a blind eye to piracy, as long as it seemed to be aimed at a rival. For men such as Teach and Roberts, robbing the Spanish or Portuguese was only profitable because they could always find an English, Dutch, French or Danish port at which they could unload and sell their ill-gotten wares.

It also mattered that the decades of piracy's golden age came at a time of flux in international relations, when no single power dominated the world's oceans. Spain was a declining imperial power but none of her rivals were yet able to truly displace her. And for most late-seventeenth and early-eighteenth-century admiralties, pirates, or what they might more politely have termed privateers, were often a useful tool rather than a menace.

It is perhaps easy to see how the conditions for piracy to flourish came about in the decades around 1700. The end of Europe's wars of religion had seen a new expansion of colonial empires and trade, the economic system that governed that trade encouraged rival powers to turn a blind eye to seaborne robbers targeting one's peers, and the lack of a single dominant navy made the enforcement of the rule of law at sea tricky. But while all of these criteria were no doubt necessary for piracy to take off in a large way, they perhaps cannot explain why it was so successful. For that one needs to look closer at the practices of the pirates themselves.

Pirates understood incentives. Let's start with the Hollywood favourite that is as much a trope of twentieth-century pirate movies as parrots, West Country accents and wooden legs: the skull and crossbones flag, or Jolly Roger. One way to think of this famous imagery is as a clear example of the economics of signalling.

The economics of piracy are relatively simple. The key to maximising profits, which is what ultimately drew men (and some women) towards serving under the black flag, was, as in many other lines of work, to minimise costs. One of the biggest potential costs pirates faced was the risk of battle with their prey.

Pirate ships tended to be well armed; if they had not been, it is hard to see how they could have taken many prizes at all. Typically they would carry two to three times as many cannon as a merchant ship and two to three times as many crew too. That not only gave them more firepower at a distance but also more fighting power in a boarding action once the range had been closed. But battles were not cost-free. Fighting to take a merchant prize was a costly endeavour. On one obvious level it could lead to death and injuries among the pirate crew. Potentially more seriously it could damage the pirates' ship, causing cruising time to be lost to repairs. Time spent performing repairs was time that was not used taking prizes, and pirate vessels were at their most vulnerable when laid up making battle damage good. But battle also risked, in the worst-case scenario for the pirates, sinking their potential prize. In that case the costs of fighting would lead to no gains at all. Pirates were often keen to trade up their own vessels if possible. If the prize was larger or faster than their ship they would usually take it for themselves. And as we have seen in the case of Bart Roberts, it was not at all uncommon for captured merchant crew to be recruited as pirates.

The ideal – and, in economic terms, profit-maximising – situation for a pirate was for a merchant vessel to surrender without a fight. To achieve this aim pirates sought to change the incentives faced by their opponents. They promised to kill any crew who offered resistance but gave complete quarter to any who surrendered without a fight. For the crew of a merchant ship presented with an approaching pirate vessel, the potential costs of resistance were extremely high and the benefits of compliance with the pirate demands obvious.

Making what an economist might call 'a credible commitment' to a surrender-or-die policy lowered the costs of taking prizes by encouraging the victims of piracy to offer no resistance. In theory at least, if the potential victims of a pirate attack genuinely believed the cost of resistance would be their massacre, they would be less likely to resist in the first place. In other words, the fact that pirates were creditably committed to carrying out what were by any definition atrocities meant that fewer atrocities would be required.

And such massacres were best avoided if at all possible – on the cold logic of profit-maximisation, let alone on humanitarian grounds. Massacring a crew was hardly cost-free. If nothing else, it would encourage the defenders of a ship who *had* resisted to fight to the last man knowing that surrender was no longer an option.

Thankfully for the pirates – and the crews of merchant vessels – not many such atrocities were required. What was really needed was for the surrender-or-die policy to be both widely known and readily believed. Pirates, in other words, needed the right sort of reputation, and what turned out to be especially helpful to them was the contemporary media. The newspapers and news-sheets of the day, especially those in port cities, understood that piracy made for good copy and were keen to write up examples of both the massacres of crews who resisted and, just as importantly, the majority of cases in which the crew surrendered and were not harmed. As the *Boston News-Letter* put it in 1723, 'good quarters to be given when craved'. Pirates had an active public relations strategy, and it worked. Indeed it worked so well that in 1721 the British Parliament attempted to make it a legal duty for armed merchant vessels to resist pirate attack. Surrender had become so common that the government wanted to make doing so a crime.

Newspapers and word-of-mouth made sailors aware of the reputation of pirates, but how was one to demonstrate that one was actually a pirate? The easiest way was to look like a pirate, and by the early 1700s that meant having the right flag.

It is unclear exactly which particular pirate was the first to hoist the Jolly Roger, although a case can be made for Black Bart Roberts and he was certainly an early adopter. Nor is the precise origin clear. It probably came from a combination of the black flags long associated with Islamic Barbary pirates operating from the coast of North Africa and the skull and crossbones which had long been used to mark crew members as deceased in ships' logbooks and records. But after its early appearance the flag spread rapidly and became a pirate calling card. It served a useful purpose. Merchant ships operating in the Caribbean in the first quarter of the eighteenth century faced two distinct threats, pirates and the Spanish coast guard (*guarda de la costa*), which while officially operating to ensure that Spain's system of mercantilism was enforced, often overstepped their authority to shake down passing vessels.

Flying a Jolly Roger was not exactly cost-free – it essentially acted as a confession of piracy if one was brought to trial. After Roberts's death, at the prosecution of his surviving crew, the court heard how the crew had sailed 'under a black flag, flagrantly by that, denoting yourselves common robbers, opposers and violators of all laws, human and divine'. But it brought benefits too. Nothing advertised that one was a pirate credibly committed to the surrender-or-die policy more than flying this particular flag. One contemporary account recounts an occasion on which Bart Roberts was being pursued by two French cruisers who had mistaken his vessel for a merchant ship banned from trading in French-controlled waters. When he hoisted the Jolly Roger 'their French hearts failed and they both surrendered without any, or at least very little resistance'.

The black flag and the contemporary newspaper reporting, as some economic historians have noted, served much the same purpose for pirates as modern Hollywood films have done for the Mafia – it built public awareness of the imagery associated with a particular manner of criminal and reinforced their reputation. If anything the resulting signalling was more powerful. Whereas flying the Jolly Roger was enough to condemn a crew to death, anyone can, in theory, attempt to impersonate a Mafioso by wearing a pinstriped suit and some sunglasses with far fewer consequences.

But pirates' understanding of incentives stretched well beyond a sound understanding of game theory intended to lower the costs of taking prizes. They organised their own ships in an exceptionally efficient manner, aligning the incentives of all on board in order to ensure smooth operations.

By their very nature they were operating outside the law and it would not be hard to imagine how a gang of criminals in a confined environment, often with valuable stolen loot to hand, could easily turn on each other. This, though, seems to have happened very rarely. Pirates organised their ships using pirate codes, several of which survive, and which some modern management thinkers have pointed to as examples of excellent corporate governance.

Black Bart Roberts's code is a fairly typical example. It contains some provisions which seem far from the popular imagery of pirates, such as a rule that all candles must be extinguished by 8 p.m. each evening and that anyone wanting to drink after that time should do so only on the open deck. It also banned gambling with dice or cards – presumably to remove a potential source of disagreement. More significantly, it explicitly organised the vessel as a floating democracy with 'every man' having 'a vote in the affairs of moment' and an equal share in provisions. Officers, like Roberts himself, were elected by the crew. And while in a naval ship of the time the captain would earn perhaps ten to fifteen times as much as the sailors and in a merchant vessel around five to eight times as much, on Roberts's pirate ship he himself only took twice as much of the booty as a common sailor. This was an egalitarian ship. The captain and the quartermaster received two shares on any prize, the master, the boatswain and the gunner one share and a half, more junior officers one share and a quarter and the rest of the crew one each. What is more, the code explicitly set out that the crew would remain together until each share was worth £1,000 (around £1.5 million in today's money) and only stop their pirating then. It even set forth a form of health insurance, with any man losing a limb in action compensated with £800 and with proportionally smaller pay-outs for less serious injuries.

The captain had unlimited authority during battle, when orders had to be obeyed and there was an obvious and necessary premium on rapid decision-making and decisive action, but at all other times their authority was held in check by a series of balances. The quartermaster – the other senior officer – took the lead in distributing booty and the crew always had the right, outside of battle, to challenge and remove their officers.

Pirates were acting in an illegal manner without recourse to contracts, laws or courts and yet managed to organise their ships into a system in which success was rewarded, talent was promoted and loyalty was built. Despite being entirely (and by definition) crewed by career criminals, mutiny was rarer on pirate vessels than on naval or merchant ships. The incentives of the men were almost perfectly aligned with each other and their officers with each working towards a specific goal.

Pirates are usually – and correctly – associated with theft and murder. Building up the 'credible commitment' to the surrender-or-die policy was hardly pleasant. But, as one recent report has put it, they could just as easily be associated with democracy, fair wages, concern for the (pirate) community and cooperation. It all rather depends on if one is viewing the Jolly Roger from the quarterdeck of a pirate ship or a potential prize.

It is perhaps going too far to call, as some management thinkers have done, for 'more pirates in the economy', but as a method of governance, the appeal is easy to see.

8

Accounting for Empire:
Why Britain Almost Swapped
Canada for Guadeloupe

In William Makepeace Thackeray's novel *The Luck of Barry Lyndon*, the titular character finds himself caught up in the Seven Years' War (1756–63), fighting first for the British Army and, after his desertion, for the Prussians. The somewhat unreliable narrator at one point opines:

> It would require a greater philosopher and historian than I am to explain the causes of the famous Seven Years' War in which Europe was engaged; and, indeed, its origin has always appeared to me to be so complicated, and the books written about it so amazingly hard to understand, that I have seldom been much wiser at the end of a chapter than at the beginning ...

Lyndon had a point. The Seven Years' War has a claim to being the first truly global war with battles fought not only in

Europe but also in North America (where it is usually known as the French and Indian War), the Caribbean, India, Africa and East Asia too. It involved all of the leading powers of its day. But it is also a rather confusing conflict to engage with. One reason that Barry Lyndon found it so difficult to explain is that it was essentially two related but distinct wars that involved some of the same powers and which happened to be fought at the same time. The war that involved Lyndon traipsing around modern-day Germany in the service of various states was essentially a clash between Austria, backed by France and Russia, and Prussia, backed by Britain, for predominance in central Europe. Meanwhile Britain fought a global war against France and Spain for control of key colonies in the Americas and Asia. The two wars were, in the end, concluded by separate treaties.

That first war, the one primarily between Austria and Prussia, is fascinating to students of military history. The rise of Prussia from being a peripheral, minor German state to one of the great powers of Europe is an important story. But in the long run, the economic impacts of this mid-eighteenth-century conflict are best traced by following the British trail.

The Seven Years' War certainly added to the British pantheon of national military triumphs. While they nowadays tend to stand in the shadows of their Napoleonic-era successors such as Wellington and Nelson, the British generals and admirals of the Seven Years' War were the heroes of their day. The fact that none of them got a 52-metre-high column in central London should not distract from this. The year 1759 became known as Britain's annus mirabilis after a series of decisive victories. Horace Walpole, a high-profile Member of Parliament, remarked that 'our bells are worn threadbare from ringing for victories'. In that year, Admiral Sir Edward Hawke took a Royal Navy fleet into the treacherous waters of Quiberon

Bay to smash French naval power. On the Plains of Abraham before Quebec, Major-General James Wolfe defeated the French under the Marquis de Montcalm and conquered French North America, despite being killed at his moment of triumph. Two years before this, at Plassey, the forces of the British East India Company had defeated the French equally decisively to cement Britain's role as the leading European power in the continent. But while Hawke, Wolfe and Robert Clive were all acclaimed as major figures in Britain's victories, there were other forces and players whose roles were just as important. Charles Palmer, Matthew Beachcroft, Merrick Burrell, Bartholomew Burton and Robert Marsh may not have won the kind of laurels heaped on their uniformed peers but as successive governors of the Bank of England during the Seven Years' War they contributed the decisive factor in the war. Britain's victory over France was achieved as much through financial strength as raw military power.

It is worth stepping back at this point and reminding oneself of the raw demographics of Britain and France in the mid-eighteenth century. The Seven Years' War occurred slap bang in the middle of a period sometimes referred to as the Second Hundred Years' War. Of the 126 years between 1689 and 1815, Britain and France were at war for sixty-eight of them. This was a battle not so much for predominance in Europe, but globally. Looking back from the vantage point of the twenty-first century, in which Britain and France are countries with similarly sized populations and broadly comparable economies – and indeed have long been so – it is easy to miss how unlikely a global leader Britain actually was.

In 1750 the total global population was around 745 million, of whom 150 million resided in Europe. France possessed a population of around twenty-five million, Britain's was closer to nine million. In other words, France was around two and a half times as populous as its great rival. Understanding how a country could compete with a rival more than twice its size means taking economic and financial factors seriously. Let's start with the economics. The eighteenth century is a key time in global economic history – possibly *the* key time, the time when the industrial revolution began to unfold.

On the grand-historical scale the industrial revolution is less a story of inventions, innovations and new forms of producing cotton or the birth of steam power – although it is certainly all of that – and more a story of a profound shift in the nature of economic growth. Broadly put, the pre-industrial world was one where natural resources presented a limit on populations. The Reverend Thomas Malthus developed a theory which became widely accepted. In his view, the natural tendency of human populations was for the number of people to grow in an exponential fashion (2, 4, 8, 16, etc.) while the resources required to sustain that population expanded in a linear form (2, 3, 4, 5, etc.). It does not take a high level of mathematical knowledge to see the rather obvious disconnect.

In the pre-industrial world there was, most of the time, an inverse relationship between the level of the population and income per head. That is to say, as the population grew, living standards tended to fall, and when the population dipped, living standards tended to rise. The Black Death was a terrible time for Europe's peasants, as one might expect when an essentially untreatable plague was painfully killing millions. But in its aftermath, the resources available to the survivors were proportionally higher and incomes rose.

The industrial revolution marked the end of this period. Fundamentally it was a story of rising productivity, or the ability to get more economic output from any given level of economic inputs. When the resource constraints eased, the grim calculus of Malthus was broken. Now it was possible – as would happen in later centuries – for both the level of population and the level of income per head to rise at the same time.

The key factor for the geopolitics of Europe and indeed the globe in the eighteenth century was that this revolution began in Britain. By 1750 British GDP (or national income) per head was already around 50 per cent larger than that of France. So while Britain's European rival might have two and a half times the population, its lead in terms of raw economic output was smaller.

Crucially, Britain was also much better placed to put its economic potential to work in the services of warfare. The key attribute to look to is tax revenues and fiscal capacity. In Britain in the 1750s, the state was able to collect in revenue the equivalent of 109 grams of silver per inhabitant; over the Channel, the French state was only able to collect the equivalent of 49 grams from its own residents. Britain's population may have only been around 35 per cent of the levels of France but its government had access to around 80 per cent as much taxation. The gap in receipts was much more manageable.

That, though, understates the case. When it came to spending power – the kind of spending power required to sustain and win a seven-year conflict fought across several continents – Britain enjoyed the lead. The straightforward reason being its ability to borrow.

Understanding why means stepping back briefly from the confusing war the fictional Barry Lyndon fought in and looking at how the British state had developed in the decades before. The English state, on roughly its current borders, had – as we saw when discussing the longbow – been unusually stable for a long time. Under the Tudors it had also become highly centralised. But more interesting than the Tudors – despite what the setters of school history curriculums and TV commissioning editors appear to believe – was what came afterwards.

Under the Stuart monarchs England took major steps towards becoming a more open-access economic order, one in which the views of violence specialists no longer dominated. The English state of the mid- to late seventeenth century, on the eve of the Second Hundred Years' War, was at least a proto-democracy. The monarch still held enormous power and the unelected hereditary House of Lords still dominated Parliament but governing was now most definitely a bargaining process. Through the House of Commons the growing commercial and prosperous merchant class, together with sundry lawyers and local notables, could make their voices heard – especially on fiscal matters. Like their Dutch rivals across the North Sea, with whom they fought several wars in this period, England was becoming an outward-looking, commercially focused maritime nation with a more open-access governing and economic order.

Nowhere was this clearer than in the events now most usually called the Glorious Revolution in 1688. While English politics displayed a notable trend towards becoming more democratic and open in the second half of the seventeenth century, the process was far from smooth. After the civil wars of the 1640s and the execution of the king, the Commonwealth eventually devolved into a quasi-military dictatorship. It did not last long after the death of Oliver Cromwell, and Charles II was restored to power mostly due to a lack of any other obvious alternatives. But he died in 1685 without a legitimate heir and was succeeded by his brother James II.

This posed a twofold problem for the English elite: James was a Catholic, having converted as a younger man, and he displayed what many regarded as absolutist tendencies, perhaps stirred by his long exile in France and service in the French monarch's armies. After James's ascension the English government therefore found itself unusually divided. The king favoured an alliance with France, believed royal powers were generally sufficient to raise revenues, and that the judiciary was subject to royal authority. Parliament, by contrast, generally favoured an alliance with the Dutch, believed it should control the state's purse strings, and supported an independent judiciary. Even leaving aside the especially vexed issue of Catholicism versus Protestantism and the particularly acute dispute over whether Parliament had any say in the question of the royal succession, there were plenty of grounds for conflict. But as long as James remained childless, these issues could be skirted over. Parliament would not be happy but could accept that James, who was already fifty-one at the time of his coronation, would not be around for ever. A decade or a decade and a half of rule by a Catholic absolutist was something they could live with. Eventually things would return to 'normal'.

The unexpected birth of a male heir, and one who would be raised as a Catholic, changed that calculation. Now Parliament had to grapple with the very real possibility of a new Catholic dynasty on the throne.

Their solution was simple enough: change the monarch. A coterie of leading merchants and parliamentarians turned to the European leader they most admired, William of Orange, the Stadtholder of the Dutch Republic and also James's son-in-law, and invited him to rule England alongside his wife Mary, the daughter of James and, until the birth of his son, his presumed heir. William consented and arrived in England at the head of a Dutch army. Tales of 1066 being the last successful invasion of England from the continent rely on ignoring the rather inconvenient fact that in November 1688 12,000 Dutch soldiers landed in the West Country and marched on London.

The Glorious Revolution is a central part of the traditional Whig history of England, which sees the national story as being a steady journey towards modernity, liberalism and progress. English writers, especially in the nineteenth century, were keen to contrast their own 'glorious' revolution with the messy French one of a century later. Even leaving aside that the English had already killed a king four decades earlier, that rousing national story is still a rather sanitised version of the truth. For a long time it was usual to portray the Glorious Revolution as everything the cross-Channel equivalent was not: orderly, legal and bloodless. None of these supposed attributes really bears much scrutiny. The legality was at best justified in hindsight only, as successful coups d'etat often are, and it certainly did not feel especially orderly at the time. The bloodless argument relies on taking a very narrow English as opposed to an overall British Isles view. The English army essentially refused to fight for James (with many of its leading officers members of the wonderfully honestly named 'Treason Club' and backing William) and so, other than a handful of skirmishes, there was no real fighting in England. But in Scotland the Battle of Killiecrankie between forces loyal to James and William left a couple of thousand dead, and in Ireland men loyal to James engaged William in a war lasting three years and marked by fierce fighting at the Boyne, Aughrim and in more than half a dozen vicious sieges. The death toll there almost certainly topped 25,000.

But whatever the historiography of the rights and wrongs of the Glorious Revolution, its economic and military impacts were to prove hugely significant in the years that followed. The constitutional revolution, which built on the events of the 1640s and firmly established the power of Parliament as well as guaranteeing the independence of the judiciary, was accompanied soon afterwards by a financial revolution.

The key to understanding the nature of English – and then British – military power lies in grasping the nature of this financial revolution. Britain could afford to contest the dominance of global trade with France, a much larger country, not just because the income per head of its subjects was higher and not just because the state could squeeze a higher proportion of this income out of them in the form of tax, but because it had a much greater ability to borrow even more money as required. Spain in the age of Philip II and his successors, and France in the later eighteenth century, were countries hamstrung by high debts that degraded the power of their militaries. Britain, though, was a country that thrived on high public debts and was able to translate the ability to borrow into hard military power.

What really underpinned this financial revolution was what an economic historian might refer to as an institutional change and what regular historians would probably call politics. Whatever the terminology, the relationship between economic and political change was closely intertwined.

Parliament in the 1690s was in a strong position. The new monarch owed his throne to their initial support – and admittedly that of several thousand Dutch soldiers on English soil. For William, though, taking the English throne was all well and good but his priority remained his native Netherlands and the threat posed to that nation by France. England's arms would be put to good use defending Dutch soil. The English, and Scottish, forces not engaged in fighting James II's remaining loyalists in Ireland were quickly in action across the North Sea fighting the French in Flanders. The Nine Years' War of 1688 to 1697 was the opening engagement of the Second Hundred Years' War.

It was also a very expensive business. In England in the 1690s total GDP (the total output of the economy) varied between around £50 million and £60 million annually. The war cost around £5 million a year initially, rising to more like £8.5 million by its closing. Those are, to be absolutely clear, big numbers. Spending 10 to 15 per cent of national income on a war might be well below the kind of levels seen in the total wars of the twentieth century (where 50 per cent-plus was occasionally hit) but outside these extreme examples it is one of the largest dedications of national income to warfare in British history.

The need to finance this kept Parliament sitting. Whereas previously Parliaments had been assembled as and when required to vote through new taxes, the financial pressures of the fighting in Flanders in effect meant Parliament became a permanent body. Specific taxes to fund the wars, raising around £5 million a year, were put in place. The English people, while no doubt grumbling at the comparatively high level of taxes, could at least agree that they had been imposed in a legitimate fashion with some degree of consent from the people – or at least the people who held economic power.

What is more, from 1690 onwards Parliament established the Commission of Public Accounts which monitored how the money raised was actually spent. Rather than simply granting revenues to the Crown, Parliament came to insist on a say on how that money was used. Specific appropriations were inserted into supply bills to limit the discretion of the monarch.

A major change came in 1698 with the creation of the Civil List which granted the monarch a pot of cash (originally £700,000) to fund their household and put a firm dividing line between the finances of the king and that of the government and country. This separation allowed for an equally crucial dividing line to be placed between debts owed by the monarch and what became known as the national debt, the collective public debt of the country as a whole which Parliament was responsible for servicing and repaying through taxation.

By the end of the Nine Years' War the English state was looking increasingly modern, or at least early modern. The ad-hoc financial and constitutional arrangements of the Tudor and Stuart years had given way to a permanently sitting Parliament, a modern national debt, regular taxation and parliamentary control of the nation's finances together with a recognised separation of powers. The institutional structure of England had been overhauled.

The last crucial institutional ingredient in the mix was created in 1694: the Bank of England itself, built on the success of the new order.

England at the end of the seventeenth century had an underdeveloped banking – and monetary – system compared to many of its European peers. In Italy and across the German lands wealthy merchants had been moving into offering banking services, often linked to the need to finance trade, for centuries. Britain, though, had no domestic equivalent of the German Fuggers or Italian Medicis. Complicating things further, the country produced pitiful and sporadic amounts of silver domestically and no gold while often running a trade deficit with her neighbours. That resulted in an outflow of precious metals leaving less in circulation domestically. It was not just that the country lacked banks, it often lacked coin too.

The seventeenth century had seen some financial innovations. In the 1640s, for example, Sir William Cavendish, a wealthy noble with interests in the wool trade, found himself needing to transport £13,500 (about £2.7 million in modern money) from Derbyshire in the English Midlands to London to pay for a shipment. This proved to be impossible to arrange at a cost that would not be prohibitive. Sir William instead utilised a bill of exchange – that is to say, he essentially paid for his goods using a signed promissory note, effectively an IOU. In the years that followed such bills of exchange became increasingly common and their form was standardised. Rather quickly they began to become a substitute for actual coinage, at least in commercial circles. Merchant A could purchase goods from merchant B paid for with a bill of exchange and merchant B could use that bill of exchange to purchase something else from merchant C. A bill might be worth less than its face value and be less secure than proper coinage but it was, if nothing else, easier to transport and often more widely available.

Banking was confined mostly to the old City of London. Banks were mostly goldsmith banks, that is to say they started out as traditional goldsmiths and later moved into offering a wider array of financial services, such as holding gold on deposit for customers and offering short-term loans. Such banks, though, lacked the resources for large-scale lending.

Modern British banking history begins at sea, and with a terrible defeat. In 1690 the English fleet, in concert with its Dutch allies, engaged the French at Beachy Head in the English Channel. Around fifty-six allied ships clashed with closer to seventy French vessels and the French came out on top. A dozen English and Dutch ships were captured or sunk compared to no French losses. The French had temporary command of the Channel and England underwent one of its periodic invasion scares. The diarist John Evelyn, a contemporary of Samuel Pepys, noted 'the whole nation now exceedingly alarmed by the French fleet braving our coast even to the very Thames mouth'.

Parliament, in these early days of William's reign, baulked at the projected £1.5 million cost of rebuilding the fleet. This gave added impetus to the drive to establish a national bank to fund such projects, and in 1694 the Bank of England was given its royal charter. The Bank raised £1.2 million in capital in just twelve days from 1,268 subscribers – the bulk of them commercial, prosperous types but with a substantial proportion coming from the old landed interests – which was loaned to the government in return for an interest rate of 8 per cent. The Bank was explicitly created to finance the wars with France and disallowed from engaging in most traditional commercial and mercantile activities. Over time, of course, it would expand into issuing paper notes, but initially the focus was purely on lending to the government.

What made the Bank work was the constitutional and fiscal credibility established by the Glorious Revolution. Parliament, or rather more formally the king through Parliament, had proved it had the means and willingness to vote through the taxes required to meet the debt payments and so lending to the government, via the Bank, seemed like a worthwhile bet.

By the end of the Nine Years' War the national debt amounted to around 20 per cent of national income – a low figure by today's standards but a worryingly high one to contemporaries. But as anyone who has ever had a mortgage or any other sort of loan knows, what matters is not just the quantum of the borrowing but its costs. As England – and, after 1707's Act of Union with Scotland, Great Britain – established that it would not miss a payment and as Parliament then demonstrated its ability to increase the tax take when needed, the interest rates charged began to fall. By the time of the Seven Years' War in the 1750s the British government was able to borrow at just 3 per cent.

In theory, the plan was always to 'pay off' the national debt at some point. Financial officials throughout the eighteenth century would often note that while Parliament had granted taxation on the basis of borrowing at, say, 8 per cent, the actual costs were often lower – perhaps 4 or 5 per cent – and the difference could be used to pay down the principal. In the late 1710s optimistic officials believed the whole thing would be paid off within twenty-two years. But that comforting arithmetic ignored the reality of Britain's long on-again-off-again war with France. By the time the Seven Years' War rolled around, following the long War of the Spanish Succession and the War of the Austrian Succession, government debt was around 100 per cent of GDP. But the costs of serving it were eminently manageable.

A country with high debts and high interest rates forced into using yet more borrowing is generally one set to suffer a decline in military power. The Britain of the eighteenth century, however, may have had high debts – higher than those which played a role in driving France into revolution – but the low interest rates, based on institutional credibility, made her debts crucially different. It was this financial framework that underpinned Britain's successful prosecution of global warfare in the 1750s. Britain could afford to maintain a top-class navy and to provide subsidies to more financially stretched allies on the European mainland to keep armies in the field against France.

For Britain, especially in the conflict's latter half, the Seven Years' War was a truly global conflict. It is important to trace here the notion of the sometimes controversial idea of a 'British way of warfare'. In the Nine Years' War, William had been justifiably concerned at the prospect of the Dutch Republic being overrun by its larger neighbour to the south and maintained a large English army in Flanders fighting directly on the continent. A similar continental commitment had occurred in the War of the Spanish Succession, fought from 1700 to 1714, with the Duke of Marlborough winning his famous victories in Europe. This was not always popular in England (after 1707, Britain). It was easy to justify the existence of the navy which not only protected an island nation from invasion but also helped to protect and expand growing British interests and trade overseas. The issue became more polarised after Queen Anne (William and Mary's successor) died childless in 1714 and the perceived need to maintain a Protestant succession led to George I of Hanover becoming king as well as maintaining his original holdings in Germany. Throughout the first few decades of the Hanoverian line, some British parliamentarians were reluctant to see British armies serving what looked to be Hanoverian interests in mainland Europe.

Epitomised by William Pitt (the Elder), a member of the Cabinet and essentially the manager of Britain's wartime strategy from 1756 to 1761, the British way of warfare downplayed the need for a large army, was suspicious of putting British boots on the ground in Europe and instead emphasised the importance of providing financial support to allies, of maintaining a powerful navy and of taking control of the colonies and overseas possessions of her opponents. Proponents of such a strategy argued that it played to Britain's strengths – a maritime culture that generated a comparative advantage in naval power and the financial strength to support allies economically. France was, after all, a much larger country and when it came to land forces would always hold the edge. One by-product of such a course of action was the opportunity to mop up French colonies overseas.

This is exactly the path Britain took in the 1750s. While a small British army did fight in Germany – as told in *Barry Lyndon* – and win great acclaim at the Battle of Minden, the bulk of Britain's war effort was focused outside Europe. As well as the victories in India and Quebec, French islands across the Caribbean were also taken, and towards the end of the conflict Britain declared war on Spain and took possession of both the Philippines and Cuba.

The intention, though, was never to hold all these gains in perpetuity. Eighteenth-century statesmen recognised that peace talks were a bargaining process that involved give and take. Indeed one feature of peace treaties in the period was that they often contained commercial clauses – the victor might not only take some colonies but also insist on favourable access for their own exports in a market controlled by a former enemy.

The aim for Britain towards the end of the war was to seize as much as possible in order to have plenty of options going into the inevitable peace talks. This did not work out quite as planned in the case of the conflict with Spain. Eighteenth-century communications being what they were, the British force that attacked Manila did so before news of the war had reached the Philippines and by the time news of their seizure reached Europe the treaties had already been concluded.

Before the inevitable haggling with the French, though, there was plenty of haggling in Britain too about exactly which prizes should be kept and which handed back in return for peace. From 1760 to 1763 a fierce debate raged which to modern ears sounds rather preposterous: should Britain aim to keep Canada or Guadeloupe? Pamphlets written by figures ranging from Benjamin Franklin to the Bishop of Carlisle weighed in on the question.

The debate was not as odd as it may appear. While Canada was physically much larger and contained a great many more people, it did appear to offer less in the way of immediate economic returns. The beaver fur trade was all well and good, but Guadeloupe was a sugar island and sugar was a high-value commodity much demanded in Europe in the eighteenth century. The immediate financial returns from Guadeloupe, though, had to be set against a clear security case for Canada: the removal of a French colony to the immediate north of Britain's own thirteen North American colonies would, it was hoped, not only secure their position but also lead to eventual financial savings from lower garrisoning costs.

The debate occasionally became bitter. The Earl of Bute, who led the government at the end of the war, was accused in the *North Briton* of not understanding the appeal of beaver pelts and he was parodied as saying, 'if any lady have be so nice as to require artificial warmth; we have cats and dogs for the purpose ... with such delicious roughness'.

In the end Britain went for the security of her North American colonies over the returns offered by a sugar island. That, though, as some perceptive commentators in the pamphlet war realised, was to have much longer-term contrary results. The presence of a large French colony in modern Canada had, if nothing else, been a clear reason for those colonies to rely on Britain for security. As one British colonist was to write in the 1760s, 'a Neighbour that keeps us in some Awe, is not always the worst of Neighbours'. The removal of the French threat changed the incentives of those colonists. Prior to the Treaty of Paris, being part of Britain's empire might have imposed some costs but it also came with the clear benefit of protection from France. After the treaty the costs remained, and indeed began to increase as Britain attempted to place more of the burden of imperial rule on to her colonies, but the benefits were much more questionable. Swapping Guadeloupe for Canada may, in the final analysis, have cost Britain North America. The country's institutions allowed her to win a global war but a failure to understand incentives made the victory hollower.

9

When Cronyism and Corruption Helped: The Royal Navy's Rise to Greatness

Admiral John Byng had plenty of time to consider his fate and many reasons to think it rather unfair. The court-martial that acquitted him of personal cowardice but found he had not 'done his utmost' to engage or destroy the enemy delivered its verdict on 27 January 1757. It was not until 14 March that he was taken to the quarterdeck of HMS *Monarch* and executed by firing squad.

Until then things had seemed to be going well for Byng in his career in the Royal Navy. He was born in 1704 to a father who was already a rear-admiral and would go on to end his own career as the Admiral of the Fleet – the highest rank in the navy – and be ennobled as a viscount. As naval pedigrees go, they do not get much better. Byng himself joined the navy at thirteen, was promoted to lieutenant at nineteen and made the rank of captain at just twenty-three. After a decade and a half of generally peaceful service mostly in the Mediterranean, he was made Governor of Newfoundland, in modern Canada, for a time before being promoted to rear-admiral in 1745 and taking up the role of commander-in-chief at Leith and effectively running the Royal Navy's operations in Scotland. This was a less peaceable time. Charles Edward Stuart, Bonnie Prince Charlie, the grandson of the long-deposed James II, landed in Scotland and led the Jacobite rebellion aiming to put his father, James II's son, on the British throne. Byng played his part in the 1745 rebellion by preventing the resupply of the Jacobite forces by their French allies and lending naval support to some of the brutal mopping-up operations after the Crown's victory at Culloden. Promoted to vice-admiral in 1747, he also became Commander-in-Chief Mediterranean. From 1751 onwards he combined that with being Member of Parliament for the Kent seat of Rochester, something not too uncommon at the time.

It was when the Seven Years' War broke out – even though it was to have a successful conclusion – that things really started going wrong for Byng. The Spanish island of Minorca had been in British hands since 1708, when it was captured during the War of the Spanish Succession. As Commander-in-Chief Mediterranean, defending the usefully placed naval base was Byng's responsibility. Sadly for him, though, as part of the usual British post-war cost-cutting regime which balanced budgets in peacetime, the Mediterranean fleet had been stripped back to just three ships of the line – that is to say, ships seen as capable of standing in a line of battle against an opposing fleet. Meanwhile the French possessed a powerful squadron based to the north in Toulon.

Byng was ordered to assemble a fleet in Portsmouth and sail for the western Mediterranean. The state of his fleet left much to be desired. It took him a month to cobble together the ten additional ships he had been promised and even then they were in a state of disrepair. When he sailed in April 1756, HMS *Defiance* was still missing two of her three masts. More worryingly, the flotilla was seriously undermanned, missing around 800 sailors. The gap was partially made good by the loan of several hundred army soldiers who could carry out basic naval tasks but lacked most of the necessary training.

Things did not get much better when the fleet arrived in Gibraltar where the general in charge refused to provide the promised Royal Marines, and naval stores, essential to refitting Byng's ships, were found to be pretty bare. After sending a dispatch to London warning of his perilous state, Byng set off for Minorca, arriving off Port Mahon on 19 May. French soldiers had already been landed on the island in force. Poor weather prevented him making contact with the British garrison, and the following day the French fleet appeared.

On one level the resulting Battle of Minorca, fought on 20 May 1756, could be regarded as inconclusive. Certainly neither side covered themselves in glory and it is not remembered as a decisive encounter. The forces arrayed appeared reasonably well matched with Byng having twelve ships of the line and seven smaller frigates compared to the Marquis de la Galissonière's twelve ships of the line and five frigates. Byng's ships were undermanned and many were still in a far from ideal state of repair but he did hold the 'weather gauge'. His fleet was upwind of the French, which was often considered a crucial edge in the Age of Sail. An upwind ship can sail downwind towards its opponents while freely manoeuvring to fire its port or starboard cannon, whereas a downwind ship trying to sail upwind finds its movement restricted and the effectiveness of its gunnery lowered.

Byng ordered his ships, as was the standard tactic of the time, to form a line of battle with their vessels bow to stern from each other and move parallel to the French fleet. Since the Anglo-Dutch Wars of a century before, this was how fleet engagements had been fought. Given that the vast majority of cannon on a ship faced out to the port or starboard, two lines of battle parallel to each other allowed the two fleets to bring the most guns into action. The idea was simply to place the two fleets alongside and pound each other until one side had had enough. The line-of-battle approach may also have brought other, less tangible benefits, to which we shall return.

But at Minorca things did not go to plan. The van (forward group) of British ships obeyed Byng's instructions immediately but the rest of his fleet found themselves in difficulties. The result was that initially the forward British ships were engaged by a superior number of French vessels while the rest of the British fleet struggled to get into position. The battle began at around 2 p.m. and was over by six that evening as the two fleets pulled back from each other. Each side had suffered around two hundred dead or wounded and while several British vessels in the van had taken some heavy damage, no ship on either side had been sunk or captured. Byng, after taking stock of the situation, headed back to Gibraltar to make repairs four days later.

At Gibraltar the fleet was reinforced by four more ships of the line and began making good the damage suffered at Minorca, but before he could take them back out to the Balearic Islands a message from London arrived, removing Byng from command and summoning him back to London. On 29 June the garrison on Minorca surrendered and the island was lost to France.

Sadly for Byng, the news of Minorca's fall beat him to London. The Ministry in London and Admiralty were keen for someone other than themselves to take the blame and Byng was tried under the Articles of War for returning to Gibraltar rather than making a second attempt to relieve the British garrison. This, it was argued, was him 'failing to do his utmost'. Once he was found guilty, the only punishment permitted was death – despite many appeals for clemency.

Voltaire in his novel *Candide,* first published just two years later, in 1759, had his eponymous central character in Portsmouth witnessing the execution and being told by a British officer that 'in this country, it is good to kill an admiral from time to time to encourage the others'.

Byng was not just any admiral, he was Commander-in-Chief Mediterranean, a sitting Member of Parliament and the son of a viscount and former Admiral of the Fleet. But that did him no good. The surprising thing is that Voltaire's partially satirical quip appears to have been true. Shooting Byng did indeed encourage the others and was part of a culture of calculated aggression that the Royal Navy sought to inculcate throughout its officers. In economic terms, incentives played a large role in the navy's effectiveness over the course of the long eighteenth century.

It is worth stepping back at this point and considering just how staggeringly successful a force the Royal Navy was from the late seventeenth to the early nineteenth century. Between the 1650s and the 1810s the Royal Navy was transformed from a mid-ranking European navy into the most powerful and successful navy in the world. Over the course of a century and a half the Royal Navy regularly defeated its Dutch, Spanish and French rivals together with a host of smaller fleets.

The numbers are striking. Through the French Revolutionary and Napoleonic Wars, between 1793 and 1815 when the Royal Navy was truly at its peak, it lost only seventeen frigates to the French – and nine of those were later recaptured. The French, by contrast, lost 229. Over the same period, and against all enemies rather than just the French,

166 British vessels were lost to enemy action or captured, of which just five were ships of the line (usually defined as those possessing more than fifty cannon). In return the Royal Navy sank, burned or captured 1,201 enemy warships of which 159 were ships of the line. In other words, for every Royal Navy loss over the course of two decades of global warfare it inflicted seven enemy losses, and for every lost ship of the line an almost unbelievable thirty-three equivalent losses. Britannia really did rule the waves.

And nor were these losses a simple case of the Royal Navy being able to bring more guns and ships to bear and outnumbering its foes. A dataset of 172 so-called 'duels' or single-ship-on-single-ship engagements over the course of the Age of Sail involving the British fleet reveals that the Royal Navy was victorious 67 per cent of the time, the battle was inconclusive on 24 per cent of occasions and the Royal Navy was defeated in just 9 per cent of those duels.

Accounting for this is not straightforward. While the Royal Navy did outmatch its opponents ship for ship, it also generally had bigger numbers to start with. Given the existence and development of the British fiscal-military state from the 1690s onwards, with its efficient taxation systems and ability to borrow, that is hardly surprising. In the 1690s, at the time of the Nine Years' War, the British fleet (or the then still English fleet) was roughly the same size as that of the French; both had a total displacement tonnage (the usual measure of the total weight of a ship) of around 200,000 tons. But by the time of the Seven Years' War half a century later, the French fleet was still displacing 200,000 tons while the Royal Navy had grown to more like 300,000 tons. The other leading fleets of the 1750s, the Spanish and the Dutch, displaced around 100,000 tons and 50,000 tons respectively. The Royal Navy clearly had a material quantitative edge over its potential opponents by the middle of the eighteenth century and one that would only grow into the early 1800s.

Warships were among the leading technologies of their day and far from cheap. A standard line-of-battle ship of the 1790s would carry seventy-four cannon. To put that in context, at the Battle of Talavera – one of the Duke of Wellington's great victories over the French in Spain, fought in 1809 – a British army of around twenty thousand men had thirty cannon. Even at Waterloo, the largest land battle the British Army fought in this period, Wellington had around 150 cannon – or in naval terms, two ships' worth. And the cannons at sea would usually be of a much heavier calibre, capable of firing balls of 24lb to 36lb compared to a normal range of 6lb to 12lb from land-based guns.

A seventy-four-gun ship – referred to as a third rate in the terminology of the time; first and second rates were larger – was a two-deck ship with a crew of five hundred to seven hundred men built to last for twenty years or more and capable of spending months, even years if needed, at sea. It weighed anything from 2,000 to 3,000 tons and required vast quantities of high-quality timber, canvas, rope, iron, pitch and tar. From the early 1700s onwards, the bottom tended to be lined in copper, adding further cost. The loss of such a vessel was, in no uncertain terms, a big deal for any state.

Britain, as an island nation, was always likely to give its navy a higher priority over its army when it came to spending and it had a state capable of spending vastly more. There is no real evidence, despite their repeated victories in ship-on-ship duels, that the quality of British-made vessels was any higher than that of their opponents. Indeed captured French frigates were prized commands for British captains who admired their sailing qualities. Different nations tended to prioritise different things when it came to ship design. The French went for speed, the Spanish for vessels capable of weathering many difficult Atlantic crossings. British vessels tended to be jacks of all trades.

But if the vessels of different navies were much of a muchness, there almost certainly was a British edge when it came to the quality of the crew. Once again Britain's place as a maritime island nation played a role here. The country simply had more experienced sailors, relative to its size, than most potential rivals. By the 1770s, for example, the British merchant fleet had perhaps 700,000 sailors with its nearest rival, the Dutch commercial fleet, having just a tenth of that number. That was a ready pool of trained personnel to draw on. Over the course of the 1790s and 1800s the British qualitative edge grew over time as the French fleet found itself spending extended periods bottled up in ports, blockaded by the British. Seamanship standards waned as a result. Britain's greater financial resources also allowed her navy to engage in more live-firing training of their cannon, which almost certainly led to British vessels achieving a faster rate of fire in action than that of those they engaged.

But while the quality of the crews certainly helped, the real British edge came in leadership. This is where incentives came into play.

The career path of a Royal Navy officer during the wider Age of Sail, and specifically during the long decades of the French Revolutionary and Napoleonic Wars, was unusual. In the British Army, and in most armies of the time, officers' commissions were purchased. A young man of perhaps sixteen or seventeen would buy an ensign's commission and after a few years he could sell that on, purchase himself the role of lieutenant and step up the chain. It was not until the 1870s that this was abolished.

Outside some specialised roles in engineering and artillery, army officers – odd as this may sound – received no formal training and were not required to hold any particular set of qualifications, other than having a large enough wallet to acquire their position. Naval officers, by contrast, had to first spend time as a midshipman – a sort of apprenticeship in the craft of being a naval officer. Boys would generally begin this at the age of around twelve or thirteen, acting as a junior officer and receiving lessons from more senior officers on the nature of navigation and how to run a ship. In theory, boys required six years at sea and letters of recommendation from their captains before being allowed to sit the lieutenant's exam, although in reality it was reasonably common for a captain to put a friend or relative's children 'on their books' for a few years without them actually serving on board.

The lieutenant's exam, which candidates could sit from the age of nineteen, was not straightforward: to pass one had to prove that:

> He can Splice, Knot, Reef a Sail, work a Ship in Sailing, shift his Tides, keep a Reckoning of a Ship's Way by Plain Sailing and Mercator; observe by Sun or Star, and find the Variation of the Compass, and is qualified to do the Duty of an Able Seaman, and Midshipman.

Which, translated out of the kind of naval jargon beloved of readers of Patrick O'Brian and C. S. Forester novels, is a fairly particular set of skills. The successful lieutenant needed not only to be capable of carrying out the technical and often tricky tasks required to handle the ship and its sails, he also needed a quite advanced knowledge of trigonometry to handle navigation.

Just passing the lieutenant's exam was also no guarantee of a lieutenant's commission. In times such as the 1780s, when

Britain was generally at peace, there simply would not be enough available roles to fit in all the qualified candidates.

Assuming, though, that one was commissioned, the next step up was to post captain. This was really where careers diverged, and things got interesting. A lieutenant might hold one of several different roles: they could serve as a mid-ranking officer on board a ship of the line or a frigate or – the juiciest jobs that many hankered for – they could even command a smaller vessel. Confusingly, while doing so they would usually be referred to as a captain although they still held the substantive rank of lieutenant.

Being a proper captain required promotion. That was in the gift of the Admiralty which could promote lieutenants to post captain as they saw fit. Once someone had made post captain then further promotion was entirely based on seniority and time in the role. In other words, if you made post captain at a young enough age and managed to avoid a premature death in battle or a nautical disaster, then you could reasonably hope to end your career as an admiral.

To further complicate things, the nature of a post captain's career could vary greatly. There were generally more post captains on the list than available commands and so many officers would find themselves stuck ashore on half-pay just waiting, and hoping, for a role to be assigned to them. If and when a role did come along, not all commands were created equally. Commanding a seventy-four-gun ship of the line which was constantly in a squadron commanded by an admiral was a different proposition from commanding a forty-gun frigate, operating independently with orders to prowl the Mediterranean and sweep up enemy commerce. Although both were no doubt preferable to commanding a run-down fifty-gun ship escorting merchant ships on the eighteen-month round trip to Australia.

On one level, the fundamental economic problem facing the Royal Navy – and all other navies of the day – was one of incentives. The Admiralty could commission and equip vastly expensive warships, it could crew them to the best of its ability and it could select the officers that would command them, but once they were out at sea there was very little it could do to ensure they were acting as it intended. Indeed a captain operating hundreds, occasionally even thousands of miles away from their commanding officer and with no way to contact them is probably just about the most difficult management monitoring task imaginable.

Whether by accident or design, the Royal Navy of the day stumbled into an effective way of aligning incentives and monitoring performance – one that rivals were slow to copy and which helps explain the qualitative edge Royal Navy ships held over their opponents.

One way to incentivise officers was financial rewards, and these, in sharp contrast to the army, were available by the bucketful for naval officers. The pay was not too shabby, but what really made the difference was the existence of prize money. Whenever a Royal Navy vessel took possession of an enemy merchant ship or warship the value of the cargo, the market value of the ship and a fee per head of the captured crew would go into a prize pot. This pot was then shared out, with the admiral commanding the vessel involved taking between an eighth and a quarter of the total (despite the fact he would rarely have been present), the captain taking a quarter, the other officers on board sharing another quarter and the remainder being dished out among the crew.

The sums involved could be substantial and spawned a whole cottage industry of prize agents and lawyers acting on behalf of naval officers who felt they had not received their fair share. To give an idea of the potential rewards on offer, an admiral during the 1790s was paid around £3,000 a year – or around £300,000 a year in today's money. But it was not uncommon for an admiral also to receive annual prize shares worth between £200,000 and £300,000, taking them into the ranks of the ultra-rich. Southern England is still dotted with the palatial country homes built by admirals with prize money. The unfortunate Byng's is to be found near Potters Bar in Hertfordshire.

There is no doubt that the rewards on offer were higher than those required to attract a sufficient number of gentlemen into the ranks of the navy. In economic terms they might be thought of as efficiency wages. By paying more than it had to, the navy left itself with a surplus of captains and admirals on half-pay and without a command at any given time. That surplus, though, was to prove useful. Because any captain at sea would be aware that if he failed to do his duty, a replacement was ready and raring to go.

The navy had to guard against two forms of behaviour by its officers, which might be termed greed and cowardice. The first was the chance that a captain, fully aware of the potential prize money involved, would prioritise taking merchant vessels rather than fighting the enemy. That path seemed to offer higher rewards and with a lower risk of being killed. The second was the fear that when push came to shove, a captain would have his ship hold back rather than closely engage the enemy.

The existence of financial rewards for success helped to align incentives, as did the pool of available replacements. But the keys to making the system work were monitoring and a firm rulebook. These rules, as set down by the Articles of War, could appear harsh – just ask Admiral Byng. But they served a necessary purpose. All British officers operated under the knowledge that failing to 'do their utmost' would be greeted with the most severe terms.

And captains, although they might serve long periods away from their admiral, were also subject to constant monitoring by their fellow officers. One major duty of lieutenants was to keep a constant log of their captain's actions which could later be inspected by the Admiralty. Lieutenants would usually be the key witnesses at any court-martial.

Even the line of battle itself – the standard way in which navies operated in battle throughout this period – can be seen as a form of monitoring device. Forming a line of ships did allow the most guns to be brought to bear but it was hardly ever the best available strategy; indeed in many of Nelson's famous victories he used radically different approaches. For a start, for it to work it relied on the enemy conveniently forming their own line to sail alongside yours. And getting the ships of a squadron into line was not an easy manoeuvre – again, as Byng could testify – and it would take time. This often gave the enemy the option to sail away. Consider, too, the Battle of Toulon in 1744. Faced with a Franco-Spanish fleet, Admiral Mathews ordered an immediate attack before forming a line of battle. This led to confusion among many British captains and a tendency, from some, to hang back. The end result was a defeat for the Royal Navy and a great many court-martials. A line of battle was not the most imaginative tactic, but its one definite upside was that it allowed for the admiral in command to keep a very close watch on his ships.

The discontinuous nature of naval promotion, the constant monitoring by underlings, the firm rules of the Articles of War, the availability of excessive prize money and the pool of half-pay alternatives all combined to create an incentive structure that worked. A British officer who 'always did his utmost' could expect promotion and potentially vast riches. One who did not could expect a court-martial at worst and long years on half-pay with no prize money at best.

It is worth comparing the Articles of War with their French equivalents. They might, especially to modern eyes, appear overtly harsh, but they were subtly milder and distinct from what went on in the French navy of the day. The key call was that an officer 'had to do their utmost', which implicitly recognised that there were times when one's utmost was not enough. Byng's great misfortune was to become a scapegoat for wider government failings and the poor state of repair of the Mediterranean fleet. When Commodore Arthur Forrest fought a French squadron to a stalemate and then failed to pursue them due to damage to his own ships in October 1757 – fewer than eighteen months after Byng left Minorca – there was no real question of him facing a firing squad. By contrast, in the French fleet of the 1790s the rule was that any captain who surrendered his ship unless that 'ship should be so shattered as to be in danger of sinking' was subject to the death penalty.

While the Royal Navy's rules incentivised captains to seek battle and try their best, the French system instead made the costs of failure too high and incentivised captains to eschew battle if possible. It was better, in the French fleet, to avoid the risk of losing a ship and so French fleets tended to adopt defensive tactics.

The final secret ingredient to the Royal Navy's astonishing success was a strange one: patronage, or as it might be termed today, cronyism and corruption.

The most important step in any officer's career was the move from lieutenant to post captain. Most lieutenants never made it, and those who did were then on a simple path to the role of admiral if they lived long enough. But while the promotion from midshipman to lieutenant involved an examination and fairly rigorous standards, the step up to post captain was somewhat more opaque. Byng, it should be remembered, was the son of an admiral. Admirals were often keen to promote their own kin where possible. The really surprising thing is that this does not seem to have harmed the navy; in fact, quite the opposite. Work by economic historians has found that the average Royal Navy ship over the course of the entire Age of Sail from 1690 to 1850 could expect to capture, burn or sink 0.8 enemy vessels a year. But if the captain had some connection to the Admiralty, that rose to 1.3 enemy vessels – a notable increase in performance.

This cannot be explained by the idea that admirals gave their relatives prime postings, easier jobs or better ships. Going back to the data on ship v. ship, it can be shown that connected captains had a certain set of attributes. The Royal Navy, as already noted, won 67 per cent of the 172 single-ship duels over the course of the period, with the enemy being victorious just 9 per cent of the time. But if one looks at only connected captains, the loss ratio remains steady at 9 per cent but the win rate rises to 87 per cent. Not only did connected captains win more duels but just 4 per cent of their engagements were inconclusive compared to 24 per cent of those of unconnected captains. In other words, connected captains were likely to fight to the end one way or another.

All of which suggests that admirals, when picking out their relatives for post captaincies, were usually looking for the combination of tenacity and risk-taking that made for a good fighting officer.

None of which of course means that patronage is a good basis on which to run an organisation, but it does suggest that nor is it always a bad one. In the Royal Navy during the Age of Sail, an institutional structure existed which incentivised captains to fight harder with large potential downsides if they did not and great rewards if they did. When placing relatives into that system, admirals had to exercise care. Perhaps if he had still been alive at the time of his son's court-martial, the first Admiral Byng might have regretted his own exercise of patronage.

10

The Economics of Rebellion and Empire in India

The year 1857 was supposed to be an auspicious one for the British in India. It was, after all, the centenary of the Battle of Plassey, Robert Clive's great victory during the Seven Years' War that broke French power in the Indian subcontinent and cemented British rule in Bengal. Or, more specifically, Company rule in Bengal. For Britain's empire in the Indian subcontinent – until the events of 1857 – was managed through the East India Company, possibly the most powerful private firm ever to have existed. By 1857 the Company commanded more than 300,000 soldiers and ruled over perhaps 160 million people. The series of events that led to the end of Company rule and the establishment of formal British governance began to spiral out of control in late March 1857.

In the early afternoon of 29 March, a rather sleepy Sunday, Mangal Pandey, a twenty-nine-year-old sepoy serving with the 34th Native Infantry, fired the first shot of what would become known to Victorians as the Indian Mutiny, which today is sometimes called the Great Rebellion or the First War of Independence. Pandey had armed himself with his musket and was pacing around the parade ground in Barrackpore calling on his fellow soldiers to revolt and threatening to shoot any Europeans he saw. He was, according to his fellow sepoys, under the influence of bhang, an edible concoction made from cannabis plants. When he did see a European, he was true to his word. As soon as Sergeant-Major James Hewson approached to see what all the commotion was about, Pandey took deliberate aim and fired.

He missed. Hewson ducked into the cover of the nearby guardhouse and ordered the sepoys within to load their weapons. He quickly became concerned at the reluctance of the soldiers to act. Minutes later, Lieutenant Henry Baugh, a young British officer, arrived on the scene. Pandey took a shot at him too, and succeeded in downing his horse.

Baugh and Hewson, armed with swords, moved to engage Pandey and a mêlée ensued. During the brief fighting Baugh took a sword cut to the neck and another which disabled his left hand. Hewson was knocked to the ground by a musket blow to his back from another sepoy, whom he later failed to identify. Pandey was only restrained from killing both Europeans by the intervention of Shaik Pultoo, a Muslim sepoy, who held him back, allowing the officer and sergeant to make good their escape. Pultoo, though, was then forced to release Pandey when other members of the regiment threatened to shoot him if he did not.

At this point Colonel Steven Wheeler, the fifty-five-year-old commander of the 34th, arrived on the parade ground. It quickly became apparent to him that while Pandey was the only sepoy openly mutinying, the situation was tense, and he could not be sure if any of the other Indian soldiers present would obey his orders. He decided to make his way to his own commanding brigadier's HQ and report on the situation.

By now word of the disturbance had already reached Major-General John Hearsey, who despite being in his sixties was a veteran of much previous fighting over the past four decades and made of stern stuff. Accompanied by his two sons, both of them officers under his command, he began to approach Pandey. When a fellow officer warned him that Pandey's musket was loaded, he shouted back, 'Damn his musket!'

Perhaps threatened by the approach of three officers, perhaps disheartened at the failure of most sepoys to provide more active support or perhaps just feeling the influence of the bhang, Pandey turned his musket on himself, bringing the immediate disturbance to an end.

But the wider drama was just beginning. Pandey survived his attempt at suicide, but it did him no good. He was tried by court-martial and hanged on 8 April. On 21 April, Issuree Prasad, a non-commissioned officer who had been on duty at the guard post, was also hanged for mutiny for failing to arrest Pandey. Nor was this the end of the matter for the 34th Native Infantry. The seven companies present at Barrackpore that day were deemed to be guilty of passive mutiny and disbanded on 6 May.

Four days later, on 10 May, the rebellion broke out on a mass scale in Meerut. Native regiments at the station there killed their European officers, and by the 11th Delhi too was in revolt. The war fought over the following eighteen months would be vicious and bloody. At least 800,000 Indians, and very possibly many more, died either directly in the fighting or as a result of the famines and epidemics that it caused.

The immediate catalyst for the uprising that killed so many, and which represented the most significant crisis the British Empire had faced in a century, was a widely circulated rumour about a new weapon due to be introduced to the Indian army. In the 1850s the British Army was in the process of switching over from older-style smoothbore muskets to rifled muskets (or simply rifles, as they were often called). The rifled barrel of the new weapon caused the ball it fired to spin as it left the weapon, greatly improving both its range and accuracy. Whereas the smoothbores, which had been in service for well over a century by the 1850s, were accurate to about 75 to 100 yards, a well-trained soldier could expect to score regular hits at 200 to 250 yards with the new Enfield rifle. During the Crimean War of the mid-1850s the rifled-musket-armed British and French soldiers had been able to outclass the smoothbore-musket-armed Russians.

In 1856 it was decided that the Indian army would begin to receive Enfields the following year. To load a musket, whether smoothbore or rifled, a soldier used a paper cartridge containing both the shot and the necessary gunpowder. Part of the process was to bite into the cartridge to open it and release the gunpowder before putting the shot into the barrel. Given that the new rifled muskets were a tighter fit than the older smoothbores, the cartridge had to be greased.

In mid-1856 a rumour began to spread among Indian soldiers that the paper for the new cartridge was greased using pig and cow fat – an obvious problem for both Hindu and Muslim sepoys. The British authorities sought to calm tensions by first ordering that the cartridges would be supplied ungreased and that soldiers could grease them themselves using whatever they preferred, and secondly by amending the firing drill so that cartridges could be torn by hand rather than bitten. Neither change did any good – indeed they seemed to confirm that the earlier rumours had some veracity.

The rising in Meerut in May 1857 resulted from the arrest of several dozen soldiers who refused to drill with the new weapon. But while the cartridge issue was the flame that sparked the insurrection, it was clearly not the full story.

The wider causes of the mutiny were as much economic as religious, so before delving further into the Great Rebellion against British rule it is worth stepping back and looking at the wider economics because India represents a fascinating case study in the global economic history of state-making and war-making.

For most of history, war and security have been the primary concern of states. Developments that strengthened the state and state capacity tended to be driven by the need to raise military effectiveness. Given broad acceptance of the crucial role of institutional development in underpinning modern standards of living and the simple fact that many of Europe's institutional developments were driven, initially at least, by military needs, there is a wide-ranging school of thought that emphasises the role of inter-state competition in explaining what is sometimes called the Great Divergence. This is a term applied to the apparent economic decoupling of Europe (and especially western Europe) and some of its New World offshoots from previously more successful economies in the Islamic world and Asia that began in the seventeenth and eighteenth centuries.

In the 1500s, China, Japan, much of the Ottoman Empire and much of what is now India were richer places than Britain, France or Germany. By 1800 that was clearly not the case, and by 1900 Europeans were several times better off than people whose ancestors would have enjoyed higher standards of living than they did.

For most of the second millennium, Europe was extremely politically fragmented. Depending on how one chooses to count them there were anything between fifty and 120 European states and statelets at any given point competing. By contrast, in China, which had a similar population to Europe as a whole, there were rarely more than a handful of states, and one of those was usually dominant. The best explanation for this may simply be Europe's relative preponderance of wide rivers and mountain ranges which provided natural frontiers and borders. But whatever the reason, Europe was an arena of political competition after the fall of the Roman Empire and China was not.

This often intensive competition between states brought economic costs, alongside the more obvious direct human cost of the hundreds of thousands who died in European wars. Political fragmentation tended to mean the existence of trade barriers and tariffs and restricted the size of markets. It also involved a large dead-weight cost in terms of the higher necessary spending on security. But on balance, it was a net gain to Europe. Warfare forged the institutions, such as banks, that later enabled economic take-off.

India is the often overlooked third man in this story. Here the pattern of political fragmentation looks closer to the European model than the Chinese and yet the trajectory of economic growth is closer to that found elsewhere in Asia.

There is evidence that, as in Europe, warfare was a driver of institutional development and ultimately higher levels of economic growth in pre-colonial India. In the early sixteenth century – the period in which Spain was making its own bid for European supremacy – India was dominated by the Delhi Sultanate, the various Rajput states, the Deccan Sultanates and the Vijayanagar Empire. These states were certainly capable of mobilising large armies and engaged in almost ceaseless warfare against each other. Over the course of the 1500s and 1600s the Mughal Empire came to dominate northern India. War, according to one recent history, 'was a constant preoccupation' of this regime. The Mughal Empire and its finances look rather like those of the most advanced European states of the time. Around 90 per cent of all revenues were spent on the military and war-making. An increasingly sophisticated taxation and bureaucratic system was developed to enable a greater proportion of national output to be used to finance fighting.

A pioneering study, published in 2022, sought to look at the impact of almost a thousand years of warfare on the Indian economy. Both the methodology and the results were fascinating. The researchers began by cataloguing every military engagement in India for which records exist between 1000 and 1757. Each was then geo-coded to a modern location. The painstaking process began, for example, with a battle fought on 27 November 1001. At this encounter Mahmud of Ghazni defeated Raja Jaipal of Punjab during the Muslim conquest of northern India. The battle was tagged as taking place at Peshawar.

Once every battle, naval engagement and siege had been coded on to modern locations across the subcontinent the researchers compared the results to current levels of economic development. In the absence of detailed statistics down to very local areas, the researchers instead used luminosity data. They gathered satellite photos of the region taken between 20.30 and 22.00 local time each night between 1992 and 2010 and looked at how much light was visible in each pixel (each pixel covered about one square kilometre). By averaging the results for each pixel over these eighteen years, the researchers had a measure of how many lights were typically visible between those times each evening on any given night in each square kilometre of modern India. As a proxy for local economic development in a relatively poor country, this really is not a bad measure. The more lights turned on in any given square kilometre, the more economically developed that area probably is.

Perhaps only a team of economic historians would ever consider comparing satellite photos taken each night over the course of two decades pixel by pixel to a list of battles over the previous thousand years. But we should be glad that they did. The link between pre-colonial military conflict and current economic development is very strong. The pattern found in Europe seems to hold: early intensive military conflict tended to strengthen local states leading, in the longer run, to more developed institutions, higher levels of domestic security and better economic outcomes centuries later.

India, like western Europe, had a comparatively high population density in this period. That mattered too. Territorial warfare to capture land mattered more and was more likely in a region where land was relatively scarce and people relatively (by the standards of the time) abundant. By contrast, in Africa during this time people were relatively scarce but land abundant. African wars tended to be fought to capture slaves rather than land and the population scarcity probably damaged state formation. In the face of rising levels of conflict between rival groups, people would often find it easier to move elsewhere rather than stay put and be dragged into collective defence efforts.

So the link between pre-colonial warfare and local economic development is strong in India, which raises the rather interesting but ultimately unanswerable question of how Indian economic development patterns would have continued in the absence of British rule. But in the end, the imposition of British control snuffed out the previous inter-state rivalries.

The East India Company had been founded in England in 1600. State-sponsored but still private companies with a remit to engage in trade, but also with access to their own hired soldiers and armed naval vessels, were all the rage in the Europe of the late fourteenth to late eighteenth century. The East India Company was hardly unique. Nor indeed for a long time was it the most successful. Its Dutch equivalent, the Vereenigde Oostindische Compagnie or VOC, was for most of the first century or so after the East India Company's initial charter the leader of the pack.

Gradually over the course of the seventeenth and early to mid-eighteenth centuries the East India Company established itself as a force in Indian politics, although still at this point merely one player among many. The big opening for the Company came in the eighteenth century with the decline and fall of the previously powerful Mughal Empire and its splitting into various entities such as those of the Maratha, Mysore and Travancore Kingdoms. After Plassey in 1757 the Company, which had access to both European weapons technology (although this was hardly unique on the subcontinent) and, more importantly, the backing of the developing British fiscal-military system which would win the Second Hundred Years' War with France, became the dominant power in the region.

Equally important, and occasionally under-appreciated when explaining Britain's dominance in India, was the role of sea power. British naval supremacy in the late eighteenth and early nineteenth centuries kept other European powers out of India and allowed British and Company forces a much greater degree of manoeuvrability over their native opponents.

Rival Europeans, such as the French and Portuguese, were either forced out or reduced to tiny enclaves, and one by one the native powers were either defeated in war and conquered or else brought into the British orbit through diplomacy, intimidation and threats.

The Company itself morphed from being primarily a trading corporation into what was effectively the government of a continent and yet still driven by the need to make a profit for shareholders. After the 1780s, the British government was forced to acknowledge that the Company was no longer just a trading enterprise and instituted what was known as a system of dual control with more official oversight of the Company's actions as well as more direct support from regular British Army and Royal Navy sources.

In India, as elsewhere, the logic of British imperial expansion was often strangely circular. Colonial governors and military types would become worried that unless a certain area was held by Britain, it posed a danger to her existing territories. So it would be seized. A few years later the same men, or their successors, would become concerned that the newly conquered area's security was threatened by a neighbouring area and so the process would continue. Given the multiple-month lag in communications between India and Britain, the men on the ground held a great deal of power. As one historian has written, 'the Company's directors in London never planned to acquire an empire, but they were powerless to prevent opportunistic employees from parasitising Asian imperial systems'. It could reach heights that seem, in hindsight, to be bizarre. To secure India, the British believed they needed to control waypoints as distant as Aden in modern-day Yemen.

The scale of the Company's conquests alone suggests that a purely military explanation is not enough. Especially by the late eighteenth century, many Indian rulers had access to European-style muskets and cannon. British and Company armies were not always successful either: in 1779 the Marathas inflicted a stinging defeat on the British at Wadgaon and in 1780 a British army was effectively destroyed at Mysore. One British general, who had fought the French in Flanders in the 1790s, wrote after a battle in India in 1803 that 'I never saw so severe a business in my life or anything like it, and pray to God, I never may be in such a situation again'. Indian armies were no pushovers for the British.

The real key to British success was its financial backing and how this crucially allowed Indian resources to be put to work in the conquest of the subcontinent.

From the 1720s onwards the Company recruited large numbers of Indian soldiers, on decent wages, and trained them in European techniques. But while the wages may have been good by Indian standards, they were low by European standards. In effect, by utilising the different price structures in place between India and Europe the Company was able to expand on the cheap.

The Company also played a clever political game. Right up until 1857 the (powerless) Mughal emperor was maintained in Delhi and the British claimed to be ruling in his name. Smaller native rulers bordering on British domains would be offered the chance to submit to British control of their foreign relations and internal security and perhaps receive a British subsidy for their court. Gradually over time these rulers lost real power to the Company. At its peak around 45 per cent of 'British' territory in India was technically ruled by native kings – the so-called Princely States. For the ever cost-conscious Company such indirect rule helped to keep the bottom line healthy.

It was this cost-conscious approach, which had greatly helped the Company's expansion, which also perhaps best explains the underlying causes of 1857. If the Enfield rifle cartridge controversy was the final spark, one must look to the wider economic backdrop to find the kindling for the rebellion. The first crucial factor to keep in mind is that by the 1850s the Indian Empire had almost reached its peak. Several intensive decades of expansion in the 1810s to early 1850s had finally come to an end.

Economic historians seeking to understand the underlying causes of the 1857–8 uprising have often pointed to factors such as a rising tax burden on Indian subjects or the decline in Indian land holdings at the expense of the British. One of the first economic analysts to write about the mutiny was Karl Marx. For him the rebellion was driven by rural discontent

caused by British economic practices. As he noted, initially
the rebels were as keen to eliminate local money lenders and
proto-capitalists as they were British officials and officers.
Interesting recent work has looked again at the class politics
of the rebellion and found that merchants, and urban dwellers
in general, were more likely to back continuing British rule.

But it is important to keep in mind that, whatever one wants
to call the events of 1857–8, it was primarily and at root a
military mutiny. That is to say, the conflict began when soldiers
refused to follow the orders of their officers, and it continued
with them killing them.

While some of India's Princely States eventually backed the
insurrection and while some civilians joined the fighting, the
vast bulk of the rebellion's manpower came from revolting
sepoys. To understand what played out, one needs to look more
at what was happening with sepoys in the 1850s rather than
with peasant farmers. Most importantly, the rebellion was
almost entirely confined to Bengal.

The East India Company ruled the subcontinent via three
'presidencies', semi-autonomous regions each reporting back to
the governor. Crucially, each of these presidencies maintained
its own armed forces. While Bengal experienced a serious military mutiny, neither Madras nor Bombay did. Indeed, troops
from the other presidencies were used to help suppress the
uprising. All of which suggests the underlying reasons for the
revolt are best understood by looking at the sepoys of Bengal
and what made them different. Why would their incentives
vary from their peers in the other presidency armies?

The Bengal army was structured very differently from its
peers in Madras and Bombay. While they both recruited
widely from different ethnic and religious groups, the British
were also keen on the idea that some tribal or ethnic groups
were 'martial peoples' more suited to soldiering. The Bengal

army was traditionally based on the recruitment of landowning Bhumihar and Rajput people around the Ganges Valley.
These, in the years between the 1760s and 1840s, were seen by
the Company as the ideal type of martial people with which
to fill its armies.

Given the basis of recruitment was high-caste Hindus, it is
no surprise that caste privileges were recognised and maintained in the Bengal regiments. Mangal Pandey was himself a
Brahman. As late as 1815, high-caste Hindus made up around
80 per cent of the Bengal Presidency infantry regiments.

Military service, and the perks it brought, was one way
of maintaining an economic distinction between the castes
in Bengal. Service with the Company offered a relatively
good rate of pay, one regularly topped up by a supplement
for serving outside the Company's territory in neighbouring
not-yet-British-governed territories, and recruitment was competitive. Pay of 7 rupees per month coupled with a pension on
retirement was unheard of in the armies of the Indian states.
The East India Company's military expansion across the subcontinent, as we have seen, was in part driven by the ability to
recruit and pay for large, well-motivated armies. And limiting
access to this well-paying, status-enhancing job was one way
in which caste distinctions were maintained.

Slowly but surely in the years before 1857 the economic
basis of this type of soldiering, and the social structure it maintained, was undermined. The Company became a victim of its
own success and its underlying cost-consciousness.

The 1840s were an active time for the army of the Bengal
Presidency as the Company fought a long series of wars against
local rivals. The need for manpower during this decade of
intensive fighting with wars in Sind, Afghanistan and neighbouring states diversified the recruitment base of the Bengal
forces, much to the displeasure of the old sepoy elite. The army

needed more men and not enough high-caste Hindus were available to fill all the roles required. The share of high-caste Hindu recruitment fell from four fifths in 1815 to around two thirds by the 1840s.

A major change came after the end of the Sikh Wars in 1849. In two very hard-fought wars the East India Company eventually succeeded in conquering the regionally powerful Sikh Empire and bringing the Punjab under British rule. British generals were impressed with their former opponents and keen to recruit as many as possible into Company service. With the Punjab now part of the Bengal Presidency, that meant recruiting more Sikhs into the Bengal army.

The Punjab fell into British hands in 1849, and in 1856 the Awadh Kingdom was conquered and became Oudh State, a Princely State within the Bengal Presidency. Even more seriously for soldiers' living standards and morale in the Bengal Presidency army, the conquests of Awadh and Punjab meant an effective pay cut: the sepoys would no longer receive the foreign service allowance for serving in these areas. Previously this had been an important supplement to their monthly earnings. That pay packet of 7 rupees a month had been set in the 1810s, and it remained at that level in 1857. Over the course of those decades the general price level doubled, implying a big fall in the real earnings of sepoys after taking account of their purchasing power. Regular foreign service payments had helped to cushion the impact. Until the mid-1850s the Bengal army had been the most active of the three presidency forces and its soldiers had received regular top-up payments. So while sepoys in all three presidency armies experienced a long and deep squeeze on their real incomes between the 1810s and mid-1850s, in the Bengal army the hit was far more sudden and concentrated into a shorter period of time.

All of which puts the outbreak of violence in 1857 in its real context. The East India Company expanded its power in India by paying its soldiers well and maintaining their loyalty. It was able to exploit differing price and wage structures in Europe and India to effectively utilise Indian resources to conquer India. But once that conquest was complete and external threats to Company rule seemed to have diminished, the natural focus on the bottom line of any company with shareholders kicked back in. Economy and savings were prioritised over the need to maintain a military edge. The lack of an external security threat helped to create the conditions that led to the greatest internal security threat British rule in India ever faced.

1857 brought together a whole host of issues, from fears that Britain was attempting to stamp out native religions in favour of Christianity to worries over social standing and ongoing challenges to traditional ways of life and customs. No rebellion or revolution ever has a single and simple cause. But 1857 was at heart a military mutiny by the Bengal army, and the falling living standards of soldiers lie at its root.

11

How the US Civil War Made the Dollar

The economists, academics and policy wonks who comment on the Eurozone are fond of declaring that Europe needs a 'Hamilton' moment. They have been saying this for years, but more so since Lin-Manuel Miranda's musical brought Alexander Hamilton, the US's first Treasury Secretary, to a wider audience.

What they usually mean by this is that Europe needs to follow in the footsteps of the United States by mutualising its national debts. The Eurozone, or so goes the argument, is in the dangerous position of having created an incomplete economic union. Countries have given up control of their own currencies and monetary policy (the ability to set interest rates) but not combined their fiscal policies – the business of taxation, spending and national debt. That creates the underlying conditions for the kind of crisis that played out between 2012 and 2015 in Greece, Italy, Spain, Ireland and Portugal. As long as fiscal policy remains in the hands of Euro member states and the common currency lacks a common national debt there will always be the risk of a replay of the previous crisis – or so the argument usually runs.

The Hamilton moment in the United States, according to this line of thought, came in 1790. In that year the fledgling United States passed the Funding Act by which the debts of the thirteen various former colonies now called states were 'assumed' by the new United States – a step which not only provides much of the fodder for Act Two of *Hamilton*, but which sought to bind the interests of the thirteen states closer together and, seemingly, create a more credit-worthy US.

But talk of a Hamilton moment obscures much of the following seventy years. The creation of the US dollar was a process not a moment, and a process that was only concluded by the needs of war – specifically the US Civil War of 1861 to 1865. The real Hamilton moment, if one insists on calling it that, came well after the first Treasury Secretary had been shot and killed in a duel with Aaron Burr. If anything, it makes more sense to talk of a Hamilton process – slow and drawn-out – rather than a single moment.

Still, Hamilton's Funding Act was a big deal and, like so many other important institutional developments, again one shaped by warfare and conflict. The American War of Independence (1775–83) was a costly business. For the major European powers, fighting a conflict halfway around the globe did not come cheap. France may have been on the winning side, but the financial costs represented a tipping point from which the *ancien régime* never truly recovered. And, after the war, Britain was left with a ratio of government debt to GDP of more than 150 per cent, the highest it had ever been, and a ratio that would only be topped in the aftermath of the Napoleonic Wars and during the total wars of the twentieth century.

Nor, as one might expect, did the victory come cheaply for

the American colonists. In economic terms, the war for independence was paid for by debt. The Continental Congress
and the various colonies which would soon become states
borrowed heavily, both domestically and in Europe, buying
supplies – and often paying soldiers – on credit, and they
issued unbacked paper money which rapidly lost its value. One
would be hard-stretched to call the Continental dollar, issued
by the Continental Congress during the war, a successful currency. Nowadays it is best commemorated by the phrase 'as
worthless as a Continental' which still occasionally crops up
in American usage. The Congress was continually forced to
print more paper notes than it had gold, or specie, with which
to back it in order to meet ongoing (almost entirely military)
spending needs. By 1778, two years after the Declaration of
Independence and three years after the outbreak of fighting, a
Continental was worth about 10 cents in the dollar; by 1780,
as the fighting drew to a close, it was worth approximately 2
cents in the dollar. Spanish silver dollars – the famous pieces
of eight – circulated widely and were preferred by anyone who
could get their hands on them, in much the same way that
those who can get their hands on US dollars in some faltering
economies today much prefer to deal in them rather than the
local official currency.

The new US government, formed in 1789, was beset by
a host of problems, but one of the most pressing was its dire
financial situation. It was highly indebted, it had little in the
way of sources of revenue (with most taxes still controlled by
the subordinate states) and its currency was essentially worthless. But Alexander Hamilton, the new Treasury Secretary, at
least had a plan.

The Funding Act was the centrepiece of this. Hamilton,
who as the musical tells us knew that 'we need to handle our
financial situation', was a keen student of economic affairs

and had closely studied the British experience over the past century. In 1781 he wrote to a correspondent that 'a national debt, if it is not too excessive, will be a national blessing'. His argument in the 1780s and early 1790s was threefold. Firstly, drawing on the British example since the 1690s, a national debt, if well managed, could be a source of national strength. Britain had shown that if a country established a reputation as a reliable borrower with solid institutions to manage the process, then even large debts could be serviced in a relatively affordable way. This acted, in military terms, as a national force multiplier. A healthy economy with decent tax revenues was useful but a healthy economy with decent tax revenues that could borrow up front when large sums were needed – say, for fighting a war – was in an even stronger position.

Secondly, as well as the impacts on the government itself and its ability to exercise power when needed, a well-managed national debt had wider benefits to the overall economy, again as shown by the example across the Atlantic. Crucially, as Hamilton wrote in 1790, 'in countries where the national debt is properly funded, and an object of established confidence, it answers most of the purposes of money'.

Not only does this statement cut to the heart of much of monetary economics, it also demonstrates Hamilton's profound earlier insights. If merchants, bankers and traders believe that government-issued securities – of the kind which make up the national debt – will definitely be repaid, then they are really not that different from actual money. For a London banker in the 1790s being paid in gold was not that different from being paid with British government debt; both acted as a store of value and could be used to purchase goods or services. A well-established national debt could oil the wheels of the wider financial system, providing bankers and lenders with a form of collateral and making transactions and exchanges easier. Even more than two centuries later, government debt still tends to sit at the centre of national banking systems.

Hamilton's arguments, though, had a third pillar, one more firmly rooted in politics than economics. A national debt, he believed, 'would be a powerful cement for our union'. This was another important insight. The thirteen states that formed the United States differed vastly in size, culture and structure, from the agrarian slave-based economies of the south to the more commercial, mercantile and urbanised regions of the north. They developed along strikingly different lines influenced by different types of settlers and, while they spoke a common language and had the shared experience of victory in the War of Independence, there was no certainty that the union they formed would last for ever. A common national debt was an example of the kind of shared institution which could bind these states together.

In the short run, it was potentially even more useful in raw political terms. Not even the very recent history of the war and victory had really been that shared an experience. Take as an example New York City. With a population of around 35,000 it was the largest urban area in the United States and the richest by far. And yet in late 1776 it had been the site of a defeat of George Washington's Continental Army and had been occupied by the British until 1781. Over the course of the late 1770s its population had grown, driven by influxes of 'Loyalist' refugees (that is to say, British-backing colonists) fleeing American victories. Economically and financially, New York essentially remained a part of the British Empire for much of the war, trading with Britain, importing British goods, dealing with British financiers and subject to a complex web of competing loyalties. While it initially acted as a sort of capital for the new United States, it was never clear exactly how onside it truly was.

Hamilton, an adopted New Yorker himself, was keenly aware of this. Subsuming New York's debts into a new form of United States debt had the added advantage of giving an incentive to New York's wealthy and powerful elite to care about the new nation. If one's fortune was tied up in debt obligations owed to the United States, one might well take a closer interest in seeing this new US succeed.

The idea behind the Funding Act became known as 'assumption' as the new United States assumed the debts of its component states. The notion was simple: the United States would take responsibility for the debts of all thirteen states and add them to its own. Creditors would no longer be holding the debt of Georgia or New Jersey but instead newly minted US debt.

The plans were certainly controversial. For a start, the fiscal position of the states varied: some had paid down much of their war debt, others had not. Some were set to be obvious short-term winners. More importantly, the step represented a centralisation of power by the federal government to the cost of the underlying states, and while Hamilton, a noted federalist, backed a strong central executive, many of his peers – especially from the south – preferred a looser arrangement with more autonomy for the states.

As any fan of the musical knows, the act was passed, with the south being bought off by siting the new US capital, Washington, in between Maryland and Virginia. More importantly, it worked. US debt that had been trading at around 60 cents in the dollar in 1789 was trading at more than 90 cents within months of the act passing in 1790.

Hamilton, then, succeeded in mutualising US debt, but he was not finished; his 'moment' was not yet done. The second stage of his financial plan was the establishment of a US National Bank, modelled on the Bank of England. This was to prove to be a major source of controversy in US politics for the next six decades.

What Hamilton wanted was something that looked like the contemporary Bank of England, a quasi-private, quasi-public institution that would sit at the centre of both the system of national debt and the wider financial ecosphere. It would act as the government's primary financial agent, serve as the link between the American and wider global (or essentially at this time European) financial centres, and through its holdings in the securities of state banks exercise a great deal of effective regulatory control over the whole banking system.

What later became known as the First Bank – and that prefix gives away much of the story – operated from 1791 until 1811 and was based in Philadelphia. On one level it succeeded, with the US financial system being generally stable throughout its operations. But politically it proved to be a headache. It was quickly seen as representing the wealthy, and in particular the financial elites of cities such as Philadelphia, Boston and New York. It pursued what it regarded as 'sound' policies but which to its critics were restrictive ones. In general, credit and bank lending growth across the United States was constrained by the new National Bank. This led to the typical result that such policies have created throughout modern economic history – a conflict between debtors and creditors. Higher interest rates and more restrictive lending practices were seen as favouring the financial creditors in northern cities over poorer debtors in the expanding western states and the south.

The First Bank's twenty-year charter was allowed to lapse in 1811. Hamilton had been killed in 1804, so just seven years later his moment seemed to be unravelling.

The timing could not have been worse. In 1812 the United States found itself at war with Britain. Without the steady hand of a National Bank, the US found itself struggling to borrow to fund the war – a war that generally went badly for the Americans with Washington itself being captured and burned. The underlying financial system fell into turmoil.

So, in 1816, Congress charted the Second National Bank.

Once more, the Hamilton moment proved temporary. The big change was again driven by war, although this time by its absence. For most of the first two and a half decades of the United States' existence, the French Revolutionary and Napoleonic Wars had raged across Europe. That had limited both international trade and global capital flows and allowed the US to develop, mostly, as a homegrown concern. Peace in Europe brought this to an end. The end of the fighting meant that the financial resources of the competing powers, and most especially of Britain, no longer had to be primarily deployed in financing the great armies and fleets that had engaged in a truly global conflict. They could now go looking for more profitable ventures.

This was also the period in which the ongoing industrial revolution, especially again in Britain, really began to pick up its pace. The cotton gin, invented a few years earlier, had the potential to revolutionise textiles production. Whereas the seed pods of the cotton plant had previously had to be separated from the fibres by hand – a painstaking and lengthy process – the cotton gin offered the chance to do this quickly and relatively cheaply. The demand for cotton soared as a result. This was followed, in the decades afterwards, by an equally important revolution in transport technology with a huge expansion in canal building followed quickly by the railway.

It was these global technological and economic developments which transformed the United States between 1820 and 1850. In 1820, the population of the United States was around seven million, with just a million of those living beyond the Appalachians, and most of them in Kentucky. Global demand for cotton, and North American grains, and the ability to transport it rapidly back to east coast ports using canals and then later railways, drove a rapid expansion to the west. The US frontier moved around 20 miles in that direction a year over these decades and people and capital poured into the newly claimed areas. By 1850 the population had reached 23 million, with half of them west of the Appalachians.

Once again, though, the old politics of creditors and debtors reared its head. While the west and much of the south was enjoying a boom driven by surging agricultural exports and transport infrastructure investment, the north – and in particular the old urban core of the north-east – was more stable. And just as in the 1790s and 1800s, this economic divergence saw a vicious political battle over how the National Bank should be setting policy.

The so-called Bank War was a major political issue in the 1820s and early 1830s which divided those mostly from the west and the south, who supported a pro-debtor, easier monetary stance, from those mostly from the north, who backed a more pro-creditor, tighter policy.

Daniel Webster, a representative of Massachusetts, made the Hamiltonian case that restrictive – or as he might have termed them 'sound' – policies firmly served the national interest in the longer run. Such policies, he believed, had 'raised armies, equipped navies, and, triumphing, over the gross powers of mere numbers, it has established national superiority on the foundation of intelligence, wealth and well-directed industry' – sentiments that one can almost imagine being delivered in a clipped British 1820s accent. His argument did him no good. In 1832 Andrew Jackson, the semi-populist President hailing from western Tennessee, vetoed the renewal of the Second Bank's charter. Hamilton's moment was once again undone. In 1837, the Second Bank was allowed to lapse.

This, then, is the part of American history that advocates of a Hamilton moment in the Eurozone tend to forget about. The late 1830s to 1850s were a time when America's monetary system looked a little like that of the modern-day European common currency area. While the whole nation used the dollar, that hid an awful lot of local differences.

The pro-debtor party had won and, in the absence of a National Bank, banking policy was once again mostly devolved to the individual states. Those favouring easier credit and monetary policy could simply charter more local banks that could get on with their business, free from a meddling National Bank in Philadelphia. In 1830 there were around five hundred banks in the United States; by 1860 there were more than 1,500. Over the same period total lending grew from around $200 million to $700 million.

But not all these banks were created equally. In states such as Georgia, Alabama and Michigan the authorities made it very easy to set up a bank and imposed relatively few restrictions on their maintenance of reserves. What is more, reserves were generally held not in the form of gold or US-issued national debt securities but instead in locally issued state debts. It is important to keep in mind here that while all outstanding state debts had been assumed in 1790, states had the ability to issue new debt after this.

Effectively during this period, while every state might be using a currency called 'the dollar', the nature and worth of those dollars varied substantially. While states such as New York or Massachusetts pursued cautious fiscal policies and kept borrowing relatively low, those such as Alabama and Georgia went on a borrowing binge. And in general each state's banking system was closely linked to its own state-level debt markets.

People quickly realised that a dollar note issued by, say, a

New York bank was in reality worth more than one issued by a bank in Alabama. The New York bank would likely have a higher level of reserves, and those reserves would be made up of the credit-worthy bonds issued by New York State. The Alabama bank was more likely to be overstretched, to hold less in the way of a cushion, and that cushion itself probably represented claims on a state government that had overborrowed itself and might not be able to pay the cash back. While neither dollar note was worth as much as a centrally issued gold-based US dollar coin, the differences between them could be substantial.

The financial press regularly updated readers on the value of notes from different institutions. In the early 1840s, for example, notes from New York and Massachusetts were trading at a discount of only 1 to 2 cents in the dollar while those from Tennessee traded a 10-cent discount and those from Alabama and Illinois at closer to a 30-cent discount.

In the panic of 1837 – a financial crisis following a fall in western land prices – eight states and one territory defaulted on their debts. The price of the bonds of all overstretched states fell heavily, pushing up the cost of borrowing. Meanwhile the political representatives of the more 'prudent' states, generally in the north, vetoed any federal bail-out of the overstretched. Much like German political leaders in the early 2010s asking why their taxpayers should bail out Greeks, New York's leaders refused to risk their money bailing out Georgia.

What brought the Hamilton moment back into the limelight and what really turned the collection of currencies called the dollar found across North America into the actual dollar was the civil war of 1861–5. War, as has so often been the case, changed the incentive structures facing those making the key decisions and drove through the creation of new institutions.

The changes in the incentive structure are easier to

understand. For much of the 1790s until the 1860s, US financial policy had been fought out in terms of a battle between pro-debtor and pro-creditor policies. By and large, the pro-creditor side also tended to favour a stronger federal executive and the pro-debtor side tended to be associated with arguments around states' rights and the need for autonomy. That battle had seen a National Bank created twice and dissolved twice over several decades. The war changed all this by removing much of the pro-debtor, pro-states' rights faction from the argument. The states that seceded from the Union were all in that camp and left the balance of power held by the pro-creditor, pro-strong central government side.

The Hamiltonians could move forward with their project, free from the usual sources of tension. And given the shape of US politics after the war, and the diminished power of the South that would last for several decades, they could bed these changes in and make them harder to reverse.

But the changes that occurred in US financial policy were not just about the unfinished business of the 1790s, they also reflected pressing military needs. In July 1861, just weeks after the fighting began, the United States issued $50 million of so-called 'demand' notes. These notes were officially classified as a form of borrowing but bore no interest. In theory they could be redeemed for actual gold 'on demand', hence the name, but in practice this was tricky. The new notes, printed with green ink backing on one side, quickly became known as greenbacks, a label which has stuck to the dollar ever since. The notes were used to pay immediate bills for munitions and to meet the wage bills of the rapidly expanding federal army.

In 1862 the government went further. As the war dragged on and expenses continued to rise, it became clear that the demand notes were not a sustainable solution. Their value declined month on month as victory looked ever less certain.

While the government could pay its soldiers in such demand notes, other suppliers were increasingly reluctant to accept them. The solution was the Legal Tender Act which really introduced the modern dollar – a paper-based currency not backed by anything at the time. As the note said until 1908, 'In God We Trust'. Although Abraham Lincoln, always a President with a sense of humour, remarked that 'silver and gold I have none, but such as I have I give to thee' would have been a more appropriate biblical quotation.

Each note was declared to be legal tender for the payment of debts and the purchase of goods and services, and the use of other forms of currency was specifically disbarred. The National Banking Act the following year went further, only allowing paper money to be issued by either the US Treasury itself – in the form of greenbacks – or by federally chartered banks that had to follow such strict regulations that their notes were essentially the same as the greenback. The US needed the ability to purchase war supplies quickly, and the greenback provided that. It also uprooted three decades of financial policies and fundamentally changed American banking.

The value of the greenback, measured in gold, continued to fluctuate over the coming years. Over the course of 1862 and early 1863 its value gradually fell until 152 greenback dollars were treated as the same as 100 dollars of gold. The Union victory at Gettysburg in July 1863 began a recovery which lasted until mid-1864. As the war ended in 1865, Congress agreed to scale back greenback issuance and put a cap on the total amount in circulation. The price continued to recover until 1878, some thirteen years after the end of the war, when it reached parity with gold. It had taken a long time, but the dollar was now truly as good as gold.

The South too tried to finance its war using the same sort of paper money, specifically through the greyback first issued in March 1861, before the fighting had even begun. It failed. Its failure is reflective of the wider imbalance of forces which characterised the whole conflict.

Almost 90 per cent of all US manufacturing was in the states which remained in the Union, with the North producing 32,000 firearms for every hundred the Confederacy managed in 1861. The North had a population of 23 million against the South's 9 million, and once the South's refusal (for most of the war) to use slaves in combat roles is taken into account, the imbalance was even greater. The Union had around 3.5 million men of military age (between eighteen and forty-five) compared to the South's total of just a million white men. While 75 per cent of that age group in the South would end up serving, just half of those in the North would – a proportion high enough to give a strong advantage in numbers while still allowing the wider economy to function. The South began the war with just 13 per cent of the nation's banks and just 29 per cent of its railway tracks.

It was not, though, only the initial distribution of resources that favoured the North. By its very nature, the political culture of the South emphasised states' rights – this was, to them anyway, the reason they had seceded – and politics was imbued with a deep scepticism of strong central government. The drastic and sweeping Hamiltonian measures imposed in the North in 1861–3 would always have been trickier in the Confederacy.

The very first paper notes the Confederacy ordered were actually printed in New York and smuggled south – such was the lack of industrial capacity. Like the North's greenbacks, the South's paper currency paid no interest and was not immediately exchangeable for precious metals. They did however promise their notes would be redeemable 'within six months of a peace treaty between the United States and the Confederate

States'. The hope was that a rapid victory would be followed by a financial settlement, which would cover the costs incurred in winning it. That promise was later stretched out to 'within two years' of the war ending.

Over the next few years the Southern states went through seventy-two different variations of dollar bills. Often badly printed, they created something of a forgers' paradise. Several states, including Virginia and Alabama, also printed and issued their own notes, adding to the general financial chaos. By the end of the war, a Confederate dollar was worth roughly 3 Union cents.

A country, such as the Union, can issue unbacked paper if it has the financial and economic strength to credibly sustain it. The Confederacy lacked such strength, especially once the chances of an early end to the war had passed in 1861. The South's reluctance to take the decisive steps needed to make a paper currency work, such as banning competing notes, added to the problems.

The Bank of England and the modern pound sterling were brought into being by the needs of the Second Hundred Years' War between Britain and France. The modern US dollar, in its recognisable form, was created by the pressures of the American Civil War. Those calling for a European Hamilton moment should always keep two things in mind: first, it was not a moment, it was the result of decades of work; and second, and perhaps more importantly, completing Hamilton's work required the accelerant of four years of vicious fighting. Europe's real challenge is to find a way to achieve this without the bloodshed.

12

The Changing Costs of War

The popular view of France's invasion of Russia has long been shaped by the popularity of Tolstoy's epic *War and Peace* and its various adaptations for television and cinema. The French occupation of Moscow, and its subsequent burning, forms part of the narrative spine of book three of the great novel. But while epilogues take the story onwards to 1820, the novel ends with the French (and allied forces) being driven from Russia in the winter of 1812. However, the war that began with the French crossing the frontier in June of that year and eventually taking Moscow actually ended two years later with a Russian, Austrian and Prussian army occupying Paris.

The battle for Paris in 1814 was fiercely fought, causing perhaps 20,000 casualties and featuring a decisive Russian charge to take the high ground around Montmartre. But Paris in 1814, unlike Moscow two years earlier, emerged from the fighting relatively unscathed. This, with some exceptions of which Moscow in 1812 was one, was the norm in warfare for centuries.

Fifty-six years later, in 1870, Paris once again found itself facing a foreign army and once again being ruled by a

Bonaparte called Napoleon. This time the ruler was Napoleon III (the nephew of the more successful Napoleon) and the foreign army was Prussian. The wider Franco-Prussian War of 1870–1 was of enormous significance to later European history, leading to a unified Germany and sowing the seeds of the Great War which would come four decades later. But it is the siege of Paris which is especially interesting to anyone looking to understand the changing costs of war.

The Prussian army surrounded and cut off Paris in September 1870 and initially attempted, almost as if in a flashback to a medieval siege, to starve the city into submission. The Parisians experienced a grim winter. Food supplies ran scarce quickly and the citizens soon resorted to eating their pets, and subsequently were forced to begin emptying the city's zoo. A café menu from during the siege lists such culinary delights as cat and mushroom stew and salami-ed rat. One Christmas menu featured elephant steak and roast camel. French cooking has always been innovative.

By mid-December, with Paris still refusing to surrender, the Prussians became frustrated. At a council of war held on the 17th and attended by the Prussian king (who would soon become the first Kaiser of a unified Germany), the Crown Prince, Chancellor Otto von Bismarck and senior generals, the military command argued that the policy of starving the city out was taking too long and asked to open a heavy artillery bombardment. Bismarck, fearful of the international repercussions of the Prussian forces shelling civilians, was against the idea but he was overruled.

On 5 January 1871 the bombardment began. Beginning at around 10 p.m. each night, the Prussians fired between three hundred and four hundred shells into Paris over the course of four to five hours.

Paris surrendered on 28 January. The bombardment was

not the tipping point the Prussians had hoped for. Indeed it proved less successful than they expected: the artillery of the 1870s lacked the range and explosive power to do as much damage as its proponents hoped to achieve. A typhoid outbreak – a direct result of the siege – and rising left-wing unrest within Paris itself which panicked the French authorities were the immediate causes of the surrender. But a decisive turning point in European warfare had arrived. In order to achieve their military goals, the Prussian command had decided that using high-explosive ammunition on civilian targets was a legitimate technique of warfare.

Seventy-three years later, and a few hundred miles north, in Hamburg, the ultimate results of that decision could be seen. On 24 July 1943 the British Royal Air Force (RAF) and the United States Army Air Forces (USAAF) launched Operation Gomorrah, a campaign of bombing that stretched out over ten days. The Americans bombed by day and the British by night. The peak of the operation came on the night of the 26th/27th and had been long planned by Britain's Bomber Command. More than 2,300 tons of bombs were dropped in a rectangle a little over 4 square miles in area over the course of a few hours. The results, for Hamburg, were catastrophic.

Bomber Command had long been intrigued by whether, in the right circumstances, the kind of smaller fires their incendiary bombs usually created could be combined into a larger blaze. Late July was dry in Hamburg that year and it had not rained for weeks. The windspeed was low. The conditions seemed perfect to put their research to the test. After an initial wave of high-explosive bombs intended not only to cause direct damage but to create plenty of kindling for what would come next, the RAF dropped 25,000 4lb incendiary bombs per square mile, supplemented by phosphorus to help the fire spread.

The firestorm this created was enough to melt metal and glass. It began around 1.20 a.m. and reached its peak around 3 a.m. It raged until 4.30 a.m. when there was simply nothing left to burn. The best modern estimates put the death toll that night at around eighteen thousand – almost entirely civilian. The primary cause of death was asphyxiation as the fire sucked up all the oxygen from people sheltering in cellars and dug-outs. Over the course of ten days perhaps forty thousand died in Hamburg and two thirds of the city's housing was destroyed.

Hamburg ranks alongside Dresden, Tokyo, Hiroshima and Nagasaki as a terrifying example of the raw destructive power of bombing in total war.

Between the nineteenth century and the mid-twentieth century the nature of warfare changed, and with it, its costs. There is plenty of evidence that before the nineteenth century warfare might actually have helped economies to grow and income per head to rise. No one would seriously make that case any more.

Europe's economic pulling ahead of the rest of the world was driven by the impact of war. This played out via two distinct mechanisms. The first is the one discussed in its varying aspects over many of the previous chapters, the way in which warfare drove institution formation among the competing European powers. The tests of war required ever stronger states and drove all sorts of financial innovations. But war helped to make Europe rich in another way too: by, counter-intuitively, killing a lot of Europeans. The world before 1800, as previously discussed, was broadly that of the Reverend Malthus, a world of constrained resources in which living standards per head tended to fall as populations expanded. The key thing to grasp about European warfare in the years before 1800 is that it tended to kill a lot of people but to leave capital, livestock, buildings and all sorts of economic infra-structure relatively unscathed.

Of course there were exceptions. Harrying, or deliberately razing the countryside of an enemy, burning crops and villages and killing livestock, was a recognised tactic used by medieval armies. It served several purposes. For a start it was a useful way to draw an opponent into battle. If a medieval ruler felt strong enough to raise an army and invade the territory of a rival, then the odds are he felt like he had a strong enough army to defeat his opponent. And his opponent, able to see this for himself, would usually prefer not to risk a battle where the odds were stacked against him. He would instead, especially from the twelfth century onwards, prefer to stay in his castles where the attackers' advantages were mitigated by well-built stone walls and well-dug moats. The attacking, though, could resort to harrying the territory of the invaded region. This was partially to keep his own army supplied but it also served as a bloody and effective way of shouting 'come and have a go if you think you're hard enough'. The ruler of the invaded region had to act to prevent the harrying if he wanted to retain the support of his vassals and peasants and have anything worth defending in the future.

Harrying could also serve as a deterrent. After a rebellion in the north of England in the late 1060s, the newly installed William the Conqueror harried the region over the course of the winter of 1069–70. He did so in an especially brutal manner, with even one pro-Norman chronicler recording afterwards that 'The King stopped at nothing to hunt his enemies. He cut down many people and destroyed homes and land. Nowhere else had he shown such cruelty. This made a real change. To his shame, William made no effort to control his fury, punishing the innocent with the guilty. He ordered that crops and herds, tools and food be burned to ashes. More than 100,000 people perished of starvation. I have often praised William in this book, but I can say nothing good about this brutal slaughter. God will punish him.'

The records of the Domesday Book, William's great inventory of his conquests, suggest a fall in the value of northern estates of between 50 and 80 per cent between the two stock-takings in 1066 and 1086. There is archaeological evidence too of the extent of the destruction. In Durham and Yorkshire in the north of England, the vast majority of villages to this day are laid out on a rectangular pattern while those in the Midlands and south of England vary much more. The best explanation for this is that these villages were burned to the ground in that long winter and restarted from scratch on a logical pattern rather than developing slowly and haphazardly over centuries.

Even towards the end of the long period under discussion, monarchs could still resort to what their ancestors would recognise as an old-fashioned harrying. In the 1680s and 1690s the French armies of Louis XIV, known as the Sun King, ravished the Palatinate region of southern Germany deliberately destroying the towns of Heidelberg, Worms, Mannheim and many others. After burning Heidelberg for a second time in 1693, Louis even had a medal struck for the soldiers involved with the Latin inscription 'Heidelberg deleta'. Still, medals aside, French actions in the Rhineland caused much outrage in the Europe of the day. During the 1500s and 1600s harrying – defined as the deliberate destruction of property and livestock as an end in and of itself – had become far less common. Armies of course still took what they needed – and more – as they passed through the countryside and a city taken after a siege could still often expect an orgy of violence and looting during a sack, but the damage was rarely that lasting or persistent.

For a start, what tended to be destroyed were wooden buildings and these wooden buildings were a straightforward matter
to replace. Stone-built buildings tended to survive all but the
most determined of sackers – at least until high explosives
arrived. One can wander around Rome today and see the
remnants of many ancient buildings despite being in a city that
has been sacked so many times there is a specific Wikipedia
page listing them.

What is more, one upside of Europe's often wet weather is
the lack of a need for the sort of complex irrigation systems
found in many other parts of the world. So while a harrying
or other form of deliberate destruction might kill livestock or
burn down wooden farm buildings it would not do the sort of
lasting damage to agricultural potential that was possible in,
say, the Middle East. Indeed, a season or two of fields being left
farrow could even increase their bounty in later years. Malthus
himself wrote in 1798:

> The fertile province of Flanders, which has been so often
> the seat of the most destructive wars, after a respite of a few
> years, has appeared always as fruitful and as populous as
> ever. Even the Palatinate lifted up its head again after the
> execrable ravages of Louis the Fourteenth.

It seems reasonable to conclude that Europe's wars before
the nineteenth century generally killed plenty of people but
left the underlying natural resources and even most of the
infrastructure intact. But did they really kill enough people to
make a measurable difference to incomes per head among the
survivors in a Malthusian world?

The answer, it seems, is yes.

One must start by recognising just how frequent
European warfare was. Even if the sample is limited to only

wars involving one of the major powers of England (later Britain), Spain, France, Austria, Russia and the Ottoman Empire, then 95 per cent of all years in the sixteenth century saw warfare. In the seventeenth it was 94 per cent of all years and in the eighteenth a still very high 78 per cent. Warfare was simply the norm. By comparison in the twentieth century a great power was at war in 53 per cent of all years.

Nor were some of these wars less costly, in terms of bloodshed, than those of the modern era. The numbers are stark. The Second World War has rightly earned its place in European history as a vicious and at times cataclysmic struggle. The Soviet Union suffered a loss of around 24 million out of a pre-war population of 168 million – a 15 per cent death rate. Germany suffered a smaller proportional death toll at around 10 per cent, while Poland endured a higher one at around 17 per cent. Britain and the United States, by contrast, never the scene of direct fighting and never occupied, escaped with death rates of closer to 1 per cent.

In the Thirty Years' War of 1618–48 the death rate in Germany, the setting for most of the fighting, has been estimated at 33 per cent. During the French Wars of Religion in the latter part of the sixteenth century that death rate hit 20 per cent. The European wars of the sixteenth and seventeenth centuries were not only more common than those of the twentieth century, they also often resulted in higher death rates than those experienced by the worst-hit countries during the Second World War.

This may sound surprising. The wars of the musket, the cavalryman and the cannonball could reasonably be expected to be less deadly than the wars of the machine-gun, the tank and the high-explosive shell. In terms of battlefield casualties they certainly were, but on a much greater scale than the wars of the twentieth century they tended to carry disease in their wake and that was the real, and decisive, killer.

Europe's many natural boundaries, as discussed previously, tended to lead to political fragmentation. One reason why the continent experienced so many wars was that its natural frontiers created many competing states. But those natural frontiers also tended to make any war all the more deadly. An army crossing the Alps or Pyrenees was not only crossing a geographic and political frontier, it was also crossing a biological frontier and bringing new germs to the local population. Plagues and pandemics were a frequent feature of European life over these centuries and commonly associated with an army on the move.

And remember, warfare that was not especially destructive of resources but was deadly for the wider population was, in the Malthusian world that existed before 1700, an economic boon. A lower total population meant higher incomes per head.

A useful cross-check comes from looking at the urbanisation rate across Europe over this period. In general, urbanisation – the percentage of the population living in cities and towns and not directly tied to the land – is a good measure of economic development. If nothing else, the fact that more people can live in cities suggests a rising agricultural surplus with farmland that can support more people than are directly involved in working it. In general, the more wars a region was involved in, the faster its urbanisation rate rose. It grew the fastest in those countries that fought the most – England, the Netherlands and France – and lagged in those which were more peaceable such as Norway, Ireland and Switzerland.

The comparison with China, which we should remember experienced centuries of stagnating income per head over this period, is instructive. Between 1500 and 1800 Europe witnessed 443 wars (almost 1.5 a year) which produced 1,071 major battles. By contrast, China experienced just ninety-one wars between 1350 and 1800 (0.2 per year on average) and only twenty-three major battles. Most of these Chinese wars, as the lack of battle suggests, were peasant revolts rather than conflicts between rival states. Nor were these Chinese wars anywhere near as death-heavy. The majority of the Chinese population lived close to the coastal plain and, the best modern epidemiological evidence suggests, the bulk of the population had formed a single disease pool as early as 1000, something that would not occur in Europe until the mid-twentieth century, almost one thousand years later. So the movement of Chinese armies did not tend to spread disease and infection to anywhere near the same extent.

Offered a chance to switch places, a European peasant of the sixteenth century would surely have been tempted to move to China. They were far more likely to live a peaceable existence there and far less likely to die after picking up a virus from a passing army. But in the longer run, all of that death drove European incomes higher over the years. By 1700 a European peasant was still more likely to experience war or suffer in a pandemic probably caused by warfare but they were also more than 50 per cent better off compared to their Chinese peers. Warfare, then, truly was a 'gift of Mars' to Europe's economy.

But Mars's gifts would be far less welcome in the nineteenth and twentieth centuries. What began in Paris in 1870 reached its climax in 1939–45 – warfare that not only killed many people but which destroyed capital, machinery, buildings and other resources at the same or even a higher rate. This kind of warfare tended not only to be bad for those who died fighting but also left survivors worse off as a result.

Take France after the Great War as one example. France was, by any measure, a victorious power, but as late as 1924 and 1925, a decade after the start of the war and six or seven years after its conclusion, its economy remained smaller than in 1914. At the end of the war, much of which was fought in northern France, 712,000 buildings, or 7.5 per cent of all buildings in the country, had been destroyed; 2.5 million hectares of agricultural land had been devastated; and 2,000 kilometres of canals, 5,000 kilometres of railway and more than 2,000 bridges had also not survived. This was destruction on a scale Europe had never previously experienced. And worse was to come in the Second World War.

Rebuilding from this type of warfare was neither easy nor straightforward. Indeed the contrasting fates of eastern and western Europe after 1945, which are often explained by the divergences between the wider capitalist and communist approaches taken to economic management, are best understood in the context of the total war fought between 1939 and 1945. None of which is to say that communism did not play a significant role in eastern Europe's slower recovery after 1945 – a topic to which we shall be returning later. But it was far from the only factor, and in the immediate post-war years perhaps not even the most important.

The nature, intensity and duration of the fighting in western and eastern Europe varied hugely. In the west of Europe, the campaigns of 1940 were relatively brief and, outside of Italy, serious fighting did not occur again until mid-1944 and ended eleven months later. By contrast, central and eastern Europe, and the western Soviet Union, was a battleground for four years from mid-1941 until mid-1945. Not only did warfare in the east last for longer, it was also on a much larger scale. The German army, in early 1945, had around a hundred of its divisions deployed fighting the western Allies against 200 fighting the USSR. The Soviet armies fought their way from their own western frontiers all the way to Berlin on a wide front across much of eastern and central Europe. By contrast, much of the west was spared the experience of actual fighting, even in 1944 and 1945.

The result was what can only be described as a demographic disaster in eastern and central Europe. Poland, Czechoslovakia, Hungary, Yugoslavia, Germany and the Soviet Union all lost 10 to 20 per cent of their populations and the hit was in all cases concentrated among young men – the traditional backbone of industrial enterprises. These countries would not recover from this until the early 1960s. In the western regions of Germany, the sex ratio (the number of men for each woman) had fallen to just over 0.82 by 1945; in the east it was 0.74. Even in Germany itself, the demographic hit was harder in the east than the west. Labour and skill shortages were common. The Holocaust (and five million of the estimated six million Jews who perished were from this region), together with the expulsion of long-settled ethnic Germans in 1945 and the fact that many middle-class types chose to head west rather than chance their arm under the incoming communist regimes, left many smaller to medium firms without their original owners and much management expertise was lost.

In economic terms, this loss of labour and wider human capital was compounded by an even larger level of capital destruction. In western Germany, the capital stock – the total value of buildings, plant and machinery – was already higher in 1948 than it had been in 1936. By contrast, in the east it was just 69 per cent of its 1936 level, almost one third lower. Germany as a whole lost perhaps 10 per cent of its population to the Second World War but 17 per cent of its industrial assets and 20 per cent of its total housing stock; it was more like 40 per cent of the housing stock in the major cities. The USSR lost 15 per cent of its population but 25 per cent of its stock of national assets. In Japan the result was even more stark, with 6 per cent of the population dying but 25 per cent of all national wealth being lost and more than a third of all industrial facilities.

Warfare in the twentieth century was different from what came before it. Battlefield deaths rose but the wider death toll, despite still hitting staggeringly grim numbers in some countries, tended to be lower than in previous centuries. On the other hand, the physical destruction brought about by first high-explosive shells, then aerial bombing and, in the case of Japan in 1945, the use of atomic weapons was much greater than anything the world had ever experienced.

On Christmas Eve 1864, Union General William T. Sherman, one of the United States' most successful generals in the American Civil War, wrote to his commander-in-chief from the newly captured city of Savannah in Georgia. He was fighting, he noted, 'not only armies ... but a hostile people'. Over the following month, while General Grant continued to square off against Confederate General Lee in Virginia, Sherman took his army on a 300-mile 'march to the Sea' through the Confederate states of Georgia, South Carolina and North Carolina to, in his own words, 'enforce destruction'. His armies destroyed mills and cotton gins, confiscated five thousand horses and destroyed railway lines and telegram systems as they passed. The War Department in 1901 would describe this as 'avenging the national wrong the Southerners had committed by dragging the country into civil war'.

This was one of the earliest examples of the kind of economic warfare that came to dominate the wars of the twentieth century – a deliberate attempt to destroy productive capacity, of which aerial bombing was the later extreme example.

Even on the move, covering 300 miles in just a month, and without the destructive tools of modern practitioners of the art, Sherman had a major impact. Modern-day economic historians have tracked the progress of his march and compared the economic outcomes in the counties he passed through to others in the same three states which were spared this nineteenth-century version of medieval harrying. In 1870, five years later, industrial and agricultural output was 20 per cent lower in the march counties than in the non-march ones. By 1880 the gap in industrial production had been made up but the agricultural impact lingered until as late as 1920, some fifty-five years after the war ended.

Unlike the twentieth century's so-called economic warfare, Sherman's army did not kill very many civilians. But in just one month, and equipped with the technology of the 1860s, he was able to have an economic impact on the areas he passed through which lasted for almost six decades. What Europe experienced in 1914 to 1918 and what Europe and much of Asia and North Africa experienced between 1937, when Japan invaded China, and 1945, when all fighting ceased, was a more destructive form of Sherman's march to the sea.

States might have been able to get rich from war and people to see their incomes grow as a result of conflicts before the nineteenth century, but in the twentieth century that changed. No longer could anyone rationally welcome the 'gifts' of Mars.

13

The Economics of Total War

The Second World War continues to be a source of fascination for many, especially among the victorious powers. In Russia, the annual victory parade marking the end of the Great Patriotic War is a major state occasion. Elsewhere the fascination manifests in different ways. As one internet meme put it, when American men hit the age of thirty-five they have a choice to make: they can become obsessed with either their civil war, the Second World War or barbecuing. The British tend to be less interested in their own civil wars but many of their bookshelves, especially those of men, groan under the weight of books on the conflict. Histories of campaigns and daring special operations feature heavily, although so too do biographies of the wartime leaders and generals such as Churchill and Montgomery. But even in a country with a seemingly abiding interest in all things to do with the Second World War, few nowadays seem especially interested in Oliver Franks. Which is a great shame, as Franks's contribution to Britain's war effort was as important as that of any general.

In as much as anyone has heard of Oliver Franks it usually relates to an anecdote about his post-war time as Britain's

ambassador to the United States. As the story goes, around
Christmas 1948 a Washington DC radio station contacted
foreign embassies in the capital and asked each of them
what their ambassador would like to see for Christmas. The
Soviet ambassador wanted freedom for all the people around
the globe enslaved by imperialism. The French ambassador
reported that he wished for world peace. And so on. Franks,
though, rather misunderstood the nature of the question and
replied, 'Well, it's very kind of you to ask. I'd quite like a box
of crystallised fruit.'

Born in 1905, Franks was of that generation too young to
have taken part in the First World War and (just about) too old
to actively serve in the Second. Before the war he had trained
as a moral philosopher at Oxford but his career had taken him
away from teaching and research and into university administration. When war came in 1939 he offered his services and
was taken on as a civil servant in the Ministry of Supply.

His first role was overseeing the movement of skilled
machinery workers from south-east England, an area seen as
especially vulnerable to German bombing, into the Midlands.
By 1940 he was Director of Labour Supply and in charge of
allocating the scarce resources available to fill a seemingly
never-ending list of factory vacancies as demand for output
rose and more and more men found themselves in uniform. By
1943 he was in charge of raw materials for the war economy
as a whole, and in 1945 he became permanent secretary of the
entire department, overseeing 65,000 civil servants and almost
a quarter of a million employees.

Franks was no great theorist and lacked a background
in economics but he was both a brilliant administrator and
a master of fine detail. His real skill, though, prefacing his
later time in Washington, was as a diplomat and a broker. At
the Ministry of Supply he managed to keep the relationship

between the Minister of Labour – Ernest Bevin, the tough ex-trade union leader – and the Minister of Production – Lord Beaverbrook, the right-wing populist former newspaper boss – functional and efficient. He was fundamentally a problem solver who looked to put the right organisation in place and ensure that the right people were in key roles. He is widely credited with playing a crucial role both in rebuilding the British Army, at breakneck pace, after the disaster of Dunkirk in which much of their heavy equipment had been lost, and in managing the fallout from German U-boat attacks when it seemed for a time that merchant shipping losses could derail Britain's war effort.

These sorts of jobs – managing and planning production, ensuring that soldiers were equipped and the civilian population kept fed, allocating finite resources between direct war-fighting capacity and the needs of the production industries – were critical to the wars of the twentieth century. In the long run, getting them right mattered more to the outcome of the war than what actually happened on the battlefield.

The First and Second World Wars saw a new type of warfare: total war. Not only entire militaries but entire societies and economic structures were rerouted towards military ends. When it comes to the share of total output devoted to the war effort, the numbers are without precedent. Take Britain, a country with a long history of global conflict before 1914, as an example. During the early 1700s, when the Duke of Marlborough was leading the allied force in the Low Countries, British spending generally amounted to around 4 to 8 per cent of national income. The Seven Years' War saw that figure rise to over 10 to 12 per cent in the early 1760s. The French Revolutionary and Napoleonic Wars required around the same level of effort, with around 10 to 12 per cent of national output being pushed towards the Royal Navy and the

British Army, and being spent as subsidies to allies in the 1790s and early 1800s to mid-1810s. By 1916, Britain was devoting 41 per cent of all national output towards the war, and in 1917 and 1918 almost 50 per cent. The story of the Second World War is remarkably similar; about 50 per cent of GDP, and actually more than 50 per cent in 1945, was the norm. One in every two pounds produced by the British went on fighting.

And while Britain was spending a higher share of its national output on warfare than the United States in the Second World War, which peaked at a 'mere' 45 per cent, it was – proportionately – spending less than some other great powers. The military burden hit more than 60 per cent of GDP in the Soviet Union and more than 70 per cent in Germany by 1943.

These are, by any stretch, colossal numbers. One advantage enjoyed by Franks and his contemporaries in the Second World War was the fact that the generation before them – and sometimes the very same people – had already done this. Indeed, Franks' first action on being appointed director of raw materials – as a good, well-trained academic – was to read the official six-volume history of the Ministry of Munitions during the Great War.

The leaders who found themselves managing the Great War of 1914 had no such reservoir of experience to draw on. Most thought the war would be over relatively quickly. The last few years of the American Civil War, especially in northern Virginia, and the even more recent experience of the Russo-Japanese War, a decade before the First World War, had, it is true, demonstrated that entrenched infantry could be very tough for an attacker to shift. But the experience of wars between European powers over the previous seventy or so years was taken to be a better pointer to how the war that began in 1914 would play out. In the Franco-Austrian War of 1859, the Austro-Prussian War of 1866 and the Franco-Prussian War of

1870–1 the fighting had generally lasted from a few weeks to a few months at most.

What many failed to grasp was how quickly military technology had shifted in the final couple of decades before 1914 and the advantages that handed to the defender. The British Army Staff College course of the 1890s, for example, which was attended by most of the colonels who would go on to command as generals in the First World War, was reasonably up to date in its understanding of modern warfare. The students studied the American Civil War of 1861–5, the Franco-Prussian War and the Russo-Turkish War of 1877–8. They learned how breech-loading rifles (where the infantry soldier was able to load his rifle without having to push the bullet all the way down the barrel as in an older muzzle loader) had increased the firepower of infantry and how rifled artillery and high-explosive shells had increased the power of that arm. But not really considered was the impact of magazine rifles (where a soldier could fire several times before changing magazine to reload), which first entered service in 1889, the role of the new machine-gun, which first saw active use in the late 1880s, or the fundamental change in destructive power which was heralded by the use of lyddite in high-explosive shells, introduced in the 1890s.

The potency of infantry acting on the defensive and the sheer difficulties in carrying out a successful offence came as a nasty shock to all sides. The popular image of the First World War leadership as donkeys leading their brave lions to slaughter has been much challenged by decades of excellent work by academics and military theorists. On the Western Front, with trench lines stretching from the Swiss border to the Channel coast and with no flanks to move around, it is still hard to see much in the way of an alternative to how the war was fought. The conflict saw a great deal of tactical and operational learning on all sides, as soldiers and officers adapted to the new reality. Infantry tactics developed quickly towards something like modern fire-and-manoeuvre techniques. The planning of artillery fire and barrages came on leaps and bounds over the course of the war. Tanks were introduced, and aircraft evolved from something occasionally utilised for scouting to the precursors of modern-day fighters and bombers.

Still, while recognising that commanders were on a learning curve and faced with a new type of warfare is certainly fairer than condemning them as mere blunderers, it is equally fair to wish that they had managed to learn faster. At the Battle of the Somme in 1916, the British imperial forces suffered 420,000 casualties, their ally in the Entente the French around 200,000 and the Germans at least 450,000. At Verdun later that same year, the French lost another 350,000 and the Germans somewhere between 375,000 and 400,000. On the Eastern Front, again in 1916, the Entente's Russian ally launched their most successful offensive of the war. The Brusilov offensive saw the Russian forces make sweeping gains in what was then Austrian Galicia and is now parts of Poland and Ukraine. They suffered perhaps 1.5 million casualties in achieving this, against around a million inflicted on the Central Powers of Germany and Austria-Hungary. All of these battles occurred in just one single year.

This kind of warfare – sustained fighting that was highly lethal to those involved and likely to last for years – was a challenge that required huge shifts in economic organisation. The war was not only thirsty for more manpower to swell the ranks but even hungrier for munitions. The clearest example of the quantitative change in the nature of warfare and its material demands can be found in artillery shells. During the Franco-Prussian War of 1870–1, which observers at the time saw as the dawn of a new and more lethal form of artillery-led battle, the Prussian army and its German allies fired around 80,000 shells per month. In 1914, though, the German army fired 900,000 shells per month. By 1918 it was firing almost 8 million shells each and every month. No army, supply organisation or government was prepared for anything on this scale. The French army went into the war with an inventory of 5 million shells and plans to produce around 100,000 a month. Their stockpile was almost exhausted by Christmas 1914.

The question facing policy-makers was how to keep up with this demand and how to achieve this without undermining other factors vital to victory. The issue was fraught with tough trade-offs. The competing powers needed to keep men in the field fighting but also needed an adequate pool of workers to keep producing ever-growing volumes of munitions. They needed to devote enough resources to direct war fighting without causing the kind of shortages in the civilian economy that would eventually lead to economic collapse or even domestic revolution. If economics is fundamentally the study of resource allocation, then total war is at heart a question of economics.

How the powers handled these issues in the Great War varied enormously, though there were always common features. As the numbers make clear, the state – in all cases – took on an unprecedented size in relation to the rest of the economy and some form of command economy, or state direction, was eventually imposed in almost all cases.

Britain began the Great War with a strong sense that this was 'business as usual'. The war would be over relatively quickly and Britain would play its traditional role of acting as paymaster subsidising continental allies while deploying only small forces to the direct land fighting and placing more reliance on the role of the Royal Navy. All of these assumptions were proved wrong over the first eighteen months of the conflict.

Initially it was indeed business as usual. The British Army and the Royal Navy bid against each other for the limited amount of shell manufacturing capacity available, driving up the price. By 1918 the British economy looked radically different from that of 1914, not least due to the efforts of the new Ministry of Munitions, the history of which Franks would eagerly read decades later. Shell production rose from half a million in 1913 to ninety million annually in 1918, annual machine-gun production from close to three hundred to almost eighty thousand. The state began building its own arms factories in 1915 as well as directing the efforts of those in the private sector. The railways, the chemicals industry, collieries and shipping were all taken under full state control by 1916.

Manpower planning was the crucial issue. The surge in armed forces volunteers in 1914 and 1915 took around 25 per cent of the industrial and mining workforce, a figure that rose to 45 per cent by 1918 after conscription was introduced in 1916 – another first for modern Britain. As early as 1915 skilled workers were being taken out of uniform and moved back into industry (and issued with special badges denoting their status to avoid accusations of shirking or cowardice back in civilian life). Some 2.5 million new workers, a third of them women, moved into industrial jobs over the course of the war.

The war left the British economy in a perilous state. What had been the world's largest creditor nation with financial claims stretching over the globe found itself transformed into a debtor, having borrowed heavily from the United States. Key industries were rerouted towards war-fighting and important export markets lost. But while the war proved incredibly costly to Britain, not only in human but also in economic and financial terms, its overall economic management should be seen as a success. Civilians grumbled about rising prices, high taxes and diminished living standards but there was never a domestic crisis. There were high-profile cases of shell shortages on the front and the army often argued it did not have all the manpower it needed, but in the end, war was sustained until the final victory. Broadly put, the painful and difficult trade-offs were just about managed.

Not every country could say the same. The clearest example of a state and regime broken by the demands of total war is to be found in Britain's ally Russia. Russia lacked many of Britain's initial advantages: its domestic industry was orders of magnitude smaller, its transport system far less developed, and its political system – still essentially an absolutist monarchy with a relatively new veneer of more consultation with domestic elites – far less well equipped to handle the kind of trade-offs total war involved, or even in many cases to recognise them as trade-offs.

The impacts were most visible in that most crucial of all markets, the one for food. During the initial mobilisation in 1914 the Russian army called up not only around fifteen million men from a predominantly peasant-based rural society but also several million horses, most of which had previously been used in agriculture. Prior to the war Russia had exported almost 10 per cent of its grain, and while the draining of workers and horses was recognised as a hit to agricultural production, it was hoped that as exports ceased the domestic food supply would be able to cope. This did not turn out to be the case.

Several things went wrong at once over the coming three years. As well as the hit to output from all those lost peasants and horses, Germany's initial advances on its front in 1914 and into 1915 in areas that are now Poland and the Baltic states captured around 6 per cent of Russia's farmland. The impact on food supply was even greater than this implies though as around 2.5 million Russians fled the advancing German forces behind the lines into territory still controlled by the tsar. In other words, the total population rose even as farmland, farm workers and plough horses were lost.

Meanwhile, in order to move soldiers and munitions the Russian army increasingly monopolised use of the country's fairly limited rail infrastructure, which had previously moved grain from the countryside to the cities. Even when food was being produced, it could not necessarily get to where it was needed.

But there was a wider economic problem too. The crops that had previously been used in the export market were not generally rerouted to the cities. Instead they mostly simply stopped being produced.

Before the war, exchange between the cities and the countryside in Russia had looked like it did across much of Europe: the cities produced industrial and consumer goods, sold these to the bulk of the population in the countryside and used the money earned to purchase, among other things, food from the farms. That is to say, farmers produced more food than their own village needed – an agricultural surplus – because they could sell that output for cash and use that cash to buy the goods they desired. That is how economies are generally supposed to work.

But as the war dragged on, more and more of Russian industry was pushed into making material directly related to the war effort. In economic terms there was a change in the terms-of-trade between the cities and the countryside. There were few manufactured goods available for civilians, and those that were tended to be taken by the consumers closest to where they were actually produced, that is to say in the cities themselves. Even if peasants had continued to produce a surplus as before, they would have little to spend the earnings on. So, in many cases, they simply stopped. The usual exchange between the rural and urban sectors broke down and food in the cities began to run scarce.

This was a problem that afflicted many of Europe's agrarian societies during the Great War, including Germany and Austria-Hungary, but it hit hardest in Russia. The tsarist state, and its provisional government successor, simply lacked the means to enforce food transfers. This was yet another example of a supposedly authoritarian state lacking the capacity to affect its will. The Bolshevik battle cry as they seized power was 'peace and bread' and much of their early programme, as we shall see later, can be seen as reimposing the exchange between the countryside and the cities, although on often brutal, state-backed terms.

If Britain and Russia represent two extreme examples of how the combatants coped with the demands of total war between 1914 and 1918, then Germany fits somewhere into the middle. As in Britain, the German move towards a command and planned economy directed towards military output came gradually and in stages but the process also varied in important ways from that which played out across the North Sea.

Initially the War Laws of August 1914 allowed the state to take greater control of transport and of some key raw materials, as well as establishing maximum prices for some activities. This was an earlier intervention than that taken by London and a sign that business as usual was not the German approach. By the autumn of the first year of the war, when it was clear that the early attempt to land a knockout military blow had failed and the war would drag on for longer than hoped, additional steps were needed. The financial incentives available to private firms for undertaking military work were stepped up, drawing more resources into the war effort. Everything changed gear radically in 1916 with the Hindenburg Programme.

Field Marshal Paul von Hindenburg and his close associate

General Erich Ludendorff had had a good war up to mid-1916. Commanding German forces on the Eastern Front they had made good gains against the Russian army, and in August of that year Hindenburg was promoted to Chief of the General Staff, taking over the running of Germany's war effort. In September, accompanied by Ludendorff, he held a conference at Cambrai, near the front line in occupied northern France, with the commanders of the armies on the Western Front. The battles at the Somme and Verdun that year, as previously noted, had been especially costly.

The problem, according to the field commanders, was that the forces of the Entente had achieved a superiority in artillery. The army on this front reported that between July and August, during the fighting around the Somme, it had received only 470 train loads of shells but fired 587 train loads. Faced with the need to increase shell production, the War Ministry assumed sweeping powers across the wider economy. Employment in the industries rose by 44 per cent as workers were redirected and that in the non-industries fell by 40 per cent. Prisoners of war were also put to work, in violation of international law.

On one level the powers assumed by the German military high command do not look that different from the kinds of economic planning and direction assumed by their opponents in London and Paris. But there were three crucial differences. First, Germany was taking an increasingly damaging hit from a British-led naval blockade which cut off some key imports. Second, unlike in Britain and France, Germany suffered to a greater extent from the kind of breakdown in traditional exchanges between the countryside and the towns of the kind which happened on an even larger scale in Russia. But third, and perhaps most importantly, Germany's war economy was almost totally military-led.

Whereas the British and French governments assumed sweeping new powers, they remained – just about – within the confines of civilian-led, democratic states. In Germany, military needs came first and foremost, with civilian requirements a distant second. Rather than helping to ensure that the military had the resources it needed to win the war, this instead, by 1918, contributed to a collapse in the German home front at much the same time that the army in the west had been beaten on the field and was in retreat.

Total war was not just about maximising military production, it was about balancing the needs for ever greater military resources with keeping the civilian economy afloat.

The Second World War, in economic terms, had many similarities with the First. This time, though, there was not even an initial pretence of 'business as usual'. Controls, direction and planning in almost every belligerent country followed on soon after declarations of war.

The production numbers for that conflict are even more staggering than those of the Great War, and so too was the bloodshed. Just take tank production as an example. In 1939 Britain produced three hundred tanks, but over the seventy-two months of the conflict as a whole it managed to produce just over 29,000. And that figure was more than overshadowed by the 46,300 tanks (and self-propelled guns) produced over the course of 1939–45 by the Third Reich.

The real difference, though, between the economics of production of the first and second total wars of the twentieth century was not just the scale, it was the location. The two great industrial powers of this second war were not, as in the first, Great Britain and Germany but the USA and the USSR. Between just 1941 and 1945, the United States produced 99,500 tanks and self-propelled guns, while the Soviet Union added 102,800.

In this war the US truly functioned as the arsenal of democracy, producing and supplying vital equipment not only to its own forces but to those of its British and Soviet allies. Seven per cent of US national income was used to supply its compatriots via Lend-Lease. In the case of Britain, Lend-Lease supported the equivalent of almost one fifth of its own GDP in 1943 and 1944. And while the Soviets received comparatively less, what they did get was crucial. Almost two thirds of the 600,000 trucks and jeeps the Soviets relied upon to keep their army supplied and moving during the long advance to Berlin in 1944 and 1945 were American-supplied.

Taken together, the two total wars of the twentieth century offer several distinct economic lessons. First, that success in a total war is about more than simply producing the most weapons – the divergent fates of Britain and Germany in the Great War point to this. More importantly, though, they prove that in total war, in the longer run, raw economic weight matters. In the short run, luck, contingency and chance all play a major role. Anything can, and does, happen on the battlefield. An army one might not rationally expect to win any given encounter sometimes does. In May 1940 very few leaders, including those in Berlin, expected the sudden and sweeping victory that the Germans won in the west, driving France out of the war and occupying Denmark, Norway and the Low Countries in a little over three months. Sometimes in war, as in sport, the favourite loses. But – and this is an important but – over the longer term chance is less important than production potential. A side that can lose a battle or campaign but stay in the war, replace its losses and try again will usually, in the longer term, win out.

This was an insight taken to heart by the British state after the Great War. The Treasury, Britain's finance ministry, went as far as to call Britain's financial, economic and industrial strength and potential the country's 'fourth arm of defence' after the navy, the air force and the army. Planning in the 1930s was premised on doing enough in the way of preparation to avoid losing a short war quickly while doing nothing that would endanger Britain's underlying economic potential, which was seen as critical to victory in a longer conflict.

Over the course of both world wars, the economic weight gradually moved away from Germany (and its allies). In 1914 the combined GDP of the Entente Powers – including their colonies and empires – was around three times higher than that of the Central Powers. By 1917, after the United States' entry into the conflict, the ratio was closer to five to one. The equivalent numbers for the Second World War tell an interesting story, tracking German gains in occupied Europe and Japanese gains in Asia and adding emphasis to the times when the Allies thought the future the most uncertain.

In 1939 the edge lay with the Allies, but perhaps not decisively so. Britain and France, together with their initial allies and empires, had a combined economic output of around $1,025 billion (expressed here in 1990 dollars) against the initial Axis powers' $751 billion. By 1942, though, Germany and Japan's sweeping conquests in 1940, 1941 and 1942 had taken the Axis's combined economic output up to $1,552 billion, while even after the entry of the Soviet Union and the United States into the war the Allies could muster just $1,444 billion. 1942, then, the mid-point of the war, was the crucial swing point at which it could go either way.

But US economic output was expanding rapidly, Soviet output was almost matching this pace, and the Axis began to lose previously conquered territories and access to their resources. US GDP grew from around $1,094 billion in 1941 to $1,474 billion in 1945 as resources underused since the depression of the 1930s were put back to work under the demands of total war. By 1944 the ratio of Allied to Axis economic output was three to one. By 1945 it was more than five to one. Economic weight mattered.

The western allies' high levels of income per head, relative to their Axis enemies and Soviet allies, allowed them to fight what some have called a 'rich man's war' by 1944, a war that disproportionately used high-explosive shells, aircraft, artillery and tanks rather than old-fashioned manpower.

In both total wars, the two competing sides not only tried to actively manage their own economies to support their war efforts but equally sought to undermine that of their enemy. The best, and most straightforward, definition of economic warfare is an attempt to destroy the enemy's fighting power indirectly, by attacking the wider supply chain of their forces. Such measures were not new to the twentieth century. Sherman's march to the sea in 1865 could be seen as a form of economic warfare, as too could Napoleon's continental system or even a medieval harrying. But in the twentieth century economic warfare expanded in scope, scale and violence. Operation Gomorrah, the firebombing of Tokyo and the eventual use of atomic weapons in Japan were all, at heart, measures of economic warfare.

The two primary weapons of economic warfare in the world wars were the submarine and the bomber.

Submarines, it was assumed in the more innocent age of the first decade of the twentieth century, would be an almost useless weapon against merchant shipping, because by the time the craft had surfaced, issued a warning to the merchant vessel and, if necessary, taken on its crew as prisoners, help may well have arrived. The whole process would just be too slow. The notion that a naval vessel, crewed and officered by the members of an official armed force, would simply sink a civilian ship with no warning, likely killing those on board, was almost inconceivable.

Under the strains of total warfare, the norms around killing enemy and neutral civilian seamen would change relatively quickly. Just as they would, more generally, when it came to the use of aerial bombers.

The first six or so months of the Great War were rough for German submariners. They had attempted to capture British merchant shipping while adhering to the usual rules of naval warfare – surfacing and demanding a surrender. The problem facing the submariners was that once they had surfaced even a lightly armed merchant ship often outgunned them. And it was – it does not really need spelling out – tricky to take a prize if the prize itself was better armed than the prize-taker.

The German response, in February 1915, was what they dubbed 'unrestricted submarine warfare'. The waters around the United Kingdom were deemed to be a war zone by the German government and submariners were given permission to sink any enemy ship in those waters without warning. Furthermore, neutrals were advised that it would be difficult to identify their shipping and any vessels at all in these waters would be at risk. This was the beginning of submarine warfare against commerce as it is nowadays understood.

British and Allied shipping losses, which had been running at around 60,000 tons a month since August 1914, spiked sharply above 100,000 tons a month in the spring of 1915, but unrestricted submarine warfare came with a high diplomatic price tag. The torpedoing of the British passenger liner *Lusitania* in May of that year killed 1,200 of the 2,000 civilians on board including 128 Americans. Faced with diplomatic pressure and threats to cut trade links, Germany's first experiment with economic warfare was halted by September 1915, just eight months after it had begun.

By late 1916 the war was dragging on and Germany's economy was showing signs of serious strain. By now the German navy, which had begun the war with a dozen submarines, had more than a hundred. Operating ranges, speed and weaponry had all improved as well as raw numbers. In December 1916 Admiral Henning von Holtzendorff, the Chief of Staff of the German Admiralty, penned one of the most important documents of the war. He argued that the advances, in terms of both quantity and quality, of the Imperial German Navy's U-boat fleet offered Germany a potentially war-winning weapon. If it was once again unleashed it could sink 600,000 tons of Allied shipping a month and disrupt Britain's food imports so drastically that it would be forced to the peace table within six months. In January 1917 the Kaiser agreed to the plan, and in February it went into operation.

On one level it worked. Allied shipping losses hit 520,000 tons that month and rose to over 800,000 in April. The British and their allies were forced to implement a convoy system which slowed down the inflow of goods but provided better protection to merchant shipping. Even so losses were still running at over 300,000 tons a month by the end of 1917. The German navy succeeded in sinking around 6 million tons of Allied shipping in 1917 as a whole – more than even Holtzendorff had thought possible.

But on a more important level, the plan failed spectacularly. Not only did the losses fail to drive Britain out of the war, but the unrestricted attacks on merchant shipping also helped to bring the United States into it.

Britain's own economic warfare against Germany was less based on the submarine, but mostly because there was simply less German merchant shipping to sink in the first place. Britain blockaded Germany from 1914 onwards, with the restrictions on trade stepping up from 1915 onwards.

Legally Germany was entitled to continue trade with her neutral neighbours, such as the Netherlands, Switzerland and the Scandinavian countries, including through buying goods there which had originated in the United Kingdom or other allied nations. There was technically nothing to stop, say, a Dutch firm importing useful war materials from Britain and then selling them on to Germany. Legal niceties quickly went out of the window, though. While the Royal Navy effectively closed down sea trade to Germany via the North Sea, an equally important role was played by accountants. From 1915 onwards neutrals such as the Dutch were set limits on their own imports equivalent to what British officials saw as necessary for their own domestic use. This indirect blockade, monitored by accountants rather than warships, was just as effective as the German use of submarines.

The numbers speak for themselves. Britain, which imported more than 60 per cent of its calories, endured no deaths to famine between 1914 and 1918. Germany, which imported less than a quarter of its calories, suffered around 750,000. Meat consumption in Britain was around 80 per cent of its 1913 level by 1914, in Germany it was closer to 20 per cent.

Disentangling the impact of the blockade from the chaotic running of the war economy – in a way that prioritised pure military needs – is tricky. As too is separating the impact of the active blockade from the simple fact that Germany harmed itself in 1914 by declaring war on its own major trading partners. But regardless of the weight placed on these differing variables, it is clear which approach to economic warfare succeeded and which failed between 1914 and 1918.

The economic warfare of the Second World War would go much further than that of the First. If the submarine was the most high-profile weapon of economic warfare in the Great War, the bomber took its place in the later conflict.

The policy-makers and strategists of the 1930s were almost bomber-obsessed. On 26 April 1937 the German Condor

Legion – a force of Luftwaffe 'volunteers' fighting alongside the fascists in the Spanish Civil War – together with their Italian allies launched a major bombing raid on the Basque town of Guernica. The raid killed somewhere between 150 and 300 civilians, inspired one of Picasso's more famous paintings and captured the attention of the world's media. This seemed to be the future of warfare; not only would soldiers on the battlefield and merchant seamen plying the shipping lanes be at risk but even civilians in their own homes, potentially far from the front lines. The British government believed in 1938 that two months of bombing would kill 600,000 British civilians and injure more than a million. The bomber, it was believed, would always get through.

The early experiences of the war did not live up to this apocalyptic fear. Germany and Britain, after an initial reluctance to land the first blow and bring potential retribution, did indeed bomb each other's cities in 1940 and 1941. The folk memory of 'the Blitz' lives on in Britain. But while the two sides traded blows, the blows were, by the standards of 1944–5, not really fatal ones. The air forces of both sides were simply incapable of living up to the pre-war hype. The bombers of the day were both fewer in number and not yet capable of carrying the heavy loads seen later in the war.

Interestingly, though, the two combatants took very different lessons from these early experiences. While the Luftwaffe essentially gave up on 'strategic bombing' as a distraction, the RAF, and later the USAAF, decided to try much harder. In late 1941 the Allied air forces were dropping around 1,000 tons of bombs a month on German-occupied Europe; by mid-1944 that would rise to more than 100,000 tons a month. Over the course of 1943, 1944 and 1945 the RAF bombed German-occupied Europe by night and the USAAF by day. Much is sometimes made of the difference between American 'precision' bombing and British 'area' bombing. But in reality 'precision' in the mid-1940s meant 'somewhere roughly near the target'.

While the British euphemistically spoke in terms of 'dehousing' German workers by destroying the housing stock, the Americans talked up attacks on specific economic targets. Even when such targets could be effectively identified and attacked, the results often disappointed the planners. Much as Holtzendorff's submarine offensive had failed to end the war within six months, even the destruction of supposedly key economic infrastructure failed to halt Germany's war effort.

In 1943, in a classic case of this, the USAAF attempted to destroy Germany's ball bearing industry, located around Schweinfurt. Ball bearings might sound like a somewhat esoteric target to pick but they were a crucial component in most kinds of vehicle and in the machinery used to produce more than half of all war equipment. The Schweinfurt raids succeeded in destroying more than half of Germany's ball bearing production capacity but, the post-war United States Strategic Bombing Survey was disappointed to report, this had almost no effect on Germany's ability to fight the war. With production halved, German industry instead ran down existing stockpiles, economised on ball bearing usage and substituted different components wherever this was possible.

In 1944, the USAAF became equally excited about the prospect of destroying Germany's synthetic oil production facilities to cut off its fuel supplies. More than 10 per cent of all Allied bombing from mid-1944 onwards was directed to this end. Once again, though, despite major successes, the actual economic effect was muted. As with ball bearings, the German economy could draw on stockpiles even as new production was sharply curtailed and the temporary shortages led only to economising and substitutions rather than actual collapse.

The real lesson of attempts to destroy ball bearing

production or oil facilities in the Second World War or to crimp Britain's food imports in the First was that modern economies are highly complicated machines with lots of moving parts. More importantly, they can adapt and change in the face of shortages.

As the economist Mancur Olson emphasised in the 1960s, there are no strategic commodities, only strategic uses. People, for example, need to be fed, but there is more than one way of doing so. The analogy of the supply chain is an alluring one – so alluring that this book has often utilised it – but sometimes a misleading one. A chain is, after all, made up of links which can be broken. Modern economies are more robust and breaking one link, or even many links, rarely causes them to fall apart. Other goods will be substituted where possible, stockpiles run down or processes adapted entirely. The impact of destroying access to even a perceived vital component of a war effort has rarely caused that war effort to collapse entirely.

None of which should be taken as saying that economic warfare did not play a major role in either war. But in each case it was a slow and cumulative effect that built up over time rather than a bolt from the blue which 'ended the war within six months'. Slowly but surely stockpiles were depleted, and the transportation system began to collapse under the weight of repeated bombing of railheads and junctions. Just as importantly, it often provoked a response. In the case of Germany in the Second World War, by 1944 more than 80 per cent of the Luftwaffe's fighters were deployed defending the Reich rather than providing support to their armies in the field. If nothing else, this handed local air superiority to the Allied armies on the Western Front and the Soviets in the east, greatly aiding their advances from 1943 onwards. The need to produce ever more anti-aircraft guns for home defence consumed half of Germany's electronic industry output by the end of the war – output that could have been put to more effective use elsewhere.

Taken together, the seemingly paradoxical lessons of the two total wars of the twentieth century are that in the long run raw industrial potential and wider economic factors are crucial to victory in a total conflict. But economic warfare – the deliberate attacking of the enemy's economy – although cumulatively effective over time is rarely the war-winning weapon it is often assumed to be.

14

The Luftwaffe: When Rewarding Bravery Was Self-defeating

Helmut Wick's career as a fighter pilot was short-lived but spectacular. On 22 November 1939, while flying his sixth combat mission, he achieved his first confirmed enemy kill, downing a French Curtiss Hawk 75 while piloting his then state-of-the-art Messerschmitt Bf 109 fighter. By the end of the French campaign, in June 1940, he had fourteen confirmed air-to-air victories and ranked as the Luftwaffe's third highest scorer. He was just getting started. Over the following months, as the Battle of Britain raged over the Channel and southern England, his total soared. On 25 August 1940 he claimed his twentieth victory. He added two more the next day. By early October he had downed forty-one enemy aircraft and was closing in on the totals of Adolf Galland and Werner Mölders, his two chief rivals. He was awarded the Knight's Cross with Oak Leaves, garlanded in the German press and promoted to major, in charge of his wing. He was twenty-five years old.

But the seven hundred or so men under his command, mostly ground crew, found him to be a poor choice of leader.

He was vain, competitive and clearly obsessed with overtaking the totals of Galland and Mölders. While he was clearly a skilled pilot, he was a terrible commander. His fighting style was highly individualistic, always climbing at full power straight from take-off and showing no regard for flying formation or the men under his command as he manoeuvred for position. Franz Fiby, his wing man, called Wick a 'real daredevil' and noted that he had excellent eyesight and was usually the first to spot the enemy, 'then he opened the throttle and simply went after them'. In the mid-afternoon of 28 November 1940, just over a year after his first victory, Wick got what he wanted. His fifty-sixth kill, a Spitfire downed over the Isle of Wight, made him the highest scoring pilot in the Luftwaffe.

Two hours later, he was dead. After returning from this latest victory to his base near Cherbourg in northern France he ordered his plane to be immediately refuelled and set off on yet another *freie jagd* (free hunting) jaunt. There was no purpose to that second sortie of the day other than to seek battle. Fifty minutes after taking off, approaching 5 p.m., Wick found himself once again nearing the Isle of Wight. Flying with Fiby and two other members of his wing he encountered Spitfires of the RAF's 609 Squadron. The four German machines faced a dozen British flyers. Wick, of course, wasted no time in moving to attack. The fight was over in seconds, with Wick's Messerschmitt taking heavy damage and forcing him to bail out into the Channel.

Afterwards a member of Wick's flight, Rudi Pflanz, who himself would rack up fifty-two confirmed kills before meeting his own death in 1942, circled the area radioing in English that a Spitfire was down to try and attract a British rescue team for his own commander. Pflanz remained in position for so long that he almost ran out of fuel himself and was eventually forced to make a crash landing on the French coast. It was to no avail.

A desperate search-and-rescue operation was launched with German boats making for the area. But it was getting dark and Wick had gone down near the enemy coast. The odds never looked good. Wick was reported that evening as missing. A few weeks later his status was officially listed as killed in action.

Wick's fifty-six confirmed victories make him one of the most successful fighter pilots of all time. But among the Luftwaffe of the Second World War he was merely an also-ran. Over the course of the war as a whole, across all the combatant nations, 409 pilots are credited with shooting down forty or more enemy planes; 379 of those, a staggering 93 per cent, served in the Luftwaffe. While the highest scoring German pilot, Erich Hartmann, racked up a score of 352 victories, no Allied pilot managed more than sixty-six.

The preponderance of German aces is not due to German overcounting. In fact, the Luftwaffe's rules for claiming a victory were relatively strict compared to its peers. To receive the credit, a pilot had to file extensive documentation, ideally with witness statements. Many such claims were rejected. Comparing German recorded victories to the war diaries of their opposing Allied squadrons shows them to be broadly accurate. By this tally, Wick's score was closer to eighty than his official fifty-six.

While the numbers are almost certainly correct, some care is still required when handling them. It was not that there was simply something in the water in Hitler's Reich that produced exceptional fighter pilots. In the early days of the war the Luftwaffe had both a technological lead over its opponents and more pilots with recent air-to-air combat experience, gained serving in the Condor Legion, sent by Nazi Germany to aid the fascist forces in the Spanish Civil War. The disparity was especially evident in the months following Germany's invasion of the USSR in the summer of 1941. Experienced German pilots in modern fighters faced an ill-trained, ill-prepared and ill-equipped Soviet air force. As Heinz Knoke, a Luftwaffe officer, recorded in his diary on the third day of the invasion, 'their knowledge of combat tactics is as elementary as their aircraft'. The Russians lost 1,200 planes in the first nine hours of the war, although two thirds of them were still on the ground when destroyed so would not have counted as aerial victories.

But the real explanation for the Luftwaffe's domination of the ace league tables is not to be found in either innate ability or in an early qualitative and technological edge. Rather it was because while most air forces in the Second World War expected their pilots to fly a fixed number of sorties before moving off active duty, the rule in the Luftwaffe was more straightforward: 'fly till you die'. German pilots achieved higher numbers of confirmed kills because they flew an awful lot more. Erich Hartmann may have won more than 350 victories (98 per cent of those against the Soviets) but he was shot down eight times himself.

Pilots in all air forces celebrated their aces, but in the Luftwaffe the cult of the ace ran far deeper. With victories came rewards. The Iron Cross, Second Class was awarded after the first confirmed kill and the Iron Cross, First Class after five. Twenty confirmed kills won the pilot the Knight's Cross, which in the early days of the war was a sufficiently rare enough achievement that it would typically be personally awarded by Hermann Göring, the Luftwaffe's commander. But as the totals of the leading aces continued to rise, new measures of success had to be invented. Oak leaves were added to the Knight's Cross for forty victories, Swords for seventy and Diamonds for a hundred. Germany found itself stuck in a strange form of the kind of grade inflation familiar to school examiners. The Front Flight Wings in either gold, silver or bronze and the Cup of Honour were new awards handed out at the discretion of Göring. Across all arms of the German armed forces around 3.3 million Iron Crosses, Second Class were awarded between 1939 and 1945 but only 7,300 Knight's Crosses and fewer than 1,000 Knight's Crosses with either Oak Leaves, Swords or Diamonds. Alongside medals, German pilots could be rewarded by a mention in the German armed forces bulletin, the *Wehrmachtbericht*. This daily publication was distributed across German-occupied territory, reprinted in newspapers and formed the basis of radio news reports. While it typically summarised the day's military events, beginning in April 1940 it occasionally praised an individual for their own exceptional service.

The point of the elaborate system of medals, mentions and other rewards for Luftwaffe fighter pilots was to incentivise better performance. The question, though, is whether this system worked as intended. Certainly it spurred Helmut Wick on to achieve dozens of aerial victories in a short matter of months. But it also got him killed.

On one level the award of the Knight's Cross with Oak Leaves is no different from a fast-food restaurant picking an employee of the month. If people value status, and the evidence suggests that they mostly do, then awarding status is a rational low-cost way for employers to motivate their staff. Whereas cash rewards for performance come with an obvious cost, so-called status incentives usually do not. By creating an artificially scarce resource, whether a mention in a daily bulletin or a bump up in a worker's title, such rewards can serve as a device to increase effort and boost output. In other words, a canny employer can exploit their workers' desire for status by using it in lieu of monetary rewards. The military has long understood this. So too has academia, which in the words of one economic study 'is awash with job titles, fellowships and prizes whose value is mostly symbolic but which convey status on their respondents'. Empirical studies have found that such rewards can work well – they can reduce absenteeism, and lead to greater effort and more accuracy in tasks – and that they come at little direct monetary cost to organisations.

But handing out such trinkets may not necessarily work in all circumstances. Exploiting people's desire for status to spur greater effort may appear all well and good for an organisation but it also risks prompting more unhelpful behaviours. Status competition can be a dangerous thing. One recent study looked at the neighbours of winners of the Canadian lottery. Understandably those lucky enough to be winning decent-sized lump sums splashed out on house renovations and new cars. But reasonably frequently, so too did their neighbours. This keeping-up-with-the-Joneses behaviour is often financed by borrowing. Strikingly, bankruptcies increase in the neighbourhoods of lottery winners and the larger the win, the higher the increase in insolvency. Competing for status is not necessarily cost-free. The introduction of an employee of the month award may result in workers trying harder to win it, or it may result in those who do not win becoming demotivated. The real world is, after all, a complicated kind of place.

There is plenty of evidence that the Luftwaffe's elaborate system of rewards may have helped produce more aces but was overall a drag on its operational performance. For a start, it led to some perverse-seeming outcomes. In September 1940, as Wick was climbing the league tables, Werner Mölders claimed his fortieth victory. Later that week he flew to Göring's hunting lodge at Carinhall outside Berlin to receive his Oak Leaves directly from the Reichsmarschall himself. Göring invited him to stay for a couple of extra days of deer hunting. Mölders, knowing that Adolf Galland had just achieved his own fortieth kill and was due to arrive at Carinhall in a few days' time, accepted the offer only on the condition that Galland would also extend his own trip by the same amount of time to prevent him having an unfair advantage in their ongoing competition to be the top ace. Göring, himself a fighter pilot in the Great War, agreed. At a time when the Luftwaffe was engaged in the most crucial days of its most intense air campaign of the war so far, the battle for status saw its two leading pilots staying on the bench for days at a time. This was hardly a rational outcome.

But the problems ran far deeper than a few aces trying to maintain a level playing field. The demographics and personality traits of Luftwaffe fighter pilots were not those of a group where the introduction of artificially scarce status was conducive to helpful outcomes. They were mostly young men, with an average age of twenty-six in 1939 and just twenty-three by 1945, of a very particular type.

The selection process was tough. Just 5 per cent of those sitting the initial entrance exam were invited on to the three-day selection stage. Here, while the candidates underwent motor skills tests and leadership games, the most important factor was performance in the interviews. The future ace Julius Meimberg was repeatedly asked what he would do if he was found not to have the right aptitude to fly fighters. Each time he answered that he knew he did have the aptitude and refused to be drawn into alternatives. This was the attitude the selectors were looking for – headstrong and competitive with boundless self-confidence. Dr Paul Skawran, a Luftwaffe psychologist, conducted a wartime study of fighter pilots. He found that most of his subjects had a dislike of crowds and responsibility over others and preferred to work alone or in small groups. Leisure time was typically spent on horse riding, abseiling, hunting or driving fast cars. Skiing was almost universally popular. There was little interest in team sports and organised squadron-level games focused on swimming,

athletics and shooting – activities where individual performance mattered and could be recorded. None of Skawran's
interviewees liked football.

Despite the pride of the fighter crews, they were far from the
most skilled pilots in the Luftwaffe. Indeed, those showing the
most promise and technical proficiency during early training
were routed towards heavy bombers rather than fighters. Night
flying, navigating by instruments alone and maintaining formation – core tasks for bomber pilots – required more in the
way of raw skill. Attitude rather than ability counted more in
the fighter squadrons.

That attitude was shaped and refined by the experience of
serving with other fighter pilots. While bomber crews would
often serve from the same base for years at a time, the fighter
squadrons led a nomadic life, regularly changing bases in
reaction to the tempo of battle and the needs of the campaign.
Mornings began with a communal breakfast before flying up
to five sorties each day. While the Luftwaffe's own physicians
and psychologists recommended horse riding, reading and
the playing of table tennis to unwind at the end of the day,
drinking, gambling over cards and visiting prostitutes were far
more common. Despite the pilots being a highly individualistic
and competitive bunch, squadrons formed a close camaraderie
that outsiders found difficult to penetrate. Attempts to transfer
bomber or transport pilots into the fighter service were rarely
successful. They were trained to work as a team rather than to
prize individual effort and they had a habit of asking questions
on arrival about things such as the recent loss rate in a squadron, which to the fighter pilots screamed of holding precisely
the wrong attitude.

In stark contrast to other parts of the German military,
distinctions of rank and social class were downplayed. While
army officers lived separately from their enlisted soldiers and

non-commissioned officers (NCOs), fighter pilots barracked and ate together regardless of rank. When Douglas Bader, a leading RAF ace, was captured after a mid-air collision over France in 1941, Adolf Galland, keen to meet a rival, went to visit him in hospital. Galland would tell colleagues he was shocked when Bader, speaking in a whisper, said, 'Please tell me I wasn't shot down by an NCO.' To Galland, and his peers, the question of whether the victor was an officer or an NCO appeared irrelevant. Galland would later tell the story to boost morale and point out the supposedly pompous nature of the RAF.

On completing training, a new fighter pilot was awarded his pilot's licence, his flight wings and a silk scarf. Most would wear that scarf even when not flying; just visible below a dress tunic or an off-duty civilian shirt, it was a visible reminder to everyone the pilot met that he belonged to an exclusive fraternity.

The overall picture that emerges is one of highly competitive, risk-seeking young men who mostly got along with each other but did not mix well with outsiders. They operated in a world where individual performance was recognised and rewarded and where collective effort counted for little. A regular worry to be found in the diaries of early war pilots, the type still in training when the Germans rolled into Poland and then France, is a deep fear that the war would be over before they got to play their part. The Luftwaffe's system of status rewards took these attributes to extremes.

The real problem was that, in economic terms, pilot skill was extremely unequally distributed. The typical German fighter pilot was credited with 0.55 victories in a typical month and faced a 3.4 per cent chance of being killed, captured or otherwise permanently prevented from flying in any given month. But there was no such thing as a typical pilot.

Complete records exist for just over 5,100 Luftwaffe fighter pilots over the course of the war. In an average month the vast majority of them, over 80 per cent, recorded no confirmed kills while a smaller minority notched up huge totals. Emil Lang recorded sixty-eight victories in October 1943 while Hans-Joachim Marseille achieved seventeen in a single day (1 September 1942).

The Luftwaffe records register 53,008 aerial victories over the course of the war. The top-scoring 110 pilots achieved as many confirmed kills as the bottom 4,900 combined. Over time that gap between the highest performers and the bulk of the fighter pilots grew larger and larger. Six years of constant aerial warfare took its toll on the Luftwaffe. By the beginning of 1942 losses already amounted to around twice its pre-war strength. Shortages of qualified air crew were more acute than shortages of planes. At the start of the war, the Luftwaffe was losing 1.8 per cent of its pilots each month; by May 1944 that had risen to a staggering 25 per cent each month. To meet the need for qualified pilots, especially as the war in the air came to be fought predominantly over Germany itself, the training period was repeatedly cut back. As late as the summer of 1942 new Luftwaffe pilots were receiving as many training flight hours as their RAF opponents, but by the second half of 1943 that had fallen to half as much time. In terms of flying time on operational war-fighting planes rather than older training models the disparity was even greater. Luftwaffe cadets received just one third of the hours of new RAF pilots and one fifth of the American total. A newly minted Luftwaffe fighter pilot in 1939 would have racked up almost eighty flight hours in a modern fighter before joining his squadron; by 1943 that was down to forty-five hours. Gunnery training, vital to dog-fighting, was almost entirely dropped. Flight training, by late 1943, involved only two to four flights, lasting under two hours in total, in which the fighter's weapons were fired. And even then the training was now entirely on firing at targets on the ground rather than in the air. The interrogation notes of a veteran Luftwaffe pilot captured in mid-1944 by the Americans are revealing. In his words, pilot training was by that stage of the war 'pitiful'. New pilots had almost no instruction at all in flying by instrument or navigating in clouds and there was no longer anyone in his unit he could trust to command a section of four planes. As he lamented, 'things are not what they were in my day'.

By early 1944 there were effectively two types of Luftwaffe fighter pilot: the veterans who had survived the early war and were easily capable of taking on rawer Allied pilots and the flow of new, increasingly ill-trained joiners who themselves were easy prey for their enemies. Of the 107 German aces who scored over a hundred victories, only eight joined the service after mid-1942. But while the nature of the pilots was certainly different, the system of status awards remained unchanged.

Figuring out how this pool of increasingly under-trained but testosterone-fuelled ultra-competitive young men responded to the status incentives on offer would usually not be straightforward. But the extensive records and documentation around claimed kills provide a large dataset, one that economists and economic historians can work with. Philipp Ager, Leonardo Bursztyn and Hans-Joachim Voth did just that in 2016.

They used the five thousand or so records of Luftwaffe fighter pilots who made at least one victory claim to try and discover if the incentives were working as intended. The status incentive they chose to measure was a mention in the armed forces bulletin, the *Wehrmachtbericht*. This is perhaps the ideal example of a status incentive: unlike a medal, the recipient did not even get something to pin to their uniform; all they got was the fleeting feeling of superiority of having been publicly acclaimed. Unlike medals, which became predictable as victory totals rose, a mention in the *Wehrmachtbericht* could, in theory at least, happen at any time to anyone. Newly qualified fighter pilots could not hope to be awarded the Knight's Cross with Oak Leaves on their first few flights but being singled out for praise in the bulletin was not impossible. A typical example ran something like that of Hans-Joachim Marseille's second mention in June 1942: 'First Lieutenant Marseille shot down ten enemy planes in a 24-hour period in North Africa, raising his total score of aerial victories to 101'.

Pilot performance is influenced by a huge variety of factors. Taking on the Red Army Air Force in June 1941 was a very different proposition from flying against the British or Americans in mid-1944. Flying conditions over the Mediterranean in the summer were rather different from a Soviet winter. The test that Ager, Bursztyn and Voth devised attempted to control for this by looking at the impact on pilots of the recognition of a former peer, someone they had served with in the past. First Lieutenant Marseille's squadron mates performed well in June 1942 at the time of his mention but that may well have reflected broader conditions in the North African desert and the ebb and flow of the aerial war in that campaign rather than any status competition with Marseille himself. A more interesting question is how did the performance of Marseille's former colleagues, serving hundreds of miles away on very different fronts, change in the immediate aftermath of his public acclaim? The detailed records allowed for a full investigation.

On one level status competition seems to have worked as the Luftwaffe intended. In the immediate aftermath of a former peer being recognised in the *Wehrmachtbericht* the victory rates of all former peers increased. But the results varied hugely by pilot quality.

Ager, Bursztyn and Voth divided fighter pilots into two

categories: good pilots, those whose previous performance put them in the top 20 per cent of scorers, and the rest. In the month after a former squadron mate was praised, the victory claims of a typical good former peer rose from just under two to just over three – a notable and statistically significant pick-up. Pilots in the bottom 80 per cent also improved their victory claims after a former peer was publicly recognised but from an already low 0.3 average monthly claim to just 0.4.

The bigger gap was in what the economists euphemistically called the 'monthly exit rate' from the sample of pilots. In war-time this usually meant death. Good pilots were always more likely to be killed in any given month than poor pilots – they were the risk-takers always closing with the enemy. Being the kind of pilot who won victories meant putting oneself directly in harm's way. But when a former colleague got a public pat on the back their chance of exiting the sample in the follow-ing month did not rise, even as their claimed victories did. By sharp contrast, the exit rate among the bottom 80 per cent of former peers of a recognised pilot increased by almost 50 per cent in the month after a bulletin mention.

The results held even when Ager, Bursztyn and Voth con-trolled for variables such as aircraft type, the experience level of former peers, the front on which they currently served and the time of year when the recognition took place.

In other words, in the immediate aftermath of a former colleague receiving some positional status, good pilots may have improved their performance substantially, but most pilots were more likely to get themselves killed. The overall impact, across the Luftwaffe as a whole, was a slightly higher victory rate but an even higher exit rate. Among former colleagues of a recognised pilot the overall ratio of victories to losses fell in the month after an award. The net impact was corrosive.

Fighter pilots in the Second World War ultimately operated

alone. In a single-seat fighter, once battle had begun, direct control by senior officers was almost impossible. In the final analysis, individual pilots made choices about whether to pursue victory or to break off contact with the enemy.

In economic terms, the Luftwaffe and its pilots were subject to what is called a principal-agent problem. The agents, in this case the fighter pilots, were making decisions and taking actions on behalf of their principal, the Luftwaffe itself. The incentives faced by the agents, in this case the fighter pilots, did not necessary line up with those faced by the principal, the Luftwaffe itself.

Principal-agent problems occur regularly, in all walks of life, although only rarely do they come with the chance of death. A typical example can be found in the legal world. The client of a lawyer, acting as the principal, may occasionally wonder whether the expensive course of litigation their agent is suggesting is really in their own best interest or whether their lawyer is simply eyeing up the fees. The real root of the problem, in economese, is 'asymmetric information' or, in plainer English, the fact that the agent holds a clearer picture of what is going on than the principal. The lawyer suggesting the expensive course of litigation has a better idea of whether or not it will likely pay off than the client weighing up the decision. The pilot in the Messerschmitt knows how closely he really engaged the enemy and the commander back on the base simply has to take his word for it.

One way around principal-agent problems is to ensure that the incentives of both the principal and the agent are aligned. That is the logic behind lawyers offering 'no win, no fee' cases. If the client does not have to pay unless the case is successful, they can be reasonably sure that the lawyer thinks it has a good shot. Well-aligned incentives should make principal-agent problems resolvable.

The Luftwaffe's system of medals and awards was supposed to do just that. The fear, from the point of view of its commanders, was that its pilots would simply not fight hard enough, that when they encountered the enemy they would be tempted to hang back and make sure they made it out alive. The incentive not to get killed is a strong one. The Iron Cross, the Knight's Cross, the possibility of a mention in the *Wehrmachtbericht*, the chance of promotion and all the rest were supposed to ensure that pilots, when push came to shove, took the risks required to win victories. Its highly competitive pilots were offered public recognition in return for performing well. But the results suggest this approach backfired. Rather than driving up performance across the organisation as a whole, the competition for status instead drove up risk-taking. For most pilots for most of the war, the public recognition of a former peer did encourage them to try harder – to break contact with the enemy less frequently and pursue victory with more zeal. But while some pilots could handle the higher risk, most could not. Public recognition reduced the average number of enemy planes shot down for the loss of one German pilot – exactly the opposite of what the Luftwaffe intended.

15

Stalin, Total War and the End of Soviet Growth

The diplomatic reception held at the Polish embassy in Moscow in November 1956 could, it is fair to say, have gone better. It was here that Nikita Khrushchev, the Soviet Premier, declared to the assembled western ambassadors that 'we will bury you'. Twelve diplomats from NATO states walked out as a result. Parts of the western press assumed this was a threat of nuclear war. That was going too far, but it was hardly a reassuring statement to make at a time of international tension. Some historians later suggested that the usual translation was not exactly right and what Khrushchev actually meant was 'we will be present at your funeral', which sounds almost as threatening. Neither version is the usual sort of pleasant small talk meant to be aired at a diplomatic soirée. Khrushchev himself, speaking in Yugoslavia five years later, remarked, 'I once said "we will bury you", and I got into trouble with it.' Although he did follow that up with 'Of course we will not bury you with a shovel. Your own working class will bury you.'

What Khrushchev, never the most eloquent of public

speakers, was trying to say was that he believed history was on the side of the Soviet Union.

The 1950s were a period of often acute Cold War tensions but also a time of rapid economic growth. After the depression of the 1930s and the total warfare of the 1940s, the 1950s seemed to be a decade in which the world economy re-found its way. In the United States and western Europe GDP was expanding at something like 3 to 4 per cent a year – the best and most sustained peacetime performance in several decades. This was the start of a three-decade run that would later be called Les Trentes Glorieuses in France, the Wirschaftswunder ('economic miracle') in West Germany, the Golden Age of Capitalism or, by economic historians who can suck the joy out of anything if they really put their mind to it, the 'post-World War Two economic expansion'. But while the western allies enjoyed the fruits of strong economic growth, the economic expansion underway in Khrushchev's USSR appeared to be even faster. Soviet growth rates at this time looked to be around 5 to 6 per cent.

In October 1957, just eleven months after the fateful embassy reception, the USSR put Sputnik, the world's first satellite, into orbit. The Soviet version of socialism seemed to be at the cutting edge of technology and was outgrowing the capitalist world, despite capitalism basking in its own golden age. Khrushchev, naturally enough, assumed that this state of affairs would continue and looked forward to the day, which his advisers expected to arrive within a few short decades, when the Soviet Union would command a larger economy than that even of the United States. More interestingly, though, the Soviets were not alone in thinking this.

Paul Samuelson not only won the Nobel Prize in Economics, he also wrote the bestselling economics textbook of the twentieth century, simply entitled *Economics*.

Beginning in the 1960 edition of that book, he included a graphic showing comparative Soviet and American growth rates and predicted that Soviet output would overtake that of the United States within around a quarter of a century. That graphic was still appearing as late as the 1980 edition, although the point of takeover was always still some twenty to twenty-five years in the future. From 1981 onwards, the graphic mysteriously disappeared. By then no one really believed that a Soviet economic takeover was possible. The real surprise is that Samuelson's graphic lasted as long as it did. The 1970s were a rough time for the global economy as a whole but especially tricky for the Soviet Union. With the benefit of hindsight, the Soviet growth spurt of the 1950s and 1960s looks to be just that – a spurt. But at the time this was still not knowable.

The Soviet economy that Joseph Stalin built had industrialised rapidly in the late 1920s and 1930s, had stood up to the test of total war against Hitler's Germany, and now it seemed to be growing quickly in a time of peace. Even those, rightly, acknowledging that Stalin had been an utterly ruthless tyrant responsible for the deaths of millions were often prepared to give him some credit for the economic model he had created.

Between the late 1920s and the late 1930s the Soviet economy was transformed. Iron production, a staple good of early- to mid-twentieth-century industry, rose from 3.3 million tons in 1928 to 14.5 million by 1937. Over the same period coal output rose from 35.5 million tons to 181 million. That rising industrial production was accompanied by a structural transformation. In the mid-1920s around 85 per cent of Soviet citizens still worked in agriculture, a figure not at all dissimilar to that found in mid- to late-nineteenth-century Russia. By the mid-1930s that had fallen to just over 60 per cent, not far off the levels seen at that point in western Europe. In the space of just a decade, a quarter of the workforce had moved from the farms to the factories.

All of this came with an incredibly high price tag in terms of human suffering and misery. The rapid forced industrial-isation of the 1930s, together with wider Soviet repression, caused between 5 and 10 million deaths. Another 1 to 1.5 million people found themselves in gulag prison camps by the end of the 1930s.

The usual terms of the later economic debate have been to ask whether all this pain actually achieved anything. On the one hand, some point to the ridiculously impressive expansion and industrialisation experienced between the late 1920s and the beginning of the Second World War and conclude that while incredibly painful, Stalin's policies at least produced tan-gible results. Others prefer to take a longer-term view. Tsarist Russia, they note, in the decade before the First World War was industrialising rapidly, although from a low starting point. The Soviet economy by 1939, some proclaim, was roughly where one would expect it to be if that pre-Great War trend had continued. What happened, by this way of thinking, was two lost decades of growth in the 1910s and 1920s followed by a rapid catch-up.

While at times fascinating, the debate sometimes misses the bigger picture. For a start, while counterfactuals are often interesting, they always remain speculative. Quite what Soviet growth trends would have looked like in the absence of Joseph Stalin, or indeed what Russian growth rates would have looked like if the 1917 revolution had never occurred, are both questions which cannot be categorically answered. More importantly, the debate often both underplays the chaos of the Great War – and civil war – in Russia and misses the funda-mental point that Stalin's programme is best understood in the context of twentieth-century total warfare.

Russia, as we saw a few chapters ago, endured a total economic, and political economic, collapse in the Great War. The usual market methods of exchange between the countryside and cities broke down under the demands of a rising military burden and the cities began to go hungry. The result, especially when coupled with military defeats in the field, was enough to drain what little political capital the tsarist regime had left and bring about a revolution.

The Bolshevik coup which seized power in the October Revolution of 1917 took Russia out of the Great War but straight into a civil war which lasted until 1923. The death toll from that fighting, together with the associated famines caused by extreme disruption, has been put somewhere between 7 and 12 million.

The economic collapse associated with a decade of warfare was far-reaching. The income per head of the survivors of the Great War and the civil war was, in 1923, perhaps 40 to 45 per cent of what it had been in 1913. Output across all sorts of industries had fallen dramatically. Annual production of basic construction materials such as bricks and glass was just 20 to 40 per cent of what it had been a decade before. Heavy industry, such as iron and steel production, had experienced a fall in output of as much as four fifths. The extent of the collapse and general dislocation is enough to render any idea that the Soviet economy was likely to return to some pre-war trend quickly rather mute. But what is especially interesting and relevant about this wartime economic disaster is the extent to which Stalin learned from it.

It is not going too far to suggest that the economy Stalin sought to build in the late 1920s and 1930s was one specifically constructed to cope with the demands of total war and avoid the problems which plagued his tsarist predecessor between 1914 and 1917.

Stalin famously declared that 'we are fifty or a hundred years behind the advanced countries. We must make good this distance in ten years. Either we do it, or they crush us.' If anything, he was understating the challenge. The best modern estimates put Soviet GDP per head at around $2,300 (expressed in 1990 dollars) in 1930. That is comparable to where the British economy had been in the early 1700s, over 200 years earlier. In the case of Germany, which is surely the rival Stalin had in mind, his rhetoric was almost spot on: German GDP per head had indeed been around that level in the 1850s.

The numbers also suggest that Stalin, judging by his own targets, made decent progress in narrowing the economic gap. German income per head was about three times larger than Soviet GDP per head in the mid-1920s but just 1.8 times as large on the eve of the two powers going to war in 1941. Of course, the best test of an economy designed to withstand the pressures of total war was not the question of income per head but rather the central question of whether it could in fact withstand the pressures of total war. Here too, the policies appear to have succeeded.

A lot of attention tends to get devoted to Soviet heavy industry. That is understandable. Steel and coal production sat at the heart of the five-year plans and the most obvious leaps forward in the Soviet economy came in just these kinds of capital-intensive projects. The ability to produce this sort of output was also crucial to the kind of mechanised warfare seen in the mid-twentieth century.

But the crucial failure of the tsarist model in the Great War was not to be found in the factories but on the farms. It was the breakdown in the usual exchange between the countryside and the cities that pushed up bread prices in the cities, led to widespread hunger and ultimately to a revolution. Stalin, and his advisers, were acutely aware of this. Hardening the regime for total war meant widespread changes in the countryside, and it was here that the tyrant was at his most brutal.

To recap, the fundamental problem with the supply of food to urban centres in the Great War – in Russia, as in many other primarily agrarian societies – was not the loss of man- and horsepower to the front (although this had hardly helped) but a breakdown in exchange. Because the industrial output of the cities was now serving the war industries, they produced fewer of the things they usually sold to the countryside. With few things to spend any disposable income on, farmers had less need to produce a surplus in excess of their own needs and agricultural output fell. The regime, in Russia and elsewhere, lacked the ability to get in and ensure that the traditional exchange continued to occur even with much of industry now devoted to the war effort.

Stalin changed all that. It is easy to think of the collectiv- isation of Soviet agriculture, the move away from peasants owning and farming their own land to a system whereby land was held by the state, as a simple and inevitable part of the transition to communism. A party committed to collective ownership of the means of production introducing collective ownership into the largest sector of the economy was hardly something unexpected. But, as well as being an ideological project, this collectivisation was seen as playing a vital role in preparing the new Soviet state for war.

In raw economic terms, in the 1920s the regime reimposed the exchange between the countryside and the cities using force rather than market exchanges. In the 1930s it systema- tised this arrangement through collectivisation and essentially making the peasants the residual claimants on food. Food would now be produced firstly for the cities – and the army – as well as for export markets, with the remainder available to those actually tilling the fields.

Of course, that all sounds rather dry and technocratic. In reality the process was brutal. The Stalinist regime certainly succeeded in extracting millions of tons of agricultural output from the farms, well in excess of what would have been supplied in the usual market-driven exchanges. It turned out that the threat of violence and death could achieve that.

Quickly, though, they took more than the countryside could actually produce. Livestock, including horses, to be slaughtered as animal feed ran short. That lowered output in the future. It did not take long for hunger in the countryside to follow. The Great Famine of 1930–3 killed between 5.7 and 8.7 million Soviet citizens. The exact numbers will never be known. It proceeded in stages over the course of the year, and while some of it was a case of extreme bad luck – poor weather leading to reduced harvests – the majority of the deaths must be blamed on human error.

A campaign against supposedly 'rich' peasants, the so-called 'kulaks', saw around a million of them 'liquidated'. This had been going on since the early 1920s but the pace stepped up from 1928 onwards with hundreds of thousands being arrested and either exiled to the gulags or executed. Their lands were seized and added to state-owned farms. From 1930 onwards the government instituted a programme of grain requisitioning, ostensibly to serve export markets. The requisitioning requirements, though, were distributed to disproportionately fall on certain regions. Ukraine, which produced under 30 per cent of the USSR's total grain output, was expected to deliver more than 40 per cent of the requisitioned total in 1932.

From 1933 onwards a system of internal passports, essentially a form of ID card, was put in place. The secret directive Stalin signed that year was entitled 'Preventing the Mass Exodus of Peasants who were Starving', which gives a chilling sense of what the measure was supposed to achieve and also belies the latter pleas of Stalin's defenders that he had no real idea of how bad things had become in the countryside.

Nowadays the real debate among historians is over whether the famine should be seen as a deliberate – genocidal – policy aimed at opponents of the regime or whether it was simply an accidental outcome of the collectivisation programme which the regime saw as necessary to harden its power. No one seriously believes the famine was not fundamentally man-made, even if this was not the intended result.

From Stalin's point of view, the collectivisation programme worked. The flow of food between the countryside and cities was no longer governed by market mechanisms and exchange, instead it was governed by central targets and backed by force. This method of feeding the cities was far less likely to break down in the future. In the Second World War, apart from in Leningrad which was subjected to a siege by the German army and their Finnish allies, there was no widespread famine and hunger in Soviet cities. The vulnerability that had brought down the tsarist regime had been removed. Although doing so had cost millions of lives.

The second stage of Stalin's economic preparation for total war was the rapid programme of industrialisation that formed the centrepiece of the two five-year plans. The scale of this industrialisation was truly monumental. Moving a quarter or so of the workforce from farms to factories in fewer than fifteen years is a pace of change that few countries have ever matched.

In terms of war planning – and this really was a central concern of Stalin's – the two five-year plans of 1928–32 and 1933–7 built upon each other. The first was about building raw industrial capacity, which was turned more explicitly towards war preparations in the second. In economic terms, the key was to increase investment in heavy machinery. Freeing up the resources to produce investment meant restricting household consumption in order to shift a greater percentage of GDP, or national income, towards it. That is an important thing to keep in mind: while Soviet national income per head grew rapidly in the 1930s, it probably did not feel like this for most Soviet citizens. Those in the countryside, as we have seen, were undergoing a terrible time for much of that decade and even those in the cities did not necessarily feel better off even if iron and steel production soared. Making more tanks and aircraft raised output but did not exactly help living standards to improve.

Alongside the rapid expansion of industry came standardisation. Before the 1930s, Soviet – and, earlier, Russian – factories had still to a great extent relied on craft skills. Rather than emphasising artisanal skills, the new focused factories of the 1930s employed mass production techniques. An important upside of this during the war would be the interchangeability of parts produced across the Soviet Union.

By 1940, arms production accounted for around 17 per cent of GDP – an almost unprecedented figure for an industrialised nation still at peace. Thirty thousand tanks rolled off the production lines in the 1930s. Even more impressive was the production of military aircraft. The Soviets had essentially no aircraft industry in the early 1930s but by 1940 were capable of producing ten thousand military aircraft a year. When war came in 1941, the USSR proved up to the challenge. Soviet output volumes in 1942 are only really comparable to those of the United States. The USSR, in that year alone, was able to produce 24,000 armoured vehicles against Germany's output of under 7,000. The USA, by contrast, managed 27,000. What makes this all the more impressive is that by this point vast swathes of the Soviet Union were occupied by the Axis powers.

The disastrous start to the Soviets' war with Germany,

which began in June 1941, meant that by the end of that year territories that had housed 40 per cent of the pre-war population were controlled from Berlin. Even worse, the 7,500 heavy factories in German-occupied areas represented about 75 per cent of industrial heavy capacity. Of the 382 ammunition factories in the Soviet Union in 1941, 303 had been captured or destroyed by the end of the year.

The real – and astonishing – success of the Stalinist system in total war came not just in the rapid industrialisation of the 1930s but in its ability to move and rebuild itself, at breakneck pace, in 1942. One and a half million railcars were loaded with factory machinery, often with the workers themselves sitting on top of the cars, and moved east. Twelve million workers and 2,600 factories moved beyond the Urals to Kazakhstan and western Siberia and restarted production.

It was here that the strengths of a centrally planned, top-down system using mass production and standardised parts were most visible. Take the example of the tractor factory in the Urals city of Chelyabinsk. As one might imagine, until 1941 it produced tractors. In the summer of 1941, 5,800 machine tools were relocated from the soon-to-be-under-siege city of Leningrad to the remote factory and installed in four giant newly built halls by the original workers who had moved with them. Production began before the halls even had roofs. By October the factory was churning out KV-1 heavy tanks even though it lacked the parts to make their starter engines. The tanks were moved by train straight to Moscow where another plant prepared the missing components and installed them, and they went almost straight into action. The following year, in August 1942, the plant was ordered to switch to T-34 medium tank production. The T-34, a fast, well-armed and mechanically reliable tank, became the benchmark Soviet vehicle of the war. Within weeks of being ordered to switch to a whole different model and class of tank, the factory was producing 1,000 a month.

The production achievements of the USSR during the war played a large role in the Allied victory. It was every bit as important to the Allied industrial war effort as was the US economy. However, the temptation to praise the ability of a centrally planned economy to meet the needs of total war must be tempered by the fact that both the freer-market US and British economies managed to achieve similar things in the early 1940s. The Anglo-American model of a large industrial base aimed at satisfying the wants of consumers in peacetime that could be rapidly shifted into meeting military needs in wartime proved just as capable of hitting the required levels of output as the centrally directed Soviet model.

The achievement of the Soviet economy in devoting a similar share of national resources to the needs of total war as that managed by the more developed western powers was, and remains, vital. Stalin was of course very keen to overclaim for this. He would later proudly boast that his regime had an economy better suited to the needs of total war and of peacetime. In the post-war decades this would be shown to be false. The Soviet boom that heralded the burying of the west and put the first satellite into space eventually petered out. Khrushchev, simply by not being as paranoid a conspiracy theorist as Stalin was, may have played a role in this.

Stalin was a man who saw enemies everywhere. Between 1936 and 1938, during the Great Purges, around 700,000 people (at least) were declared to be enemies of the people and killed. Any potential rival to the Boss, as Stalin was known, was a potential victim. More Red Army generals and colonels were killed in the 1930s than in the entire Second World War.

Oddly enough, the purges may have played a role in keeping Soviet growth healthy. Stalin had already demonstrated that violence, repression and the threat of force could effectively replace market mechanisms in the supply of food, although at a huge human cost. The purges too may have provided an incentive structure which was costly in human terms but gave some economic benefits.

In a market-based economic system, competition between firms provides the key to economic dynamism. Managers who fail to adequately serve their consumers risk losing business. Firms can go bust and managers can be sacked. All of this, to an extent, helps to align the incentives of those managers with their firm and forces them to compete for business. Resources, whether money or people or commodities, eventually flow towards the firms that are more productive, more innovative and which can make best use of them. Stalin's widespread use of terror also offered an incentive system for managers. The direction of his paranoid gaze could never be exactly guessed and even success was no guarantee of safety, but failure was worse. Managers who failed to meet their targets faced imprisonment or even execution.

Khrushchev, who broke with Stalin and condemned his wide-ranging paranoia, scaled back the use of terror and made the Soviet Union a more humane place. But in the absence of either market-based incentives or the ruthless enforcement of the economic plans, managers and bureaucrats found themselves with few reasons to achieve. Their firms could not go bankrupt, their salaries were not based on their performance, and their promotion was based on political connections.

More important, though, was the impact this had on the wider political economy of the Soviet Union. Under Stalin, leaders – both mid-ranking and more senior – faced the regular threat of death, imprisonment, internal exile or just being rotated into a different position. This came with an economic cost in terms of preventing expertise being built up but with two distinct economic benefits. First, as noted, it provided a compelling set of incentives to meet targets. But second, the rapid rotation of leaders and officials helped to keep corruption and patronage networks – always a danger in an economy without market incentives – in check. The 'stability of the cadres' which began under Khrushchev and reached its zenith under Leonid Brezhnev did bring the benefit of replacing potential chaos but also allowed exactly those kinds of semi-corrupt patronage networks to develop.

By the 1970s and 1980s Soviet economic policy-making was dominated by special interest groups, and the industrial-bureaucratic takeover was all the more damaging because the leadership of these groups was part and parcel of the one-party communist regime. Ruinously high agricultural subsidies to inefficient farms could not be stripped back because the farm managers were part of the one-party state with their own coteries and allies. Soviet policy-making became a series of trade-offs between the different parts of the Communist Party-industrial nexus. Gorbachev inadvertently summed up the situation when he remarked to President George H. W. Bush that 'we need to reduce arms in a way that won't make the army rise up'. Bush of course did not have to worry about his army rising up. And neither did Stalin. But decades of stable cadres had made the Soviet military into a self-sustaining interest group which competed with other parts of the state for resources and had to be carefully managed. As one recent history of Gorbachev's attempts to revive the Soviet economy in the 1980s put it, 'the dilemma, in a nutshell: to reform the economy without angering the energy industries, the farm bosses or – most dangerous of all – the security services'. In the end the absence of terror and purges would not only stifle the one clear incentive structure the Soviet economy had in the absence of market discipline but also create a range of bureaucratic interest groups that would put the needs of the army, the energy industry, farms or whatever sector they happened to represent first.

Stalin created an economic system which was capable of meeting the needs of total war. The model he chose, though, was not the only one available and it involved a staggering level of brutality and suffering. In the end it turned out that without the terror, it no longer worked.

16

Economists Are Not Always Right: Walt Rostow and the Vietnam War

Economics is, when used well, an incredibly powerful tool for understanding human behaviour. A keen awareness of the role of incentives, and an understanding of the importance of institutions, helps to explain how things happened as they did and can make even the most seemingly illogical behaviour make more sense when placed in its proper context. That has, hopefully, been the core message of this book so far. But an equally important message is that economists are not always right.

The experience of economists serving as their nation's finance minister has been, at best, a mixed one. Joseph Schumpeter went on to be known as one of the twentieth century's major economic thinkers and ended his career at Harvard. His work on creative destruction is studied to this day and his book *Capitalism, Socialism and Democracy* is one of the most important works of political economy of the century. He once claimed to have set himself three goals in life: to be the greatest economist in the world, the finest horseman in Austria and the greatest lover in all of Vienna. Sadly, he noted, there were too many fine horsemen in the former Habsburg lands for him to achieve all three. Despite being the youngest full, professor of economics in the German-speaking world before the First World War, his ventures into practical rather than theoretical economics proved fraught. He lasted less than a year as Austrian finance minister and the bank he ran in the mid-1920s collapsed. Not an especially strong track record for the world's self-professed greatest economist.

But the worst damage done by economists working in public policy has often come outside the sphere of economics. The shining example of this is Walt Rostow, who was one of the most famous and bestselling economic thinkers of his day.

Walt Whitman Rostow was born in Manhattan in 1916 to a family of relatively recent Jewish Russian immigrants who were both socialists and lovers of America. His siblings, like him, were given names celebrating his parents' American heroes. While Walt got the great American poet, his brothers were named after the socialist leader Eugene Debs and the essayist Ralph Waldo Emerson. From his parents he took a love for their adopted country, a desire to work hard and excel and, despite their own socialism, a hatred for Soviet communism. In later life he would recall a visit to his childhood home by a Russian immigrant working as a purchasing agent for the Soviet government. Afterwards his father told him: 'These communists took over the Tsarist police and made them worse. The Tsarist police persecuted the political opposition but never touched their families. These people touch families too.' Hard work, a fierce ambition and a hatred of communism would define his life.

He won a full scholarship to Yale at fifteen, graduated at nineteen and then crossed the Atlantic to become a Rhodes

Scholar in Oxford. By 1940 he was back in New York, as a professor of economics at Columbia at the age of just twenty-four. When the war came, this patriotic and ultra-smart young man offered his services and soon found himself at the Office of Strategic Services in Washington before being posted to London in September 1942 to work in the Enemy Objectives Unit, helping to pick targets for the strategic bombing offensive. He would spend the next three years closely involved in this form of economic warfare.

He was at times a controversial figure during the Second World War. While widely acknowledged as bright and persuasive, he also had a tendency to focus sharply on one thing at a time and become utterly convinced of his correctness. Colleagues occasionally found him difficult to work with as a result. All of this would still be true two decades later.

By 1943 he had become convinced that oil was the Third Reich's Achilles heel and that a sustained bombing attack on the German oil industry would cause the Nazi war effort to collapse. It took him months to convince the Eighth Air Force's leadership of this, but eventually his Oil Plan was put into operation. But not in a way that pleased Rostow. While the heavy targeting of oil facilities began in May 1944, the USAAF carried out the attacks in conjunction with their Transport Plan to hit German rail capacity rather than focusing entirely on energy resources.

Rostow never really got over this. While the consensus view, as we have seen, of later historians is that the Transport Plan did more damage to the German war effort by preventing goods being moved to where they were needed and that the Oil Plan failed as the Germans were able to utilise stockpiles, to substitute other materials for oil and generally to economise on energy use, Rostow remained convinced that a single-minded focus on bombing oil facilities would not only have ended the war sooner but fundamentally changed the nature of the Cold War that followed. If, in his view, the Oil Plan had started sooner and been given more resources then the German collapse would have come about before the major Soviet advances into eastern Germany and central Europe. If only people had listened to Rostow, the war would have been won quicker and many central and eastern European nations would have spared Soviet occupation and communist rule.

Rostow, as a respected economist and a key player in the bombing campaign itself, was offered a place serving on the post-war Strategic Bombing Survey but turned it down in favour of returning to the United States to work briefly for the State Department before moving back into academia. That bombing survey did find, as Rostow had predicted, that the Oil Plan had inflicted a major blow to the German war economy. But it also noted that German war production had peaked in December 1944, months into the major and sustained bombing campaign, and cast doubt on the overall effectiveness of the bomber offensive itself. Its broad view was that strategic bombing was a powerful tool of economic warfare, more than capable of wearing down an enemy's ability to stay in the fight, but also that this was a slow process which played out over years rather than months. Rostow never accepted this.

Rostow spent the rest of the 1940s and the bulk of the 1950s combining a career in academic economics with public-facing newspaper articles, think tank reports and occasionally dispensing political advice. In 1960, however, he made the transition from occasional public commentator to bestselling author.

The Stages of Economic Growth: A Non-Communist Manifesto has not aged well despite selling around 250,000 copies in the first dozen years or so after its publication, making Rostow one of the most famous economists in the world and, in the words of one contemporary newspaper, 'the most famous economic historian since Karl Marx'. Rostow would no doubt have especially enjoyed that accolade because, from the title on down, *Stages of Economic Growth* is an explicit attempt to provide a differing account of national economic development from that proposed by Karl Marx a century before.

Rostow, when he was not planning bombing campaigns, was an historian of the nineteenth-century British economy. He was something of an Anglophile, not only attending Oxford as a Rhodes scholar in the 1930s but teaching there at times after the war. His real genius was to combine his interest in and knowledge of British economic history with the vogue in American social science in the 1950s, that of 'modernisation' theory. The denizens of sociology and political science departments at the time, as well as a fair few of the inhabitants of economics departments, were obsessed with categorising both contemporary and historical societies as either 'traditional' or 'modern' and studying how the transition from one to the other occurred. Modern, of course, was essentially seen as what might be termed 'like the America of the time' – prosperous, fast-growing, secular, and with widespread civic engagement. It was the end state of history, the goal everyone should be trying to attain. Communism, by this way of thinking – and especially to Rostow – was an aberration, a system that lured countries away from the path to progress.

Rostow essentially combined his view of the idealised society – that of the America he lived in – with his understanding of how the British economy had transitioned from a traditional to a modern society during the industrial revolution and sought to turn this into a universal model of economic progress. The moment of 'take-off' as Rostow saw it would only come about after certain preconditions had been met. Secular education had to be established, banks had to be formed, and an entrepreneurial class had to come into existence. Ten to fifteen years after these necessary components were in place, the take-off itself – which might take another century to fully play out – would get underway with economic processes taking over from traditional social norms, and productivity – and therefore income per head – beginning an upward trend. The post-industrial revolution state would then go through several stages of growth – hence the title of the book. Eventually it would arrive at the supposed nirvana, which was an age of mass production coupled with mass consumption. Britain, in this understanding, was the paradigm case study and the United States of the late 1950s the ultimate destination.

The timing of the book, as with all bestselling works of social science, proved crucial. The world of the late 1950s and early 1960s was one in transition. It was a time of widespread decolonisation as the European empires which had dominated the world for two centuries retreated, albeit at differing paces. Using United Nations membership as a proxy illustrates the point. Formed by fifty-one initial members in 1945, the UN had eighty by the mid-1950s, but by 1960 that number had climbed to ninety-nine and by 1965 to 117; by 1973 it comprised 135 member countries. In the year in which *Stages of Economic Growth* was published, Nigeria achieved independence from Britain, Congo from Belgium, and half a dozen African states from France.

At just this time of a growing number of newly independent countries, the USSR seemed still to be motoring ahead economically and to be providing a blueprint for how new nations could industrialise quickly and raise their national incomes. Rostow's *Stages of Economic Growth* offered a competing path.

There is plenty to criticise in the book. It is, for a supposed work of economic history, strangely ahistorical in that it begins with the known end state of modernity and simply works back from there. Contingency and chance play only small roles in a story of growth that is strangely linear, almost mechanical at times, and which proceeds in easy to understand stages. The role of natural resources and geography, such as Britain having easy access to the coal that was the key fuel of early industrial processes, is seriously underplayed. More importantly, the work attempts to generalise a mostly European experience into one suitable for any country on earth.

It was a Rostow fresh from this public success and acclaim who came back to Washington to work at the White House of John F. Kennedy. He seemed initially to be the ideal man for this new era. In an administration that wished to portray itself as intellectual, new and modernising, here was one of the world's most famous thinkers. And at a time when the Cold War was mostly seen as being waged in the developing world, among the newly decolonised states of Asia and Africa, here was the man who had quite literally written the book on how these countries could develop in a non-communist manner.

He did not last long. As Kennedy said, 'Walt is a fountain of ideas; perhaps one in ten of them is absolutely brilliant. Unfortunately six or seven of them are not merely unsound, but dangerously so.' One of the final straws that ended his short tenure at the White House came during the Berlin crisis of 1961 when the Soviet Union enforced a blockade on West Berlin, the western enclave cut off in East Germany. The stand-off was eventually resolved by a huge NATO airlift which kept the isolated city supplied until the Soviets backed down. Rostow's alternative proposal had been to up the pressure on the Soviets by seizing an East German city – he suggested Magdeburg – and holding it until the Soviets stepped down their blockade. Kennedy, thankfully, decided that using US armed forces to invade East Germany could well provoke a nuclear war.

Rostow was shuffled off to the State Department in a

planning role where, it was hoped, he would have less of a day-to-day say on policy but would still be able to generate longer-ranged ideas. He became, while there, gradually more and more obsessed with the issue of Vietnam.

The United States was involved in Vietnam well before Rostow became interested in the country. The French could not have attempted to cling on to their Indochina colony in Southeast Asia after the Second World War without US military and financial aid. About one third of the direct financial costs of France's ultimately unsuccessful attempt to hold on to the colony were paid for through United States support.

The situation facing the incoming Kennedy administration in January 1961 was tense. Vietnam, after its independence from France in the mid-1950s, was now split into two countries: a communist North, backed by the Soviet Union and China, and an authoritarian South which faced an insurgency by northern-backed guerrillas wanting reunification under communist leadership and which was financially reliant on the United States. Over the coming years, first under Kennedy and then under his successor Lyndon Johnson, US involvement would step up again and again in a war which eventually caused 58,000 US casualties and killed an estimated 2 to 2.5 million people in the two Vietnams and neighbouring countries by the mid-1970s.

Rostow would play a significant role in this US escalation, beginning with him returning to the White House as National Security Advisor under President Johnson. The key aspects of his personality and previous experience came to the fore here – a fierce opposition to communism coupled with an equally fierce conviction that he possessed an alternative vision and a belief in the power of bombing. His appointment was initially well received, with the *New York Times* editorialising that he possessed 'an independent and cultivated mind'.

The Domino Theory, that if Vietnam went communist then so too would its neighbours, had first been articulated by Dwight D. Eisenhower in the 1950s, and it was firmly gripped by Rostow in the 1960s. From the start of his period back in the White House, Rostow's advice was straightforward: the key to ending the war in Vietnam lay in bombing. Initially he wanted merely to bomb strategic targets in North Vietnam in order to demonstrate to the North's leadership that supporting the Vietcong guerrillas in the South was not a cost-free option. They would, he hoped, end their logistical support as the price of continuing to provide it rose. When that failed, he instead advocated large-scale bombing in order to destroy the North's economic potential and cause its war effort to collapse. Throughout the war, and his involvement with it, he fundamentally refused to accept that the guerrilla movement in the South was in any way indigenous or based on any sort of legitimate grievance at the harsh rule meted out by the Saigon dictatorship. To Rostow it was also a pawn of the North which Hanoi could stop at any time.

The scale of the bombing that took place over the 1960s and 1970s is without precedent in history. Between 1964 and 1973 the US Air Force dropped 6,162,000 tons of bombs on Indochina. The US Navy and Marine Corps added another 1.5 million tons. That is approximately three times as much bombing as the United States carried out in the European and Asian theatres of the Second World War combined. As one study has noted, it represents about 100 kilograms of explosive per head of population in the region. To put that another way, the weight of all the ordnance dropped on Vietnam over the course of a decade was higher than the combined weight of the entire population. This was bombing on a sustained scale, far heavier than anything Germany or Japan experienced between 1939 and 1945.

The bombing was also, in general, more accurate. Weapons technology in the 1960s allowed for far greater and more precise targeting. The Rolling Thunder campaign of 1965 to 1968, of which Rostow was a key planner, destroyed 65 per cent of the North's oil storage facilities, 59 per cent of its power plants and 55 per cent of its major bridges.

During these years the controversy over the impact of US strategic bombing in the Second World War was essentially relitigated in the debate over the bombing of Vietnam. Notable doves in the US administrations of those years – men such as the economist J. K. Galbraith, who served as ambassador to India under Kennedy, Arthur Schlesinger, who served as a special assistant to Kennedy, and George Ball, a senior State Department official under both Kennedy and Johnson – had all taken part in the post-war bombing survey and all harboured serious doubts about bombing's effectiveness as a tool to change North Vietnamese policy. Rostow and the senior leadership of the US Air Force – who were disproportionately former bomber men – refused to accept this.

Like any good economist, Rostow understood the power of incentives. Sadly for Vietnam and the United States, his own assumptions about the incentives of the enemy were found to be incorrect. In 1964 he explained to Secretary of State Dean Rusk that the Vietnamese communist leader Ho Chi Minh 'has an industrial base to protect; he is no longer a guerrilla fighter with nothing to lose'. By bombing North Vietnamese industry and infrastructure, Rostow assumed the US could force them to negotiate. He turned out to be doubly incorrect.

On one level the whole assumption was misplaced. The primary goal of the decision-making Politburo in Hanoi was winning the war and reuniting, as they saw it, their country. Protecting the industrial base of the North – limited as it was anyway – was never a major goal. Losing more than half of the country's major bridges and power plants no doubt hurt, but it was not enough to force a change in policy.

But Rostow also failed to engage with how the North's communist allies in the USSR and China would react to the bombing. The short answer is that as the US escalated its own involvement in Vietnam, so too did they. Direct Soviet military involvement never approached the scale the United States and its own allies reached, but there were up to three thousand Soviet military advisers aiding Hanoi's war effort at times, much of the country's anti-aircraft armaments at times were Soviet-crewed, and Soviet economic involvement was high. A Central Intelligence Agency report in mid-1968 spelled this out, and may well have underestimated the numbers. By the CIA's reckoning, between 1954 and 1964 the wider communist world provided $1,090 million worth of military aid and economic aid to North Vietnam. But between 1965 and mid-1968 that more than doubled to $2,175 million. Civilian aid ranged widely from processed petroleum and trucks to raw foodstuffs and consumer goods such as processed linens. That aid, worth a total of around $2 billion over the course of thirty or so months, should be put in the context of a North Vietnamese economy with an annual output of perhaps $1.5 billion at the time. Hanoi was receiving aid worth about 50 per cent of its economy each year in the mid-1960s from its allies. That is comparatively about twice as large as US Lend-Lease assistance to Britain in the Second World War, and more importantly, the size of the aid flows was directly increased in line with the US-led bombing campaigns.

This had two effects. First, the flow of finished industrial goods (including consumer goods) and food from the USSR and China allowed the North to devote a far greater proportion of its manpower to the war effort than would otherwise have been the case. But equally importantly, it also completely undermined Rostow's assumptions about the likely impact of the US campaign. The idea was that by ramping up bombing Hanoi would face so much economic dislocation that it would be forced to negotiate. What actually happened was that as the bombing stepped up, so too did the communist aid to the North, plugging the gap.

That 1968 CIA report put the cost of the bombing damage to Hanoi's economy at around $300 million – in other words, less than half of the value of the civilian aid received alone. Rather optimistically it went on to argue that the costs to the Soviet Union of supporting North Vietnam were higher than the costs to the US of supporting South Vietnam and bombing the North. That may have been true, and it is certainly debatable, but that also fundamentally misses the point. The aim of bombing North Vietnam was not to drain Soviet resources, and support wider Cold War efforts, it was to end the war in the South. And as long as the Soviets made good the losses, that was not going to happen. The North Vietnamese economy was larger in 1969 when Rostow left the White House than it had been in 1964 when he entered it. Despite several million tons of high explosive being dropped on it.

Not only did North Vietnam's economy weather the largest bombing campaign in human history surprisingly well, it also seems to have had an unusually muted longer-term impact. The United States' armed forces kept detailed records of where they dropped those millions of tons of ordnance in the 1960s and 1970s. That allowed economists to look back from the vantage point of the early 2000s and see if they could view any signs of lasting damage.

The province that received the heaviest bombing, even more so than Hanoi itself, was Quang Tri, which was then right on the North/South border in the so-called Demilitarised Zone. Just eleven of the province's 3,500 villages escaped the bombing. The authors of a later study took the district-level bombing data and calculated which ten modern Vietnamese districts received the heaviest bombing between 1965 and 1975. Alongside Quang Tri and Hanoi, the results were as expected, with most high explosives dropped on either North Vietnamese industrial centres, the region around the old border or the western border of the old South Vietnam, adjacent to Laos and Cambodia, through which the North had supplied guerrillas in the South via the Ho Chi Minh trail. But – and this is where it becomes more surprising – controlling for geographic and demographic factors, those regions showed no difference from the rest of modern Vietnam by 2002 when it came to local poverty rates, infrastructure levels, literacy or population density. Less than three decades after the heaviest bombing campaign in history it was not visible in the economic data.

That mystery can be resolved through a combination of three interrelated factors. First, there was the other side of the balance sheet, the already discussed communist aid which helped make good much of the damage at the time. Secondly, the post-war united Vietnamese government seems to have done a good job directing national resources to areas where they were most needed. The researchers also postulate another possibility: it may well have been that the experience of the 1940s to the 1970s of, as they saw it, two long wars against foreign involvement – first the French, then the Americans – left Vietnam with a strong sense of nationalism and that that energy was ploughed into rapid post-war reconstruction.

Of course, the lack of an economic scar decades later does nothing to diminish the extent of the human suffering at the time. Nor did that achieve its goals. As US bombing failed to end the war, the number of US ground forces deployed into South Vietnam gradually, and then quickly, stepped up. The aim of the ground forces was never to 'win' the war militarily – that was the task of the bombing. Rather it was to prevent defeat by holding off a collapse of the South.

Rostow stuck to his guns until the bitter end of the Johnson administration, becoming, in the words of one political scientist, 'a byword for a specific kind of Washington virtue; offering terrible advice but at least doing so consistently'. He was certainly consistent. In 1995, when Robert McNamara, Secretary of Defense under Kennedy and Johnson, published his memoirs and declared 'we were wrong, terribly wrong' to have engaged in the policies of the time, Rostow responded with a scathing review in the *Times Literary Supplement*. Under the headline 'The Case for War' he argued that the United States had actually won the war on the grounds that the economies of Southeast Asia had tripled in size between 1961 and 1980 and would not have done so in the absence of US involvement.

Rostow's Vietnam is a cautionary tale. Having an awareness of economic reasoning and a view rooted in how incentives work is no bad thing. But it is never enough. Thinking you understand your opponent's incentives – or, worse still, assuming that they are the same as your own – is often worse than not considering them at all.

The problem with Rostow's work on economic history was that it was too deterministic; it always seemed to assume that action x would result in outcome y. At times it almost reduced the course of economic development to a simple checklist that policymakers had to tick off. Once the prerequisites were assembled, then growth would play out in stages. The problems with his national security policy-making turned out to be similar. Bombing could change the behaviour of Hanoi almost as easily as pulling a lever. He failed to understand both what Hanoi was trying to achieve and what the North Vietnamese really cared about. He also failed to see how US escalation would be met by an escalation in aid from its Cold War opponents. And when bombing failed to achieve its goals, the answer always seemed to be even more and heavier bombing.

Economists often need to be reminded that they are not always right.

17

Planning for War, Ukraine and the Incentives for Analysis

On 11 July 2014, as the version of events which entered western military thinking ran, two Ukrainian mechanised infantry battalions gathered in the pre-dawn darkness a few miles to the west of the town of Zelenopillya in eastern Ukraine. The war in the Donbas that had been raging since April was now going well for Ukraine. What the government still called the Anti-Terror Operation had seen a joint police and military offensive rolling back the Russian armed separatist forces across eastern Ukraine. The soldiers arriving near Zelenopillya were a mixture of veterans and often battle-hungry younger men. They were equipped with a hodgepodge of mostly older equipment and, their commanders would later admit, in no state to fight a regular army. Their war, they believed, probably only had a day or two of action left. Soon they would roll into the last separatist checkpoints and put down the insurrection in this part of Ukraine. The Russian occupation of the Crimea to their south was another problem and a thornier one to resolve. There, regular Russian forces were deployed and the Ukrainian government had acknowledged, although not formally recognised, the Russian occupation. But here in the Donbas at least the fighting would soon be over.

The Ukrainian battalions paused to get their bearings and make their final pre-battle checks. Suddenly the unmistakable sound of drones was heard overhead. This, in and of itself, was not unusual. The pro-Russian separatists had been using drones for reconnaissance purposes since the war began. Still, even if not entirely unexpected, the presence of enemy drones over the open fields was unwelcome. The Ukrainians had been hoping for the element of surprise in their early morning attack.

It was what happened next that was truly unexpected. When they sought to confirm the presence of enemy drones to their brigade command, the Ukrainian forces found their communications blocked and jammed. And then the artillery fire started. The two battalions suddenly came under a heavy bombardment in the form of both shells and rockets which in less than a minute devastated their forces. Many of their accompanying armoured vehicles were destroyed, some of them with their crews still inside. Soldiers who had got out to stretch their legs during the short break in operations were even more exposed.

The battle was over before it had even begun. Ukrainian losses were around thirty men killed, hundreds more wounded and two battalions' worth of armoured vehicles knocked out of action. The Ukrainian army would not get this close to the Russian border again. Among other things, the Russian army had just demonstrated, for the first time in the conflict, that it was prepared to directly intervene in the fighting over the border in the Donbas with the full force of its arsenal.

But it was the nature of this Russian arsenal which really sent shockwaves through the western European and US military establishments. This was a nightmare scenario for any modern army. The Russians had demonstrated an ability to pair up drone reconnaissance with exceptionally strong conventional artillery. They had identified a Ukrainian armoured force on the move, jammed its communications and then essentially destroyed it before it had the ability to move again. The US military of 2014 would have had trouble achieving a similar feat. The fact that the Russians had this capacity, and even more so were prepared to use it, gripped analysts across NATO militaries. The Russian attack, they believed, had not only demonstrated a sophisticated use of drones both to identify the Ukrainian position and to jam their electronics, it had also shown the potency of new Russian artillery munitions: thermobaric ammunition, weapons composed almost entirely of fuel which burn longer and more intensively than conventional high explosives.

The US Army established the Russia Next Generation Warfare study to learn the lessons of what was happening in eastern Ukraine. One US analyst who returned from a field visit to Ukraine told an assembled group of senior US officers in 2016 that 'If you have not experienced or seen the effects of thermobaric warheads, start taking a hard look. They might soon be coming to a theatre near you.' General H. R. McMaster, who later served as National Security Advisor from 2017 until 2018, directed this Russia Next Generation Warfare study and certainly sounded concerned in 2016 when he reported:

We're out-ranged by a lot of these systems and they employ improved conventional munitions, which we are going away from. There will be a 40- to 60-percent reduction in lethality in the systems that we have. Remember that we already have fewer artillery systems. Now those fewer artillery

systems will be less effective relative to the enemy. So we
need to do something on that now.

The Russians now not only had more artillery than
the NATO militaries but much more effective munitions,
improved coordination with drones, and the ability to deploy
this firepower in a way western militaries could not match.

This version of the Battle of Zelenopillya is crucial to
understanding what the conventional wisdom looked like in
February 2022 when Russia invaded Ukraine. Putin's Russia,
ran the argument, was a regional power that had invested
heavily in its military for two decades. What is more, that military had been battle-hardened by fighting in eastern Ukraine,
in Georgia and in Syria. It possessed, as well as raw numbers,
cutting-edge equipment and the knowledge to deploy it. The
west had sought to deter a Russian invasion of Ukraine via the
threat of imposing economic sanctions, but when that did not
work, there was nothing they could do. This Russian jugger-
naut would surely overwhelm Ukrainian resistance within days
at least, weeks at most. The one good thing that could be said
was that at least the war would not last long.

What happened next came as a surprise to most, although
not all, western analysts. The war did not end in a matter of
weeks. Ukrainian resistance was fierce, but just as importantly,
the Russian army simply failed to carry out its core tasks with
anything like the efficiency, technique and skill that observers
had expected.

In 2015 and 2016 western analysts had been talking up
the raw threat of Russia's 'next generation' warfare. By the
end of 2022 they were almost equally damning. The Atlantic
Council, a US think tank, summed up the new attitude in
an end-of-year report on the war in Ukraine. 'The Russian
military', it noted, 'has not mastered certain complex tactics

such as combined arms operations and suppression of enemy air defences. For example, armoured columns entered urban areas unsupported by dismounted infantry, while Russian air power stays largely over Russian-controlled territory for fear of being shot down by Ukrainian air defences. This adds to other problems endemic in Russia's military such as poor leadership, poor morale, and poor logistics.' Furthermore, the Russian sector and armed forces turned out not to be immune to the wider corruption endemic in Putin's Russia. The reactive armoured plates on modern Russian tanks that were supposed to detonate when hit and deflect an incoming shell turned out sometimes to be filled with rubber rather than explosives. And rather than being the terrifying weapons that had grabbed the attention of thinkers after Zelenopillya, 'the Russian military received precision-guided weapons that often miss targets or otherwise fail'.

The analysis had probably swung too far the other way. Russia, in the eyes of western military thinking, seemed to have transformed from a superman to a weakling in the space of ten months. As the Russian army proved itself capable of fighting a battle of attrition throughout 2023, views once again began to shift.

But the mystery remained. How could the army that fought the Battle of Zelenopillya be the same army that failed so spectacularly in basic military tactics and which was proved to have serious equipment problems in early to mid-2022?

The answer may be simple: the western version of Zelenopillya never actually happened.

Analysts began to reconstruct the chain of events that unfolded on 11 July 2014 by going back to the primary sources – in this case the Ukrainian survivors. The picture they painted of the battle differed sharply in many significant respects from the one that entered the lexicon of western militaries. The core story – an unexpected attack by a Russian artillery unit, firing across the border on to a Ukrainian mechanised force with great effect – remained the same. But all of the important details varied.

In the usual western account the fields to the west of Zelenopillya were a temporary resting point for the Ukrainian battalions, a jumping-off point for their planned attack. By contrast, Ukrainian veterans spoke of it as a depot rather than a brief waystation. Accounts varied as to whether the encampment had been in place for days or potentially even several weeks but they all agreed it was a regularly used resting and provisioning point for Ukrainian forces engaged in fighting the separatists in the Donbas and attempting to secure the border crossings. There were no entrenchments or dug-outs and vehicles were parked in neat rows as if awaiting an inspection. The whole place had the feel of a peacetime garrison rather than a wartime base near the front.

A then nineteen-year-old sergeant who was wounded in the attack reported that he was shocked when he first arrived at the camp for a meal break. He told later interviewers that 'a soldier greeted me in shorts. I asked, "Don't you have a war here?" And he said, "There's fighting, but it's far away." The feeling in Zelenopillya was that the war did not apply to them. It looked like an ordinary training camp, like something in the rear.'

Another Ukrainian soldier, this one a Red Army veteran who had experienced the reality of warfare in the dying days of the Soviet Union in Armenia and Azerbaijan, reported that the camp consisted of 'big green tents that weren't even hidden. Just in the middle of a big open field.' Whenever his unit had stopped over at the camp they had chosen to stay away from the main area and to dig their own trenches near a tree line towards the end of the fields. When he heard about the attack, he was not surprised by what had played out. 'The officers in charge of the camp must have thought that they were safe. But everyone who already had fighting experience all knew that the camp was a very unsafe place.'

This, then, is the first crucial point of departure. Rather than Zelenopillya being a case of a temporary halted mechanised unit being destroyed before it could get moving again, it becomes an artillery strike on a long-established position that had not taken the usual precautions to protect itself from such an attack.

What is more, according to survivors the vehicles of the two mechanised units that were hit on 11 July were piled high with supplies, including spare ammunition. As the Russian shells and Grad rockets hit, that ammunition exploded. As a veteran of the attack put it, 'there was so much ammunition on the vehicles, there wasn't room for people. That caused more casualties than the Grads themselves.'

This is the second crucial difference in the accounts. Rather than the Russians using top-of-the-range, cutting-edge technology to give their artillery the destructive power to destroy two mechanised battalions' worth of equipment, that destructive power came from the Ukrainian ammunition that was stowed on their own armoured vehicles.

In April 2019, five years after the incident, the then commander of the Ukrainian armed forces described Zelenopillya as a tragedy but an avoidable one. The problem, he believed, had been negligence on the part of the local Ukrainian officers in not taking adequate precautions to safeguard their units, coupled with surprise that Russia would choose to escalate the conflict by firing directly on Ukrainian regular units with its own conventional forces.

The Russian attack itself, by this telling, had been unexpected. But there was nothing especially unconventional or ground-breaking about it. Nor did it demonstrate any particular capacity that most western armies could not match. One former US artillery officer told a researcher that equipped with a pencil, a protractor, a map, a battery of rocket artillery and ten minutes to prepare he felt confident he could knock out two mechanised battalions parked in uncamouflaged, unentrenched rows in an area the size of a football field. This was the kind of thing artillery had been doing since at least the 1940s.

Given the rather different views on how Zelenopillya played out, it becomes important to ask where the western version originated, if not from Ukrainian veterans and eyewitnesses or from the Ukrainian political and military leadership. The surprising answer appears to be a white paper produced by an American think tank which was never intended for wide circulation. Even there, Zelenopillya appears not as a central case study but as an anecdote among much wider coverage of the fighting between 2014 and 2015. And yet it was seized on by others and even featured in the US Army's own official publications of doctrine by 2020.

The two differing accounts of the Battle of Zelenopillya result in the same end point: heavy Ukrainian losses. But they also offer rather different solutions. The solution to the Ukrainian account lay in firstly accepting that the Russian military would be prepared to actively engage in the fighting itself and secondly in doubling down on the basics of military training and operating procedures. Soldiers had to be trained that during a movement to and from the front, whenever they were stationary they should disperse, dig in and where possible camouflage their position. This is exactly what they did. Over the following months as the fighting escalated in eastern Ukraine and Russian artillery regularly engaged, there was no repeat of Zelenopillya.

But better training and a doubling down on caution when stopping near the enemy was no solution to the version of Zelenopillya as seen in western eyes. The problem by this reckoning was not a lack of basic operating discipline by the unit under attack but the sheer capacity of the Russian army in terms of new munitions, advanced drone technology and new electronic warfare techniques. The solution favoured in the west was vast new investment in building its own version of these capacities.

In other words, the western response was to invest billions of dollars into building countermeasures to fight a capacity which might never have existed in the first place.

This is where an examination of incentives once again proves vital – as is the cautionary note that those of differing institutions do not always align well. The militaries, the analysts and the focused think tanks which wrote reports on their version of the Battle of Zelenopillya had their own preferences for policy. Militaries in democratic states, especially in peacetime, are always fighting for resources against other spending priorities. Being able to point to a threat that must be contained is no bad thing for them in their dealings with the setters of government budgets. Meanwhile, a great deal of money from the industry tends to find its way into funding research on policy and, a cynic might note, anything which suggests more needs to be spent on the products of that industry is more likely to be emphasised.

Peacetime militaries, and the civilian industry which supplies them, have always had at least the temptation to talk up the nature of the potential threat they face. The best example is probably that of the so-called 'bomber gap' in the 1950s and early 1960s. The US enjoyed a brief monopoly as a nuclear power after deploying its atomic weapons in 1945. But by 1949, aided by spies and communist sympathisers in the west, the USSR had its own functioning atomic weapons. Before the introduction of intercontinental ballistic missiles and the increasing use of submarines as the planned launch vehicles for a nuclear attack, it was assumed that any nuclear war would see the weapons being delivered as they had been in 1945 – by bombers.

In the mid-1950s, a widespread fear emerged that the Soviets had taken the lead in terms of long-range aircraft capable of delivering a nuclear attack directly on the opposing superpower. It started in 1954 with an article in *Aviation Week* that was reporting rumour as much as fact. The piece described new Soviet jet bombers – the M-4 Bison – capable of taking off in the USSR and delivering a nuclear attack directly on to American cities. That led quickly to wider reporting and handwringing in the American press and concerned questions being asked in Congress.

In 1955, in a display of (with the benefit of hindsight) wonderfully simple deception, the Soviets upped the ante. On Soviet Aviation Day that year, ten of the new Bison bombers flew past the review stands and then quickly turned around before flying past again. The trick was repeated a second time in quick succession, although this time with only eight Bisons flying into view. This was enough to convince most observers that twenty-eight rather than ten Bisons had been on display. The US Air Force, working from the false assumption that the Soviets had managed to produce twenty-eight of these new bombers in a matter of months, calculated that the Soviets would have six hundred of them by 1960. The actual run rate of production at the time would have put the total closer to two hundred. The US Air Force was in the process of introducing its own super long-range jet bomber, the B-52, and argued that it was going to face a shortfall relative to the USSR – the bomber gap.

Much like the Royal Air Force in the 1930s, the broad assumption of US Air Force planners two decades later was that air defences were likely to prove ineffective and be a drain on resources and cash. The bomber, it was still thought, would always get through. The best defence, by this way of thinking, against a large Soviet fleet of long-range bombers was to have even more US ones. Deterrence and the possibility of a devastating counter-attack was the name of the game.

President Eisenhower, who would use much of his farewell address as President to bemoan the growth of the military-industrial complex and fret about the possibility of future arms races, was sceptical of the claims. But he did approve the deployment of the new U-2 high-flying, long-range reconnaissance aircraft to overfly Soviet territory and gather evidence. This began in 1956.

One early such flight spotted thirty M-4 Bison aircraft on the ramps at Leningrad air force base. Multiplying those thirty confirmed sightings at one bomber base by the number of known and suspected Soviet bomber bases was enough to convince the US Air Force that the Soviets were indeed well on the way to having six hundred Bisons by the early 1960s. The US B-52 programme would have to be stepped up. In fact, those thirty Bisons photographed at Leningrad represented the entire Soviet fleet of such planes at the time.

Further reconnaissance flights over the coming three years eventually allayed American fears over the extent of Soviet production but the air force remained sceptical. After the loss of a U-2 and the capture of its pilot by the Soviets, the flights were eventually outsourced to British RAF pilots in order to maintain US plausible deniability of violating Soviet airspace. It was a British pilot who in December 1959 took what the then director of the Central Intelligence Agency later described as a 'million dollar photograph'. The image of the Kuybyshev

bomber factory, supposedly the heart of Soviet Bison production, showed no signs of bombers undergoing work or even of
much preparation.

The great irony is that the much-feared M-4 Bison never
actually had the range to reach much of the continental United
States and return to Soviet airspace. Only ninety-three of them
were ever produced and the programme was wound down in
the early 1960s. The majority of those that were manufactured
found themselves being used as tankers rather than bombers.
The US Air Force, though, got its 750 B-52s as a counter-
measure. They were used heavily in the bombing campaign
in Vietnam and are still in service today.

The story of the 'missile gap' as nuclear weapon delivery
moved to intercontinental ballistic missiles in the 1960s was
much the same. Once again, this gap – despite showy eye-
catching graphics in the press and much political angst – never
really existed. Kennedy used it as a campaigning issue in his
1958 bid to hold his Senate seat and again in the presidential
campaign of 1960. When he took office as Defense Secretary
in January 1961, closing the gap was an early priority of
Robert McNamara. He later said that he devoted his first
three weeks in the job to working closely with his deputy and
the intelligence community to get a fuller picture of the facts.
He concluded that 'there was a gap, but the gap was in our
favour'. That left him in the somewhat awkward position of
having to find a way to back off from a claim which had been
a key election battleground for the incoming administration
just weeks before.

A similar series of inflated estimates were associated
throughout the Cold War with all aspects of the Soviet military. The US assessment of the Soviet defence budget is a case
in point. Working out the exact size of this budget was a core
component of estimating Soviet military prowess and also far

from straightforward. There was an annual number published by the Soviet government, but could it be taken at face value? And even if it could be assumed to be broadly accurate, which was clearly a questionable judgement, how should that number be translated into US dollar values to allow for a comparison with US defence spending? The Soviet Union was, after all, a command economy in which prices did not operate in the same way as in the capitalist west. For example, if the Soviets wanted their military to have more tanks, would they pay the true market price for them or would they be getting them simply at cost? Or, as some believed, might they actually be getting them at below production costs with the losses being swallowed up by the also state-owned and -directed armaments industry? Similar issues were encountered on something as basic as manpower and wage rates. With living standards and wage rates lower than in the United States, any given level of spending on soldiers, sailors and airmen would surely result in more soldiers, sailors and airmen than a comparable level of defence spending in the US.

As a result of these uncertainties, at any one time there would be several different estimates of Soviet defence spending doing the rounds even within the US government. Throughout the 1960s, 1970s and 1980s the Central Intelligence Agency's estimates of Soviet defence spending were consistently higher than the estimates produced by outside analysts but – and this will surprise no one – lower than those produced by the Defense Intelligence Agency which was directly responsible to the Pentagon itself. Any debate on Soviet defence spending would produce a bewildering array of competing numbers, and in general, those who desired lower US defence spending favoured the lower estimates while those supporting a higher US defence budget plumped for the higher estimates. A further upward pressure on US defence spending throughout the

Cold War came from the tendency of all three major armed services to engage in their own direct lobbying of Congress, often making the case for pet projects that the administration as a whole had decided against.

But when it comes to over-egging a potential threat, there is a real risk that faulty intelligence – or intelligence too coloured by potential future budgetary settlements – risks bad decision-making. To return to the example of Zelenopillya, what would materially have been different if western militaries had chosen to favour the Ukrainian account of the battle rather than the one which focused on ground-breaking new Russian capabilities? One might argue that had the western version of Zelenopillya never entered wider military thinking, then western militaries might be in a worse position. The fears of Russian military capabilities may have been proved groundless in 2022 but they provided the necessary political motivation to secure a leg-up in western spending on artillery which allowed, among other things, an increased flow of military aid to Ukraine once the war began.

Similar reasoning can be applied to the 1950s bomber gap controversy. Yes, there was never a bomber gap, and yes, objectively the case that was made for those 750 B-52s turned out to be incorrect. But, from the point of view of the US armed forces, those B-52s played a major role in the Vietnam War (leaving aside questions about how they were used) and are still in use at the time of writing. It is hardly, by this logic, as if the money was simply wasted. Faulty or exaggerated threat analysis led to an increase in real resources in terms of new hardware which was subsequently put to effective (and occasionally ineffective) use.

In reality, though, such arguments are thinner than they appear. The money that was used to produce a huge fleet of B-52s in the late 1950s and 1960s could have been spent elsewhere – either on competing defence equipment, other types of public spending, or for cutting taxes and handing the choice over that spending back to consumers and firms. The decision to spend on one type of military gear comes with what economists call opportunity costs.

But there is a wider critique of this reasoning than simply arguing that because something eventually found a use there was no harm in exaggerating a potential threat. Before the Russian invasion of Ukraine in February 2022, the US administration spent weeks warning the world that such a moment was coming. They attempted to deter Russian aggression by threatening a new round of sanctions if Russian soldiers crossed the frontiers. That deterrence, as we know, failed.

Was there, though, an alternative scheme of deterrence that might have had a greater chance of success? One option would have been to provide the Ukrainian armed forces earlier with the kind of western weapons and training that they began to receive in great numbers from the spring of 2022 onwards. Might a visibly more potent Ukrainian army have deterred Putin's attack? The answer is of course unknowable but there are plenty of reasons to believe he would have weighted the chance of a major military setback higher than the potential for economic damage to Russia.

But one important reason such an option was not on the table in late 2021 and early 2022 was the widespread belief that any Russian invasion would succeed, and succeed quickly. The exaggerated fear of Russian military capacities almost certainly shaped western policy in those crucial moves.

Colouring estimates of intelligence to help in internal fights for resources is understandable. All organisations indulge in this in some form or another. But when faulty intelligence begins to shape wider strategic planning, real costs become involved. Incentives always matter.

Conclusion

In the nineteenth century the Prussian, and later German, general staff became a source of envy to other militaries around the world. It emerged initially from military disaster. The Prussian army of Frederick the Great had forged a reputation for success. Prussia, once a backwater among the small states of the German lands, had become a great power under Frederick through force of arms. But in 1806, after initially sitting out the Emperor Napoleon's wars against Austria and Russia that culminated in his great victory at Austerlitz, Prussia entered the fray and saw its armies humiliated and smashed at the dual Battle of Jena-Auerstedt in October of that year. Despite outnumbering their opponents by perhaps ninety thousand to sixty thousand and despite fighting closer to their home depots, the Prussian forces suffered a catastrophic defeat. The Prussian reputation for military prowess was shattered in a day, and the French were now the masters of central Europe.

It was from the ruins of that defeat that what became the Prussian general staff, at first an unofficial body and from 1814 onwards an official one, emerged. The aim was to 'support incompetent Generals, providing the talents that might otherwise be wanting among leaders and commanders'. A coterie of reforming officers, including a young Carl von Clausewitz, formed the dual institutions of the Army War College and the general staff.

At a time when most military officers lacked any sort of formal training, the approach was almost revolutionary. Through the nineteenth century the general staff evolved into an elite body with the Prussian, and then German, military. The brightest young officers would be selected at an early age to undergo intensive special training and serve as staff officers. Entrance was highly competitive and the total number of general staff officers rarely rose much above a hundred. The members of this small body spent peacetime thinking about war strategy and preparing for the shape of future conflicts, and in an actual battle would be dispatched to serve on the staff of more senior field commanders and provide direction and input.

What made the Prussian general staff the envy of other militaries and led to dozens of attempts to copy many of its essential features in later years was its apparent success when tested in battle. In 1866 the Prussian army defeated the Austrian army in a war which lasted just seven weeks. Key to this victory was the use of the rail network to assemble an army of around 285,000 men in just twenty-five days while it took the more ponderous Austrians forty-five days to assemble just 200,000. Prussia was confirmed as the leading German power. In 1870–1 the supposedly mighty French army was brought down in a campaign which saw the French field forces defeated in a matter of months.

In increasingly technical and larger-scale wars, where armies could be moved rapidly by rail and communicate by telegraph, the German system seemed to offer a route to producing the kind of highly trained, technically proficient professionals that wars now required, the kind of officers who could plan a large move by railway well in advance and solve many military problems before they were encountered in the field. This system was reasonably – by the standards of the nineteenth century at least – meritocratic and rewarded talent. It also took great pride in being, as much as possible, above politics and isolated from outside pressures.

It was a system that worked very well indeed in the nineteenth century but which failed spectacularly in the total wars of the twentieth century. In a limited war, such as that fought by Prussia against Austria in 1866, a system that allowed true military technocrats to run the business of fighting was a virtue. In the total wars of the twentieth century it proved to be a disastrous handicap.

The fundamental problem, and a repeated failing of the German general staff in the first half of the twentieth century, was a consistent approach of trying to find military solutions to grand strategic problems which did not have a simple military solution. The plans it drew up were often militarily sound, at least in the short term, but almost always ignored the wider political, diplomatic and, crucially, economic context.

The now infamous Schlieffen Plan put into operation in 1914 was, in the words of one recent history, more of 'an opening gambit' than a real long-term plan for war. Germany's strategic problem was that it faced powerful enemies to the west and to the east. There was no straightforward route out of this problem in purely military terms, but this did not stop the general staff from trying to find one.

Its eventual answer was a rapid campaign to knock France out of any war before turning to face Russia. It essentially bet the house on a quick victory, and what is more, the plan to achieve this end involved violating Belgian neutrality with no real consideration of the fact that this would almost certainly be enough to bring Britain into the war. As the war progressed, the same sort of mistakes reappeared. The military solution to getting Britain out of the war was unrestricted submarine warfare. This not only failed to do its job militarily but actually brought the United States into the war. As the general staff assumed ever greater economic powers, it threw an unsustainable volume of resources towards serving direct military needs and eventually helped to collapse the entire German economy, the whole war effort and indeed even the regime of the Kaiser it was supposed to serve.

In the Second World War it planned and carried out an almost entirely unnecessary invasion of the Netherlands with little thought given to the important role that shipping to that neutral neighbour had played in helping to keep the impact of the British blockade at bay, for a time, in the previous war. Despite later attempts by German generals to blame everything on Hitler, it went along with the plans for the ultimately catastrophic invasion of the USSR. In both of the total wars of the twentieth century the eventual victors pursued an ultimately successful grand strategy. One which integrated and traded off where necessary military and operational planning with economic factors and resources, diplomatic objectives, and one which kept at least a wary eye on domestic politics and the need to maintain civilian morale. This is how total wars, which are far more than simple military contests, are won. In the German case this was achieved in neither conflict. The temptation of the technocratic general staff was always to put military needs first and attempt to draw up a military plan to overcome any problem. This approach was doomed to failure.

The rise and fall of the German general staff as an institution for running wars is a telling example of how warfare changed between the 1860s–70s and the 1910s–40s. But this, as this book has hopefully demonstrated, was just the latest in a long series of shifts and changes in the nature of warfare, and the economics of that fighting, over the centuries.

War and violence have shaped human institutions for as long as human institutions have existed. The earliest political entities were probably formed by those who happened to be physically tougher than their fellow early farmers realising that using threats to get food from others was a lot easier than growing their own.

The relationship between institutions, incentives and warfare has constantly evolved. Warfare has shaped institutions and states, and those states and institutions have in turn shaped the course and form of warfare. Given that, over the longer run, the development of institutions has been a key determinant of economic outcomes, it is not too much of a stretch to say that the economic history of warfare and conflict is a key part of understanding why some countries are rich today and some are poor.

Two major turning points in the economic history of warfare have occurred over the last millennium.

The first was the military revolution of the early modern world, which fundamentally changed the direct fiscal costs of wars. Spain could be a leading power in the sixteenth century with an army numbering in the tens of thousands, but needed 300,000 regulars backed by half a million militia to maintain its position by the 1650s. Armies became even larger after the French Revolution with its concept of the entire nation in arms and the *levée en masse* allowing it to put millions of soldiers into the field. This was an important stepping stone to the mass warfare of the twentieth century. As wars became ever larger, states – the key economic institution – had to evolve and change to fund them. What became the modern forms of taxation, of public borrowing and of the wider financial system really began to develop in the aftermath of the military revolution. That military revolution ushered in fiscal and financial revolutions which in turn helped to create an even wider economic revolution.

The second turning point came later. In the nineteenth century warfare became even more destructive. While earlier wars had killed many people, the damage to property, buildings and infrastructure was generally limited. Cities were occasionally sacked after a siege, but they were rarely levelled by fighting. From the 1850s onwards the growth of high-explosive artillery shells saw wars starting to mean the devastation of a nation's capital stock. Aerial bombing supercharged the trend. The victorious side before the early 1800s could generally hope to meet its costs by forcing the loser to pay, but by the twentieth century even the victors would usually be worse off as a result of the conflict.

Wars between states, as opposed to civil wars, have become rarer over time. That partially reflects their rising costs and the fact that they almost never now pay for themselves, but it also reflects changing norms. Norms are an important concept in the social sciences in general, usually referring to a socially enforced set of standards of behaviour as opposed to written-down legal rules. It is a law that you do not steal from shops, but a norm that you wait in line to pay rather than pushing to the front of a queue. In economic terms, norms – as part of the rules of the game of behaviour – can be thought of as a form of institution. Over the course of the twentieth century, the norms around the use of war as a tool of policy have shifted considerably in much of the world.

In December 1861, Spanish ships seized the Mexican port of Vera Cruz. The following month, British and French soldiers arrived to reinforce the Spanish position. Britain, Spain and France's Tripartite Expedition was intended to enforce claims for repayment on a republican Mexican government which had defaulted on its international loans. In Europe, few batted an eyelid at this use of military power to enforce a debt contract. More than a century and a half later no one ever seriously suggests using armed forces to extract payments from countries which miss international bond payments. The norms have simply shifted over time. The bar for using military force, at least against a comparable state, is now much higher.

One reason that Russia's invasion of Ukraine in 2022 provoked so much shock in western capitals was because it represented a brazen violation of the new norms around warfare in Europe. States in Europe did not simply invade other states in Europe any more – or so they thought.

Norms, though, as with any institution, can change again.

Large-scale inter-state warfare between major powers is hard to imagine in the world of the twenty-first century. That is partially because of the norms of behaviour but also because of an awareness of the human and economic costs. But it is worth remembering how hard it was to imagine in the world of the early twentieth century too.

Norman Angell, then a journalist and later a Member of Parliament, first published *The Great Illusion* in 1909 – initially as the less catchily titled *Europe's Optical Illusion*. It was an instant bestseller which was translated into eleven languages. Written at a time of rising global tensions and with the European powers dividing into the two great power blocks that would fight the Great War, it was a careful study of the costs of modern warfare and the nature of an interconnected global world. The great illusion of the title was that nations could still profit from even successful warfare and conquest. The costs of war, argued Angell, were now so high that any war would herald an economic disaster and be over quickly. He was half right. The Great War was an economic disaster for almost every nation involved, but it did not end quickly.

Much of Angell's book is an argument on the interconnected nature of the global economy on the eve of the First World War. Financial markets, trade patterns and supply chains had become so interlinked and crossed so many borders that they could not be disentangled. This alone, Angell hoped, would help to safeguard against an outbreak of fighting.

Global trade in 1914 was running at levels which would not be seen again until the 1980s. The total value of goods crossing borders, as a share of total global GDP, had risen from around 5 per cent in the 1840s to 14 per cent on the eve of the war. Global capital flows, mostly in the form of cross-border lending, had risen over the same period from around 7 per cent of global GDP to 20 per cent – again, a level that would not be reached again until the 1980s.

It is easy to forget just how (to use the modern term) 'globalised' the world economy was in 1914. Looking back from 1919 on the pre-Great War world, the economist John Maynard Keynes wrote that 'the inhabitant of London could order by telephone, sipping his morning tea in bed, the various products of the whole earth – he could at the same time and by the same means adventure his wealth in the natural resources and new enterprise of any quarter of the world'. That's something that sounds very familiar to modern ears.

But this global economic interconnectedness, despite the beliefs of Norman Angell and many others, did not make large-scale inter-state war between the great powers impossible. It certainly did make it, when it came, even more costly in terms of both blood and treasure. It may have been by any definition economically irrational but, as any student of history should know, something being economically irrational does not mean it will not happen.

Notes on Further Reading

This is not, I am afraid, a full bibliography but instead a collection of the books and papers I found most useful in pulling this work together. Readers wishing to delve further into any of the material covered in the preceding chapters are advised to start here and then follow the references in the works listed below.

For general reading on the history of warfare, *The Cambridge History of Warfare* edited by Geoffrey Parker is a superb place to start. As a general guide to the economic history of the last one thousand or so years, the monumental work of Ronald Findley and Kevin H. O'Rourke in *Power and Plenty: Trade, War, and the World Economy in the Second Millennium* is without peer. It takes power and warfare as seriously as plenty and trade.

Charles Tilly's *Coercion, Capital and European States* underpins much of the thinking behind this book, as does Ian Morris's *Why the West Rules – For Now*. Walter Scheidel's *Escape from Rome: The Failure of Empire and the Road to Prosperity* helped to clarify my thinking on several key points. *Why Nations Fail* by Daron Acemoglu and James A. Robinson is the best introduction to the economics of institutions. Mark Koyama and Jared Rubin's *How the World Became Rich* is the best single read on historical political economy, and *Global Economic History: A*

Very Short Introduction by Robert C. Allen is the best starting point for anyone interested in global economic change over the longer term.

On the Vikings, *The Oxford Illustrated History of the Vikings* edited by Peter Sawyer and *The Vikings* by Martin Arnold offer the best introduction. *Beyond the Northlands* by Eleanor Rosamund Barraclough is a fascinating look at the non-violence specialist side of the story. Mancur Olson's article 'Dictatorship, Democracy, and Development' is the best single read on the theory of stationary bandits and can be found in the *American Political Science Review*, volume 87, number 3. Guy Halsall's *Warfare and Society in the Barbarian West 450–900* is indispensable on early medieval warfare.

The Horde: How the Mongols Changed the World by Marie Favereau is an excellent read on the Great Khan and his successors. Timothy May's *The Mongol Art of War* fleshes out the military detail for those especially interested. 'The First Globalization Episode: The Creation of the Mongol Empire' by Ronald Findlay and Mats Lundahl, a chapter in *The Economics of the Frontier* by the same authors, is the single best read on the economics of the empire.

Longbow: A Social and Military History by Robert Hardy is a very useful and fascinating read. On medieval warfare more generally, *The Oxford Encyclopedia of Medieval Warfare and Military Technology* edited by Clifford J. Rogers is excellent. Douglas Allen and Peter Leeson's paper 'Institutionally Constrained Technology Adoption: Resolving the Longbow Puzzle' was published in the *Journal of Law and Economics* in August 2015.

Emperor and *Imprudent King*, Geoffrey Parker's biographies of Charles V and Philip II, are both exceptionally good, while his *The Military Revolution* is recommended on the wider developments in European warfare. Fernando Cervantes's

Conquistadores: A New History is superb on Spain's empire in the Americas. David Fischer's *The Great Wave* is useful on the European Price Revolution, while *Lending to the Borrower from Hell* by Hans-Joachim Voth and Mauricio Drelichman is indispensable on Philip's fiscal arrangements.

The Witch in History by Diane Purkiss is an excellent read. *Witchcraze: A New History of the European Witch Hunts* by Anne Barstow is the best single volume on the height of witch mania. Diarmaid MacCulloch's *The Reformation: A History* is the best read on the wider religious conflict. Peter Leeson and Jacob Russ's 'Witch Trials' article can be found in volume 128, issue 613 of the *Economic Journal*.

The Light of Italy by Jane Stevenson is a superb biography of Federico da Montefeltro. F. L. Taylor's *The Art of War in Italy 1494–1529* is mostly concerned with the later period but very useful on what came before. 'The Economy of Renaissance Italy, the Preconditions for Luxury Consumption' by Richard Goldwaite was published in *I Tatti Studies* in 1987.

Under the Black Flag by David Cordingly is an excellent introduction to piracy. Joel Baer's *British Piracy in the Golden Age* is a more detailed examination of the pirates mentioned. Peter Leeson's excellent paper 'P*irational* Choice: The economics of infamous pirate practices' was published by George Mason University in 2010.

The best single-volume history of the Seven Years' War, or at least of the Anglo-French global contest, is Daniel Baugh's *The Global Seven Years War*. John Brewer's *The Sinews of Power* on the British fiscal-military state that developed after 1688 is a fantastic read. Steven Pincus and James Robinson's excellent working paper 'What really happened during the Glorious Revolution?' was published by the National Bureau for Economic Research in 2011.

N. A. M. Rodger's *The Command of the Ocean*, the second

volume in his planned trilogy on British naval history which covers 1649 to 1815, is an exceptionally good book. Andrew Lambert's *War at Sea in the Age of Sail* is a useful introduction to the wider period and non-British fleets. Douglas Allen's 'The British Navy Rules: Monitoring and incompatible incentives in the Age of Fighting Sail' was published in *Explorations in Economic History*, volume 39, issue 2. Hans-Joachim Voth and Guo Xu's 'Patronage for Productivity: Selection and Performance in the Age of Sail' was published as a CEPR discussion paper in 2019.

Saul David's *The Indian Mutiny* is an excellent modern one-volume history. Rudrangshu Mukherjee, Shobita Punja and Toby Sinclair's *A New History of India* is excellent on the bigger picture. William Dalrymple's *The Anarchy* is superb on the key period in which British power was established. 'Pre-Colonial Warfare and Long Run Development in India' by Mark Dincecco, Anil Menon, James Fenske and Shivaji Mukherjee was published in the *Economic Journal* in 2022.

Bray Hammond's *Banks and Politics in America from the Revolution to the Civil War* is the single best book on early American financial history. Gordon Wood's *Empire of Liberty* and *What Hath God Wrought* by Daniel Walker Howe are excellent on the United States from 1789 until 1848. *Battle Cry of Freedom* by James M. McPherson is the best single-volume history of the civil war. Roger Ransom's chapter 'The Civil War in American Economic History' in *The Oxford Handbook of American Economic History, Volume 2* is very useful. Jeffry Frieden's 'Lessons for the Euro from Early American Monetary and Financial History' was published by the think tank Bruegal in 2016.

Alistair Horne's classic *The Fall of Paris* is still the best read on the siege of 1870–1. 'Gifts from Mars: Warfare and Europe's Early Rise to Riches' by Nico Voigtländer and Hans-Joachim

Voth was published in the *Journal of Economic Perspectives* in 2013. 'Capital Destruction and Economic Growth: The Effects of Sherman's March, 1850–1920' by James Feigenbaum, James Lee and Filippo Mezzanotti was published in the *American Economic Journal* in 2022.

The literature on the economics of total warfare is voluminous. Good starting points, though, are two ebook collections of essays on the economics of the two wars edited by Stephen Broadberry and Mark Harrison and published by the CEPR in 2014 and 2019. William Philpott's *Attrition: Fighting the First World War* is excellent, as is Phillips O'Brien's *How the War Was Won* on the Second. Richard Overy's *Blood and Ruins* takes the economics of the Second World War seriously. Adam Tooze's *The Wages of Destruction* is a must-read on the Nazi war effort, and Randall Hansen's *Fire and Fury: The Allied Bombing of Germany* is a useful read on the bomber offensive.

Williamson Murray's *The Luftwaffe, 1933–45: A Strategy for Defeat* is the best single-volume history of the Luftwaffe. Philipp Ager, Leonardo Bursztyn and Hans-Joachim Voth's working paper 'Killer Incentives: Status Competition and Pilot Performance during World War II' was published by NBER in 2016.

Robert Allen's *Farm to Factory* is an excellent economic history of Soviet industrialisation. Mark Harrison has written extensively and well on Soviet economic policy; *The Soviet Home Front 1941–45* is especially good. Chris Miller's *The Struggle to Save the Soviet Economy* is the best read on the later years and especially good on the ending of terror as a factor undermining Soviet political economy.

It may be old, but David Halberstam's *The Best and the Brightest* is still the best single (long!) book on US policy-making in Vietnam. *Dereliction of Duty*, a more up-to-date book by H. R. McMaster, is a useful supplement. Edward Miguel and Gerard

Roland's 'The Long Run of Bombing Vietnam' was published in the *Journal of Development Economics* in 2011.

Despite its dry title, *Soviet Defense Spending: A History of CIA Estimates, 1950–1990* by Noel Firth and James Noren is a good read. The research on the Battle of Zelenopillya can be found at The Local Blind Spot blog.

Peter Wilson's magisterial *Iron and Blood: A Military History of the German-speaking Peoples Since 1500* is one of the best books on the military (and political, economic, social and diplomatic) history of any nation I have ever read.

Acknowledgements

Richard Beswick has once again been everything I could have asked for in an editor. This final version is a much better book than it would have been without his input. I am also grateful to Nithya Rae at Little, Brown, who shepherded the book to publication in a very smooth manner, and very appreciative of Daniel Balado's excellent copy edit. Many thanks are due to my agent Kate Barker for playing the roles of both good cop and bad cop as and when required and ensuring that this work eventually made it to the finishing line.

I could not have hoped to touch upon events spread out over more than a thousand years on multiple continents without leaning very heavily on the hard work of others. The notes of further reading are intended as both a guide to the best starting points for further reading and also as a form of acknowledgement of the most helpful books and papers I have read when pulling this work together. But the work of many scholars has been incredibly useful and I apologise for lacking the space to list all of their works.

Professors Mark Harrison and Stephen Broadberry were kind enough to invite me to a three-day seminar series on the economics of war in Venice at which I got to meet many of the scholars on which some chapters of this work draw. I learned a great deal from those discussions. I also learned that the quality of catering at an Italian-hosted academic event is leagues above that found in Britain.

Finally, I owe an incalculable level of gratitude to my family for putting up with me writing another book. Natalie – I could not have done this without you.

Index